A PLACE AT THE TABLE

a participant° guide
MEDIA

A PLACE
AT THE
TABLE

THE CRISIS OF
49 MILLION
HUNGRY AMERICANS
AND HOW TO SOLVE IT

Edited by **Peter Pringle**

PUBLICAFFAIRS

New York

PublicAffairs books are available at special discounts for bulk purchases in
the U.S. by corporations, institutions, and other organizations. For more
information, please contact the Special Markets Department at the
Perseus Books Group, 2300 Chestnut Street, Suite 200, Philadelphia, PA
19103, call (800) 810–4145, ext. 5000, or e-mail
special.markets@perseusbooks.com.

Book Design by Brent Wilcox

The Library of Congress has cataloged the printed edition as follows:
    A place at the table : the crisis of 49 million hungry Americans
and how to solve it / edited by Peter Pringle.
        p.   cm.
    Includes bibliographical references and index.
    ISBN 978–1–61039–181–8 (pbk. original)—
ISBN 978–1–61039–182–5 (electronic)
    1. Hunger—United States.   2. Food supply—United States.
3. Food relief—United States.   4. Public welfare—United States.
I. Pringle, Peter.
TX360.U6P584 2013
363.8—dc23

                                                                2012029475

First Edition
10 9 8 7 6 5 4 3 2

CONTENTS

CONTENTS

Part II
Feeding the Hungry

It's not easy for Americans to imagine tens of millions of people going to bed hungry in their rich country. The lines outside soup kitchens have grown during the recent Great Recession, but the faces of those waiting for charity food, unlike the faces of the starving in Africa, do not show hunger. In the media there are no images of famine in the poorest states. Indeed, many low-income Americans appear overweight. So hunger in the land of plenty needs its own definition.

Fifty years ago, in his book *The Other America,* Michael Harrington identified the nation's "invisible poor." Even though they lived "better than the medieval knights or Asian peasants," Harrington wrote, they were poor by American standards; they were denied "the minimal levels of health, food and education that our present stage of scientific knowledge specifies as necessary for life as it is now lived in the United States."[1]

Harrington's book shocked the nation. The media documented cases of real hunger, mostly in the South. Politicians hurriedly constructed a new safety net, including a new, more effective food stamp program. Hunger soon disappeared, at least from the front pages. But two decades later it was back—brought on by a recession and the welfare cuts of the Ronald Reagan era. A presidential commission concluded that the word *hunger* had "come to mean rather different things to different people." A new clinical definition favored by the medical community defined hunger as a "weakened, disordered condition brought about by a prolonged lack of food."[2]

Researchers trying to put together a program to take care of the problem found a lack of reliable data. In the late 1980s and early 1990s, the Food Research and Action Center (FRAC), the nation's leading hunger advocacy and lobby group, launched a series of national surveys on hunger in America. The figures were startling. They found that 4 million American children under age twelve were permanently hungry; they were missing school or falling asleep in class, tired, and often ill. Another 9.6 million were deemed to be at risk of hunger.

Anti-hunger groups used those numbers to lobby Congress to enact legislation requiring the US Department of Agriculture (USDA) to collect and publish data on the extent of hunger in America. With a new questionnaire, researchers began to classify Americans as either "food-secure" or "food-insecure." Food security was defined as "access by all people at all times to enough food for an active, healthy life." At a minimum, it included the "ready availability of nutritionally adequate and safe foods" and "an assured ability to acquire acceptable foods in socially acceptable ways (e.g. without resorting to emergency food supplies, scavenging, stealing or other coping strategies)."[3]

Households were then further subdivided into "food-insecure *with* hunger" and "food-insecure *without* hunger"—depending on whether the members of the household occasionally skipped proper meals and snacked on less nutritious foods or went for long periods with no food at all. True hunger was defined as severe physical discomfort or mental stress—"the uneasy or painful sensation caused by a lack of food," or "the recurrent and involuntary lack of access to food."

Today American households are characterized as having food security, low food security, or very low food security. The latest estimates from the Department of Agriculture are that 48.8 million people in America live in food-insecure households, half of them children; 46 million participate in the Food Stamp Program; and about one in four Americans participate in at least one of the domestic food and nutrition assistance programs run by the USDA.[4]

In describing hunger in America and thinking about how to end it, most contributors to this book have used the terms "food security" and "food insecurity," sometimes specifying high to low levels depending, again, on such factors as the number of times a month a parent eats less in order to feed his or her children, or a household's inability to buy nutritious foods because it's located in a place without grocery stores—a so-called food desert.

This book is the eighth in a series of companion volumes to documentary films produced by Participant Media on the most important social issues facing America today. It follows most closely in the footsteps of *Food, Inc.*, which is about the nation's food production system and its impact on our health; *Waiting for "Superman,"* which calls for radical reform of America's failing public education system, and *Last Call at the Oasis*, which is about Earth's imperiled water supply.

As in the previous books, this companion to *A Place at the Table* features essays by experts who expand on the key issues raised in the film, and following the format of the film, the book also includes personal stories of the participants—the activists as well as the victims—in America's war on hunger and obesity.

The foreword is by Jeff Bridges, the Academy Award–winning actor and longtime anti-hunger activist. He is national spokesperson of the No Kid Hungry campaign. In the introduction, the film's producers, Kristi Jacobson and Lori Silverbush, explain how and why they decided to make the documentary.

The rest of the book is divided into four parts. Part I, "On the Frontlines of Hunger," begins with Dr. Mariana Chilton, a professor of public health, telling the story of an amazing group she founded consisting of young mothers trying to raise themselves out of poverty. She recalls how she took them to the U.S. Congress to participate in the dialogue on hunger and poverty. Pastor Bob Wilson and teacher Leslie Nichols tell their stories of distributing food to those in need in a small town in Colorado. Hunger researchers Allison Karpyn and Sarah Treuhaft examine the "food deserts" that now exist in some communities and suggest ways of eliminating them. And Tom Colicchio, the producer of the television show *Top Chef*, lobbies Washington politicians for increases in funding for child nutrition programs. Ken Cook, the president and cofounder of the Environmental Working Group (EWG), a public-interest research and advocacy organization, writes a powerful essay explaining the shocking inequities in the new 2012 Farm Bill and its effect on America's hunger crisis.

Taking a close look at the fascinating history of food stamps, Gus Schumacher, Michel Nischan, and Daniel Bowman Simon add to our perspective on the hunger crisis by reminding us of the origins of that idealistic safety net in the New Deal era and detailing how much has changed since then—for the worse. Marion Nestle, the New York University nutritionist and acclaimed critic of the food industry, writes about the explosion of calories in our diet in today's "Eat More" environment; Jennifer Harris, of Yale University's Rudd Center for Food Policy and Obesity, uncovers the new hidden persuaders of web food advertisers, and Janet Poppendieck, the New York sociologist, best-selling author, and well-known historian of poverty and hunger in America, presents overwhelming arguments for school lunch reform.

Part II focuses on those who provide food for the hungry: Matt Knott, CEO of Feeding America, the nation's largest food bank charity, explains the origins and work of that organization; David Beckmann, the Lutheran minister and head of Bread for the World, and Sarah Newman, the chief researcher on *A Place at the Table*, write about the intersection of faith and feeding the hungry; and Sharon Thornberry tells her personal story of how and why she became a senior manager at the Oregon Food Bank, America's first statewide food bank. Scott Stringer, the Manhattan borough president, and his director of communications, Josh Getlin, suggest what local government can do to help the food-insecure, and Andy Fisher, a veteran activist in community food projects, argues that we must get off what he calls the "anti-hunger treadmill"—the charity-based emergency feeding program and its ties to the food industry.

In Part III, three well-known and widely published anti-hunger activists, Bill Shore, Joel Berg, and Robert Egger, suggest bold and diverse strategies for solving the problem that go "Beyond Feeding the Hungry."

Finally, in Part IV, as in other Participant Media books, steps are offered that you can take as a consumer and a citizen to help end hunger in America. It starts with Kelly Meyer's inspiring story of how she became involved as an accidental activist in hunger in America. Then the Food Research and Action Center presents its seven-step plan for ending child hunger by 2015. The FRAC program is followed by a directory of NGOs through which you can become involved nationally, regionally, or locally.

We hope you will follow the lead of Kristi Jacobson and Lori Silverbush, the producers of *A Place at the Table*, their colleagues at Participant Media, their publishing partners at PublicAffairs, and the committed authors who contributed to this book in seeking solutions to the plight of the poor and the hungry in America. However we label hunger today, to have almost 50 million citizens uncertain where their next meal is coming from or wondering whether they can afford to buy food for the day is unacceptable in a society so rich and productive as ours. As Jeff Bridges writes in his foreword, "We can't be bystanders. We can't be okay with this situation. We can't be missing."

Peter Pringle
New York, September 2012

Peter Pringle is the author and coauthor of ten books on science and politics, including the *New York Times* Notable Book *Food, Inc.*; the bestselling *Those Are Real Bullets: Bloody Sunday, Derry, 1972*; and a mystery-thriller about food and patents, *Day of the Dandelion*. His latest book is *Experiment Eleven: Dark Secrets Behind the Discovery of a Wonder Drug*. For thirty years, he was a foreign correspondent for British newspapers. He lives in New York City.

The Missing Element

JEFF BRIDGES

Like most Americans, I have never personally been at risk of hunger. But also like many Americans, I am very disturbed to see a growing number of Americans, especially children, face hunger as an uninvited visitor every day.

In the 1980s, I learned that more people were working than ever before, but even then millions of Americans were hungry or didn't know where their next meal was coming from. Public charities and food banks were doing more than ever before, but they couldn't keep up with the growing need. Charity is an important provider of emergency assistance, but it is not a way to feed a nation. We don't protect our national security through charity, and we shouldn't protect our families that way either.

What could be more important for our nation than finding a solution to this important problem with such an impact on our future? If another country was doing this to our children, we'd be at war. As Americans, we have stepped up to many challenges: fought tyranny, landed on the moon, put a stop to polio, and built the most prosperous nation in history. We can do stuff, really well. And we already have the knowledge and infrastructure to ensure that no family—no child—ever goes hungry in this country. But we haven't done it. So what's missing?

Here's what I've learned: First, the political will to end hunger is missing. We need to make ending hunger important enough that our political leaders get the message from us, powerfully, and start acting accordingly or they don't get reelected. Second, dissatisfaction is missing. Humans have an amazing ability to absorb bad news, adjust to disabilities, and "get along" in less-than-ideal situations. We can't "get used" to having persistent child hunger as part of the American experience. Third, I was missing. Each of us has a unique ability to make a difference, to make our world a better place because we were there. Like everyone else, I could do things and I know people. As an actor, I could do Hollywood things, attract media, and bring attention to the issue. But everyone has unique talents, skills, and relationships that can make a difference in ending hunger. The challenge is always moving from "I could do. . . ." to "I will do. . . ." Making that step was one of the most rewarding things I have ever done.

I cofounded the End Hunger Network to help focus the power of the media on hunger. In 1985 we helped produce the historic Live Aid concert, and we went on to create a number of programs that engaged the music, prime-time television, and video industries in creative initiatives that brought wide public attention to the issue of hunger.

In 1996 we produced *Hidden in America,* a dramatic film that tells the story of one family's struggle with hunger. My brother Beau played the lead role of a recently unemployed father who finds himself jobless, uninsured, and barely able to feed his family. As part of his preparation for his role, Beau tried to apply for food stamps. No one recognized him as he was shuffled for hours from one line to another. He could imagine someone in that position saying, "Oh God, I don't want to do this. I'd rather go out and beg."

But sixteen years later, the movie is just as relevant as the day we made it. Hunger is once again "hidden in America." Even though hunger seems to be a factor for an increasing number of families these days, it's largely an invisible epidemic.

Over the years I've been fortunate to meet many hungry families. The malnourished parent may be the cashier at your supermarket who isn't earning much, has three kids at home, and faces difficult choices every night. It may be the child with her head down on her desk in school . . . with her body in the classroom but her mind elsewhere, even if she's missed only one or two meals.

These are our neighbors, struggling in a fight just to survive. Many of them are living in our own neighborhoods and may never have had to face hunger before. But they shouldn't fight alone. We can't be bystanders. We can't be okay with this situation. We can't be missing.

Victor Hugo wrote: "Nothing is as powerful as an idea whose time has come." Ending hunger's time has come. You have a voice and a vote, and you can help make it happen.

～

Jeff Bridges is an Academy Award–winning actor and father of three daughters. He is national spokesperson of the No Kid Hungry campaign (www.nokidhungry.org).

The Producers

A Place at the Table

KRISTI JACOBSON AND LORI SILVERBUSH

In the summer of 2006, Lori Silverbush, the New York writer-director, released her first feature film, about the lives of young girls in juvenile detention. While making the film, Lori mentored a twelve-year-old girl who had problems in school and kept falling asleep in class. One day the principal of the school called to say he had found the young girl foraging in the trash—for food. Lori learned that part of the girl's problem was that she was not getting enough to eat. She was one of the 17 million kids in America who face what the government calls "food insecurity": they are at risk each day, not from drugs or family abuse, but from their family's inability to buy enough food so that they can have an active, healthy life.

Lori teamed up with Kristi Jacobson, an award-winning documentary filmmaker who has immersed herself in challenging subjects and deeply human stories. Lori and Kristi quickly found that hunger in America is not confined to children, and that it is not necessarily found only in the places they had assumed. Food insecurity affects one in six of the U.S. population— and since the recession of 2008 the problem has gotten worse.

Together, Lori and Kristi spent the next two years crisscrossing America, researching and filming. The result is the first full-length documentary about hunger in America in a generation. This is their story of how they made the film.

We cast a wide net. We met people in government agencies, charity workers, religious leaders, doctors, advocates, frontline fighters, all engaged in a massive, mostly hidden war on hunger, distributing food to the young, the middle-aged, and the old, in rural communities, downtrodden inner cities, and leafy suburbs across America. We visited food pantries and food banks. We saw millions of pounds of canned and packaged food, the surpluses and seconds of our nation's corporate food producers, being trucked to food banks and pantries. Yet despite this, there are still 49 million people who end the day lacking the nutrition necessary to keep their bodies and minds functioning well enough to cope and thrive. Some are so badly in need of nutritious food—the kind American farmers are known for the world over—that they are unhealthy, suffering from the nation's most prevalent, and devastating, modern disease: obesity.

Over the two years it took to make the film, we were constantly surprised by the extraordinary dedication of those who work to fight hunger. They inspired us to tell their stories. Early in our research, we were fortunate to meet Dr. Mariana Chilton, a public health professor, who was often asked to appear before congressional committees in Washington as an expert witness on the health problems of the hungry. The more appearances she made, the more she felt that the politicians were not really listening: to them, she was just another talking head from the medical community. So Chilton turned to activism, founding the organization Witnesses to Hunger. Recognizing that we are a nation where policies for the poor are decided without their participation, she distributed digital cameras to forty mothers in North Philadelphia and asked them to document their struggle to feed their families. This simple act would have profound implications, giving the women a voice that has since become part of the national dialogue about hunger. As filmmakers, we were inspired to follow Dr. Chilton's example in the making of our own film—to let the victims of hunger speak for themselves.

It was through Dr. Chilton that we met Barbie Izquierdo, a spirited single mother of two, who became the film's first protagonist. We found Barbie caught in a welfare trap that is well known to those in her world, but which we found shocking. She was one of the 49 million Americans whose lack of income qualified her for food stamps to help feed her family. She could have remained a welfare mom, but every day she looked for a job, trying to climb out of poverty. Her efforts and her anti-hunger advocacy paid off with a job at the Greater Philadelphia Coalition Against Hunger. Her new job left her, however, facing a new, devastating reality: with an income that was insufficient to provide nutritious food for her children but too high to qualify for food stamps, she was less capable of feeding her family than before.

To document the extent and range of the hunger problem we visited not only inner cities like Philadelphia but also small towns. One was Collbran, Colorado, a quaint, proud cattle ranching community of a thousand people nestled in a valley in the Rocky Mountains—the kind of place where people look out for each other. When we arrived there in the summer of 2010, virtually everyone in town was feeling the impact of food insecurity in some way. The local pastor explained that the problem had spiraled in recent years: even two-income families were relying on his church's weekly communal meal and after-school feeding program for children. The police chief and a fiercely independent cattle rancher told us how they visited the church's food pantry or used the after-school children's meal program to make it each month.

In Collbran, we met Leslie Nichols, a fifth-grade teacher who delivered bags of charity food throughout the community in her spare time. And it was here we met ten-year-old Rosie, who said she often found it hard to fall asleep at night because of the hunger pains in her stomach. Her daily struggles to focus and stay engaged at school were further testimony to what it means to be a food-insecure child in America today.

In Jonestown, Mississippi, a sultry Delta town with two thousand people, we confronted the phenomenon of "food deserts"—places where residents must travel a mile or more in a city, and still greater distances in rural areas, to buy fresh meat, dairy products, and vegetables. Often found in the middle of America's industrial farmland—where just a generation ago people farmed and ate off the land—these food deserts are a true obstacle for the many people without access to transportation or sufficient income for gas. The federal government estimates that 23.5 million people live in a food desert. One of them is Ree Harris, a short-order cook at Uptown Brown's, Jonestown's only restaurant. She told us that the nearest supermarket to Jonestown was a forty-five-minute drive—each way.

On a good day, she said, Jonestown's store might have a banana or two for sale, at a price she could afford.

Everywhere we went, the most affordable and plentiful options seemed to be fast food and packaged processed food, the building blocks of an unhealthy diet. We couldn't help but ask ourselves: why does a cheeseburger—whose multiple ingredients must be processed, cooked, packaged, marketed, and advertised—cost less than a fresh peach? The answer is so tightly wrapped up in government farm policy, political horse-trading in Congress, commercial interests, and misguided social planning that unraveling it is more than the media is generally willing to take on, and certainly more than the average voter is able to comprehend without help.

∽

We were witnesses to the shameful way in which America treats its most vulnerable. The grim statistics and the shocking events we were confronting led us to consult the experts—on agriculture, health, nutrition, and social planning. These experts pointed to the link between the preferential policies enjoyed by big agriculture and the nation's hunger and obesity crisis. We learned that agricultural policy had been forged with the intention of helping farmers weather the dust bowl and Great Depression of the 1930s, but had evolved into an entitlement system, with unforeseen and tragic consequences. As Ken Cook of the Environmental Working Group says in our film, "Most of that subsidy money, about 70 percent of it, has gone to just 10 percent of those beneficiaries. The biggest, largest, best capitalized farms. They're hauling in this taxpayer money." And yet Americans are being told we have insufficient resources to make school meals nutritious or to provide an adequate safety net so that everyone can eat.

We saw firsthand the efforts of the food banks and other charity-run agencies that now distribute food to the poor as a result of the decades-long shift of responsibility from the government to the private sector. Although food banks and soup kitchens provide invaluable help to people in need, the ever-growing numbers of hungry people indicate that charities clearly are not providing a long-term solution. If our goal is to eliminate hunger, malnutrition, and obesity in America, then we need to take action on the larger systemic problems that have caused them in the first place.

Janet Poppendieck, a noted author and professor of sociology at Hunter College in New York, says in the film that our charity model has evolved into a highly efficient and sophisticated "secondary food system for the poor." She comes to the conclusion in her seminal book *Sweet Charity* that major players in the corporate food world—among the most generous donors to food banks—are more interested in the "halo effect" of their charitable donations than in truly ending hunger. And that is how it seemed to us. The big food companies, which ultimately benefit from our flawed food system and the unlivable wages that compel people to turn to charity, lobby intensively in Washington to maintain the status quo. By donating their surplus food to charities, corporations manage to avoid substantial dumping fees while earning big tax write-offs—and at the same time, they can brag about their philanthropic work.

Millions of ordinary Americans are being encouraged to donate cans of food and volunteer their time at food pantries, believing that these efforts will make a significant difference in ending hunger. A food bank employee quietly confided that canned food drives and volunteer days are more valuable as public relations gambits than as anti-hunger measures. The real business of food banking involves trained warehouse employees, scanning systems, and trucking companies to move millions of pounds of surplus corporate food. Nevertheless, she explained, can drives are useful: they make people feel good and get them engaged in the issue.

People may be engaged, but we couldn't help asking ourselves—to what end? If the majority of Americans with a desire to help are being led to believe that they can fix hunger with a few cans of food, is that true engagement? Is the current charity model allowing us to assuage our consciences without asking the really hard questions? *Why, in a nation that has the means to feed everyone well and plentifully, are 49 million people not getting enough to eat?*

Over the next two years we dared to imagine a system in which food banks become obsolete. If federal agricultural subsidies went toward fruits and vegetables rather than overproduced commodities, would that peach be cheaper than the cheeseburger? Could the substantial expertise of food bankers and the pioneering efforts of community food activists be marshaled to help set up local and regional systems of delivery to food deserts? Could we explore community-based growing solutions through public funding rather than rely on the quixotic arm of charity? If we were to modernize highly effective programs like food stamps and base them on the reality of need, not the punitive and outdated current method, parents like Barbie, we imagined, could focus their considerable energies on parenting, studying, and their family's upward mobility rather than the draining and demoralizing daily quest for food.

These ideas led us to the really big idea—what if we were to create a Department of Food Policy, as many experts have called for? Such a department, comprising federal and state agencies, would take over the distribution of the food discarded by America's food industry and carry out federal and state policies that provide incentives for supermarkets to open up in food deserts and regulate the advertising of junk food to children on the Internet and all media platforms, as it does with television. Why do we have policies that keep liquor stores away from schools but allow junk food into them?

Why can't school meals be highly nutritious and free for all students, like textbooks, thereby erasing the stigma for the millions of kids who need government-subsidized meals? Maybe then young people like Rosie in Collbran, Colorado, would have the energy they need to learn. And why not have teachers like Leslie Nichols teach healthy food choices and preparation? If we can teach algebra, why not food smarts?

All these changes would cost money up front, but it seems clear that in the long term we'd recoup our investment in the form of decreased health care costs and a surge in productivity. After all, what could be a greater stimulus to an economy than a healthier, more productive population? Doesn't the free market prosper when people take fewer sick days, have dollars to spend in the marketplace, and know how to make real, healthful food choices, thus increasing demand for those items? With increased demand comes greater production, leading to lower prices. Lower prices for fresh food would benefit the very people who need it most.

In Jonestown, Mississippi, the indomitable second-grade teacher Odessa Cherry said it best when speaking of her students at a Mississippi primary school: "Awareness is the first step." That was the case a generation ago, when the unsparing program *CBS Reports: Hunger in America* moved Senators George McGovern and Bob Dole to speak out against the problem. They understood that the true cost of hunger is measured not in dollars but in human suffering and loss of human potential. What they did next was our biggest inspiration for making this film: they acted, not in the interest of their parties, but in the interest of millions of Americans who did not have enough to eat. And it worked. We truly believe that when Americans are made aware of injustice in their own backyard, they will demand change from their leaders. When Americans equate ending hunger with patriotism, we know we will kick this thing once and for all.

⌇

Kristi Jacobson is an award-winning filmmaker and director/producer whose work has screened in theaters and festivals worldwide and has been featured on HBO, PBS, Channel Four/UK, ESPN, ABC, CSB, A&E, and Lifetime. Jacobson's 2007 film *Toots* won the National Board of Review's Top Documentary Award for 2007 and was selected as a critics' pick by the *New York Times,* the *New York Post,* and *New York Magazine.* Kenneth Turan of the *Los Angeles Times* called Kristi's debut feature, *American Standoff,* "deeply human . . . surprisingly heartbreaking." The film, examining the role of unions in modern times and the legacy of Jimmy Hoffa, premiered at the 2002 Sundance Film Festival and aired on HBO's award-winning *America Undercover* series later that year. Jacobson has tackled a wide range of subjects, including violence against women, HIV and AIDS, and the extreme sport of BASE jumping, and among her television credits are the 2004 Emmy-nominated and Cine Eagle Award–winning PBS series *Colonial House; Together: Stop Violence Against Women,* broadcast on Lifetime Television as part of its nationwide campaign to stop violence against women; and *E:60* for ESPN. Jacobson is a member of the Directors Guild of America and New York Women in Film and Television, and she was a 2009 Sundance Institute Creative Producing Fellow. She graduated summa cum laude from Duke University, where she studied sociology.

The *New York Times* called writer-director **Lori Silverbush**'s first feature film, *On the Outs,* "shockingly fresh" in its July 2005 review. *New York*

Newsday dubbed the film "a small miracle" and likened it to the films of directors Mike Leigh and Ken Loach. The film stemmed from a workshop she and her creative partners had led with incarcerated juvenile girls in New Jersey. After learning from her work with at-risk kids that many of them had experienced hunger or food insecurity throughout their young lives, Lori was motivated to learn more about the relationship between hunger and dysfunction in children. What she learned—that a clear link exists and that nearly 17 million kids in America are experiencing regular hunger in a nation with enough food and resources to feed them all—inspired her to action and led to *A Place at the Table,* her first documentary film. Lori has since adapted the German box-office hit *FC Venus* for Focus Features and is preparing to direct her next feature film, *Babylon,* about the drug culture and nightlife of American teens. Lori received her master's degree from New York University's Tisch School of the Arts and was chosen in 2000 to participate in the American Film Institute's Directing Workshop for Women, whose graduates include Maya Angelou and Joanne Woodward. Her thesis film, *Mental Hygiene,* won the Jury Prize for Best Short Film at the 2001 Deauville Festival for American Cinema and first prize in the *Marie Claire* Magazine Stop the Violence Film campaign, which traveled around the United States to help end violence against women.

Hunger in America, 2013

FOOD RESEARCH AND ACTION CENTER

Food Research and Action Center (FRAC) is the leading national nonprofit organization working to improve public policies and public-private partnerships to eradicate hunger and undernutrition in America. FRAC works with hundreds of national, state, and local nonprofit organizations, public agencies, and corporations to address hunger and its root cause, poverty. Here FRAC reports on hunger in America in 2013.

Millions of Americans struggled with hunger even before the Great Recession hit the United States. In the years 2000 to 2007, the country experienced an economic expansion as real GDP grew 18 percent. But this national prosperity did not "trickle down" to middle-income and low-income Americans. Middle-class incomes were largely stagnant over these years, and poverty rates rose from 11.3 percent to 12.5 percent.

During this time of overall economic growth, the shockingly high percentage of Americans living in what the government calls "food-insecure" households hardly changed. Even as the economy was growing up to 2007, large numbers of people were still struggling with hunger.

After the Great Recession hit in late 2007, many more Americans lost their financial footing and their ability to take care of basic needs, such as putting enough food on the table. According to the Economic Policy Institute, 8.4 million jobs were lost in the recession—"the most dramatic employment contraction (by far) of any recession since the Great Depression." Family incomes dropped, poverty rose, and many parents and children lost health insurance. In 2010 a startling 16.1 percent, or 49 million Americans, lived in households that were struggling with hunger.

Americans who are at risk of hunger don't live in just a few very rural or large urban areas of concentrated poverty; they live in places as wide-ranging as Dayton, Ohio; Asheville, North Carolina; Tulsa, Oklahoma; Riverside, California; and Orlando, Florida. In fact, these communities are all among the twenty-five top metropolitan areas in the United States with the highest percentage of people reporting to Gallup that there were times in the last twelve months when they couldn't afford enough food for themselves and their families. That's according to a 2011 FRAC report on food hardship that analyzes the Gallup data. This same report found that 15 to 25 percent of respondents in seventy-nine large metro areas and in forty-two states said that there were times in the past year when their household did not have enough to eat. The problem is also widespread throughout the country's congressional districts: 15 percent or more reported food hardship in 323 congressional districts in the 2010–2011 period. All told, the 2011 report finds that nearly one in five households struggle with food hardship.

Food hardship and food insecurity are technical ways of saying that people aren't getting enough to eat and that their health is being compromised by an insufficient diet. Here are a few things that might be happening in a household experiencing food hardship or food insecurity:

A mother who can't afford enough baby formula to last the month dilutes the baby's formula with water or expands it with rice cereal, and her infant is deprived of the full complement of nutrients that she needs for optimal development.

Two parents divide their own dinner to give their children a second helping so that the children don't go to bed hungry.

Families buy starchy, processed foods and forgo fresh produce, which is more costly and may not even be available in the markets or grocery stores in their neighborhoods.

The country's strongest and largest defense against hunger is the federal Food Stamp Program.

At earlier periods in US history—particularly through the Freedmen's Bureau after the Civil War and in the 1930s during the Great Depression—the federal government distributed food vouchers. But the modern Food Stamp Program began when President Lyndon B. Johnson signed the Food Stamp Act of 1964. He called the program "one of our most valuable weapons for the war on poverty." The program gives financially strapped households—including families, senior citizens, singles, and people with disabilities—more purchasing power so that they can buy enough food to eat balanced meals throughout the month. About half of those who benefit from the program are children.

During the 1960s, television documentaries, reports from civil rights workers, and testimonials by writers all shone a spotlight on largely invisible communities of hungry Americans and the ways in which chronic malnourishment had ravaged their health and bodies. For instance, civil rights workers in the Deep South found several communities of African American sharecroppers and tenant farmers living on the edge of starvation, surviving on diets of sugar, fatback, and starch. These diets resulted in the spread of nutritional diseases such as childhood rickets and pellagra—diseases formerly thought to exist only in the developing world. The 1968 CBS investigative report *Hunger in America* documented instances of severe child hunger and malnutrition among Mexican Americans in San Antonio, Texas, among families in rural parts of Loudoun County, Virginia, among Navajo households in the Southwest, and among African American families in Hale County, Alabama. *CBS Reports* also brought cameras, and viewers, into the pediatric units of hospitals. The cameras captured footage of babies who were so undernourished that they had hollowed-out, sunken cheeks, boney bottoms, skeletal arms, and skin that fell in wrinkled creases around their knees. Some of these infants were so underfed that they had even lost their ability to suck or to cry for food.

The outburst of attention in the 1960s and 1970s to America's hunger problem spurred Presidents Kennedy, Johnson, and Nixon to work with Congress to create or strengthen a wide-ranging mix of nutrition programs (including the Food Stamp Program). These programs have made a profound difference in the lives of many poor and near-poor Americans. Since the 1960s and 1970s, presidents, Congresses, states, and cities, recognizing the Food Stamp Program's capacity to respond quickly and robustly to human need and to local and national economic hardship, have invested the program with greater authority and flexibility so as to reach more eligible people, including more working families and more senior citizens. (There have been some exceptions: in 1981 and in 1996, Congress made harmful cuts to eligibility and benefits, some of which have since been restored.) Similarly, in the past few decades the national school breakfast and lunch programs have received the backing and support to grow in size and scope. Twenty years ago, only 30,000 schools offered school breakfast, but now nearly 90,000 schools work with the federal government to offer breakfast meals to children. Much of this effort to expand the reach of nutrition programs has been done on a bipartisan basis.

THE FOOD STAMP PROGRAM

In 2008 the Food Stamp Program became the Supplemental Nutrition Assistance Program (SNAP). SNAP provides those who are eligible with an electronic benefits transfer (EBT) card to purchase a specific amount of food. Individuals or households are generally eligible for the benefits if their income from sources like work or Social Security or unemployment insurance is below the cutoffs set by a mix of federal and state rules. The EBT card that participants receive looks like a typical credit or debit card. People can use it at participating grocery stores and farmers' markets to buy basic items such as milk, grains, fruit, meat, vegetables, and dairy products. They cannot, however, buy alcohol, cigarettes, preprepared meals like those sold in a grocery store "hot bar," vitamins, or household items like cleaning supplies.

The amount of benefits that a household receives is based on a complex set of rules that evaluate how much money the household has available to spend on food considering its income and expenses for items like child care, medical costs, and rent. The current maximum allotment is $200 a month for a single person and $526 a month for a family of three.

SNAP is a robust, responsive program because of its structure. Like Medicaid or unemployment insurance, it has no fixed cap on expenditures. It is an entitlement program that can grow to meet the needs of everyday people during financial crises and also during natural disasters. For example, disaster food stamp assistance was dispatched quickly to 770,000 households in 2005 after Hurricane Katrina slammed into the Gulf Coast. When Hurricane Irene and Tropical Storm Lee hit parts of the country in 2011, more than one million people received disaster food stamp assistance.

The Food Stamp Program also acts as a rapid and direct boost to the economy. The money is spent quickly on food, and so it is injected immediately into the economy, with positive multiplier effects. Mark Zandi, chief economist of Moody's Analytics, calculates that each dollar of added SNAP benefits adds $1.73 to the economy.

Of course, SNAP is more than an economic boost—it is a lifeline to seniors who live on a small fixed income, to those who have lost jobs, to those who are underemployed, and to those who work full-time but are not paid enough to support a household; in 2010, 41 percent of SNAP participants lived in a household with earnings. By giving people more purchasing power for food, SNAP helps protect the terribly limited funds of such households so that they can take care of other basic necessities such as rent, electricity, phone service, and medicine.

SCHOOL BREAKFAST AND LUNCH PROGRAMS

The magnitude and reach of the National School Lunch Program and the School Breakfast Program, which serve free or reduced-priced meals to children in public schools, make these enterprises critical partners in the national fight against hunger.

During the 2010–2011 school year the lunch program served meals to 20.3 million low-income children on an average day, and the breakfast program served 9.8 million low-income children. All of the meals are subject to federal nutrition standards—standards that were raised even higher by the "Healthy, Hunger-Free Kids Act of 2010." The updated guidelines require that the meals include more fruits and vegetables, more whole grain foods, less sodium, and low-fat, or fat-free milk.

SUMMER AND AFTER-SCHOOL NUTRITION

Many school districts also offer after-school nutrition through a federal program that provides snacks or meals for students who take part in after-school enrichment programs, academic clubs, and other activities. This food is offered at many schools and at public agencies like parks and recreation programs, as well as in other community settings such as boys' and girls' clubs and YMCAs.

A different federal program, the Summer Food Service Program, brings meals to children during the summer months. Like the after-school meals program, summer meals are provided through school districts, recreation centers, boys' and girls' clubs, and other children's programs.

WIC AND CHILD FOOD CARE

Whereas the school meals programs make sure that children have enough to eat at school, the WIC program helps ensure that there's enough for young children and babies to eat at home. WIC (officially called the Special Supplemental Nutrition Program for Women, Infants, and Children) helps pregnant women, postpartum women (whether using breast-feeding or infant formula as sustenance for their babies), infants, and young children have a sound nutritional diet. Women enrolled in WIC receive nutritional counseling and breast-feeding support, and they and the children receive vouchers for healthy foods.

The nutrition support offered by WIC is critical because young children, infants, and babies soon to be born are in a phase of rapid and tremendous brain development and growth. For example, by helping pregnant mothers eat right and eat enough, WIC helps reduce the number of low-birth-weight babies born to low-income women. Geraldine Henchy, director of nutrition policy with the Food Research and Action Center, explains why this effort is so critical: "Low-birth-weight babies are more likely to face lifelong complications such as learning delays and physical impairments. This is a high-risk condition with serious health consequences." The WIC program also helps decrease the incidence of iron deficiency anemia in children. "If you have anemia, you don't have enough oxygen-carrying capacity in your blood," says Henchy. "It means less oxygen being carried to your brain. Anemic children are more at risk for developmental problems."

The Child and Adult Care Food Program (CACFP) pays for food for low-income children in Head Start, child care centers, and family child care. It improves preschoolers' nutrition, reduces obesity, strengthens the quality of care, and, in some states, is the only monitor of family child care for many children. CACFP also makes child care more affordable for low-income parents who rely on these programs to provide a safe and healthy place for their children. The program serves about 3.3 million children on a typical day, but should be reaching many more.

We examine each of these government programs in greater detail later, especially Chapter 6 (the Food Stamp Program) and Chapter 9 (school meals).

PART I

ON THE FRONT LINES
OF HUNGER

CHAPTER 1

Witnesses to Hunger

DR. MARIANA CHILTON

FROM *A PLACE AT THE TABLE*

Since last March did you ever cut the size of your meals or skip meals because there wasn't enough money for food? How often did this happen?

> —*From Dr. Mariana Chilton's list of eighteen official*
> *government questions to establish whether a young*
> *Philadelphia mother should be considered food-insecure*

Mariana Chilton is the founder of Witnesses to Hunger, which works to in-crease women's participation in the national dialogue on hunger and poverty.

Some people might think that hunger is a moral problem. Some think it's political. Some consider it a mere economic problem. Although hunger is each of these, it is also a major public health problem. Not only does hunger hold us back today, but it will burden us for generations if we don't take bold action to treat and prevent it.

In the film, you see me interviewing a young woman with her son. I am asking her questions about depression, about her child's health, and about food insecurity. One of the questions is, "In the last twelve months, did you ever cut the size of your meals or skip meals because there wasn't enough money for food?" It's one of eighteen questions in the Household Food

Security Survey Module, taken from the US Department of Agriculture's Economic Research Service (ERS).[1] I was carrying out an interview for our Children's HealthWatch study, which is a multi-site research and surveillance study that investigates how public policies affect the health and well-being of young children under the age of four. The answers to my questions tell us whether the mother is "food-insecure" or has experienced depressive symptoms. Our research shows that, compared to young children in food-secure households, infants and toddlers in food-insecure households are:

- Thirty percent more likely to have a history of hospitalization
- Ninety percent more likely to be reported in fair or poor health
- Nearly twice as likely to have iron deficiency anemia
- Two-thirds more likely to be at risk for developmental delays[2]

These are just a few of the health consequences. (For more information on the effects of hunger on very small children, please see the Children's HealthWatch website, www.childrenshealthwatch.org.) The most significant of these is the impact that food insecurity has on child development. Any kind of nutritional deprivation, however short, in the first three years of life can have lifelong consequences for children. It affects their cognitive development and ability to get along with others, their stature, their weight, and their brain at a much deeper level.

In those first one thousand days of life, the foundation and architecture of the brain is built at a rapid pace. In fact, during the first few years of life, seven hundred new neural connections (or synapses) are formed each second. (For more information, visit the Center for the Developing Child website, http://developingchild.harvard.edu/.) Because good nutrition provides the building blocks for brain development, any type of nutritional deprivation can slow down or truncate brain growth, causing lifelong consequences. In addition, research shows that a child's development is not based on nutrition alone but also on the amount of interaction between the caregiver and the child. So if a family is food-insecure and the mom is depressed, the child is deprived of both essential nutrients and the social stimulation necessary for social and cognitive development.

After age three or four, that window for cognitive, social, and emotional development begins to close. Economists show that it will be far more costly to bring a child up to speed after that window of opportunity is gone.[3] Imagine the public health problems that are unleashed because of poor child development. Not only are such children more liable to poor health, but add the other grim possibilities—poor school performance, higher dropout rates, lack of job skills, low wages, depression, maybe prison, and/or more likely high-risk teen pregnancy, which begins the cycle of hunger and poverty anew.

In America, approximately one in four (nine million) young children under the age of six lived in food-insecure households in 2010. House-holds experiencing even more severe forms of food insecurity are those where parents limit the size and quantity of their children's meals or their children do not eat for a whole day because there is not enough money for food. Very few families ever admit that their children "go hungry," by these USDA standards. And some research shows that families do try to protect the youngest children from experiencing food insecurity, at the expense of others in the household. Back in 2006, approximately 0.4 per-cent of children under age six (140,000 children) were reported to be food-insecure at this level of severity.[4] During the economic downturn, this rate of severe food insecurity increased by 250 percent. Now there are 533,000 very young children who are at severe risk.[5]

All this happens without much public outcry or substantive political discussion and with no public acknowledgment from US government agencies. The American public can't "see" the problem, and the moms who know about it are so busy struggling to pull out of their predicament that they can't take the time to figure out how to advertise their plight. This is why the story of Barbie Izquierdo—one of the young mothers we took to Congress and the first mother to join Witnesses to Hunger—is so important. Consider her son Aiden, age two when filming started, who has displayed signs of speech delay. Barbie described her hunger to us, and how the struggle manifests itself in her children's behavior and in her depression. Thankfully, our social work team encouraged her to seek early intervention services, and Aiden is doing much better. So is Barbie. But imagine the millions of women like Barbie, and the nine million children under age six, who are in food-insecure homes.

Hunger doesn't happen just by itself, when everything else is fine. It happens when a family has to make a trade-off—pay for rent when they need to pay for food, or pay for heat rather than groceries.[6] Children's HealthWatch has shown that housing insecurity and energy insecurity (not being able to pay utility bills) are harmful to children's health as well, but our latest research shows that food insecurity is also related to making what we call health care trade-offs. Too often food-insecure families are not seeing a doctor, or not buying medicine, in order to be able to have money for food, or vice versa. Parents sacrifice not only their food in order to feed their kids but their own health.

In our work with Children's HealthWatch, a Philadelphia woman described the trade-offs she had to make to prevent her children's acute asthma attacks. After one of her children was hospitalized, she had to buy a nebulizer to deliver the asthma medication through a mist, yet had no funds. She said in her interview in January 2010 that she had to make the terrible choice of paying for a nebulizer, which insurance would not cover, or paying for food. She said she had to ask herself, "Do you want to breathe? Or do you want to eat?"

～

We started Witnesses to Hunger out of frustration at the way people continue to ignore hunger, try to deny it exists, or worse, are indifferent. The women we met through Children's HealthWatch and other research among the emergency food cupboards of Philadelphia were trying so hard to make it and to provide the best for their children. What our science didn't capture in the interviews was the anguish and sometimes the tears that a mother showed when she was answering our questionnaire. There was a lot of pain there. There was also a lot of energy, enthusiasm, grit, entrepreneurial spirit, and street genius. Yet these positive characteristics were being ignored and shut out from the halls of Congress.

As part of Witnesses to Hunger, my team and I gave digital cameras to forty-two women in Philadelphia, several of whom we met in the emergency room through our research with Children's HealthWatch. We asked them to take the lead in describing their experiences of raising their children and to give us their ideas for improving the systems meant to help them.

Now we have a traveling exhibit of their photos, a website searchable by woman, child, topic, or policy issue, and an expert speakers bureau of women who know hunger and poverty best. We visit politicians on Capitol Hill in Washington, DC, provide testimony, speak at press conferences, and run webinars.

Through Witnesses to Hunger, low-income mothers utilize their photos as a way to open the door to serious conversations on a topic so few people seem to want to discuss. Who best to inform the public and policymakers about how well the programs work than the participants in these programs and those who know hunger and poverty firsthand? And they do so without shame. They engage us with a strong dose of naked truth, expertise, and hope. As an organizing tool to get low-income people to solve the problems most important to their families and communities, Witnesses to Hunger can be started anywhere. It's also a way for the rest of us to pause, listen, witness, and engage.

The moms involved in Witnesses to Hunger have insisted that beyond speaking about policy change, they want to provide encouragement and support to other women and girls. We have started a woman-to-woman peer mentoring program to navigate the chaos of the social services systems in Philadelphia. In addition, the women have developed a tool kit that anyone can use to start Witnesses to Hunger in their own communities. Witnesses to Hunger currently reaches across the state of Pennsylvania—to Scranton, Harrisburg, Johnstown, and Clearfield County. Witnesses has also spread the word to Providence, Rhode Island, Martha's Vineyard Island in Massachusetts, and most recently Baltimore, Maryland, and Boston, Massachusetts.

Anti-hunger organizations can do more to ensure the participation of those who know hunger and poverty best, but it's hard work. It demands that nonprofits pay attention to those things that may not be part of their particular mission, but may be central to the larger mission of human development—the mission of experiencing a life worth living. When the women speak about nutrition assistance, they may also have other related troubles. For example, in the film you see Tianna Gaines, now the chair of the Witnesses to Hunger advisory board and a Witness herself, testifying at the Russell Senate Building about poverty and hunger in 2009. You might remember the way she looked out at Senator Casey, Senator Harkin, the other ladies of Witnesses, and the Senate staffers and said so simply and so powerfully, "This is . . . un, this is unnecessary."

Tianna was homeless at the time. So while some people may have thought she was doing amazing things, such as providing testimony to the Senate, Tianna was still returning "home" to her three young children and her husband in a musty, broken hotel room on the outskirts of Philadelphia. And if a woman so poised, so smart and savvy, could speak out in Congress, it *is* unnecessary—unacceptable—that such a person should be homeless.

At the opening of the photo exhibit of Witnesses to Hunger in December 2008, we had a full house despite torrential, freezing rains. Barbie Izquierdo was so thrilled to speak at the exhibit, but she went home afterward to an unsafe house that was imploding. Barbie lived in a house she could not afford to fix, a house located on a warring drug dealers' street, and that night rainwater from the leaks through the roof was spilling over the buckets she'd put out to catch it. In her basement was two to three feet of water. Her children's laundry was floating about in plastic bags, and the washing machine was covered in mud.

Such are the stories from Witnesses to Hunger that go way beyond hunger. They reveal the full experience of what it means to be a human being living in poverty. And they make us question our very humanity when we simply accept that so many among us, through no fault of their own, are so hungry and so poor.

Remember how Barbie's speech ends the film: Do you feel my hunger? Do you feel my pain? What she is saying is, I am no different than you. You and I are the same. We are a part of the human family. How can this not grip you? It's like looking in the mirror.

SOME URGENT PROPOSALS

Hunger knocks the breath out of you. But that doesn't mean we can't solve it. The primary solution is a comprehensive anti-hunger policy that can stimulate economic growth and protect our most vulnerable citizens.

The safety net works but needs urgent improvement. Children's HealthWatch has strong evidence that the safety net programs can help improve child health and well-being.

1. The Supplemental Nutrition Assistance Program (SNAP), the food stamp program, is an effective and efficient way to address and pre-

vent hunger. Children's HealthWatch research shows that SNAP benefits help protect child health.

- SNAP improves the odds that a child will experience healthy development.
- SNAP reduces the odds of severe and moderate food insecurity.
- SNAP is associated with a reduction in the odds of having to make a health care trade-off.

For more information, see our report "The SNAP Vaccine: Boosting Children's Health" at www.childrenshealthwatch.org.

2. The Special Supplemental Nutrition Program for Women, Infants, and Children (WIC) is a program for pregnant and lactating moms and for young children up to age five. A family must be at 185 percent of the poverty level or lower to be eligible. Shockingly, child poverty in our country is so high that 53 percent of babies (up to their first birthday) born today are participating in the WIC program.

- Children under age three who receive WIC benefits are more likely to be in excellent or good health compared to eligible children who do not receive WIC benefits.
- Receipt of WIC benefits is linked to a decrease in the risk of developmental delays in young children.
- WIC is associated with decreased levels of stress—a composite measure of food insecurity and depressive symptoms.

For more information, visit www.childrenshealthwatch.org.

3. Just as housing insecurity and energy insecurity are related to food insecurity and fair to poor child health, our research shows that programs that help to alleviate some of those stresses have a positive public health impact. The Low-Income Home Energy Assistance Program (LIHEAP) is associated with a decreased risk of food insecurity and poor child health, and children receiving housing subsidies have better growth outcomes than children in families who do not receive this benefit.

For more information, visit www.childrenshealthwatch.org.

So these programs can work—but they should be expanded, not pinched back. For instance, housing subsidies have long waiting lists, and the Housing Choice Voucher Program (Section 8) is so strapped for funding that even the waiting lists are closed in some cities. So while the "net" is there, it's hardly within reach of many of those who need it.

As Barbie explains in the film, SNAP allotments do not adequately cover the cost of food. Our research shows that in Philadelphia a family of four receiving the maximum allotment of food stamps—assuming no other income—would find it impossible to buy the items on the USDA Thrifty Food Plan on which the allotment allowance is based. For more information, see our report "The Real Cost of a Healthy Diet, 2011" at www.centerforhungerfreecommunities.org.

⌒

Many of us are trying hard just to protect the safety net that's there, but it's also time to re-envision a safety net that truly works and that doesn't penalize a family for trying to get out of poverty. Consider our most recent research that shows that families who are cut off from the SNAP program owing to a reported increase in income are more likely to experience child food insecurity. This happened to Barbie when she was offered a full-time job. No longer able to get food stamps, she said she was hungrier when she was working full-time than when she wasn't working at all. We don't give families enough time to adjust to working full-time and still look after their children, nor does the current policy give women any opportunities to begin saving money to build enough of a safety net of their own.

This is how we can have so many people working yet still going hungry in the United States. The minimum wage doesn't cover the cost of what it takes to keep a family healthy. So many large corporations and small businesses pay such low wages that their workers are still eligible for public assistance programs. And who foots the bill? American taxpayers.

Today this is the new American Promise: if you are born into poverty, your chances of getting out are slim.

MOVING BEYOND HUNGER

Nothing will change if our key government decision-makers do not recognize their duty to all Americans. The place to start is with a national plan conceived with the help of scientific experts and those who have experienced poverty firsthand. Until then, we'll just be feeding the problem, not solving it. To command that level of accountability, all of us must become more involved. We must not let up until we see a radically positive change in the amount that workers get paid and the way our public assistance programs work to help those living on the lowest wages. We must not let up until our political leaders respond to our requests to end hunger and allow our most vulnerable children to grow and to thrive.

We need to develop a national plan to end hunger in the United States through effective and efficient government programs, public and private partnerships, corporate accountability, and information-sharing with benchmarks and publicly accessible reporting mechanisms. This national plan should engage multiple players: government, corporations, the philanthropic community, health care professionals, nonprofit leaders, public assistance participants, unions, journalists, media personalities, teachers, and regular citizens. Considering the breadth of the knowledge and expertise of those who experience deep poverty and food insecurity, there should be a mechanism for allowing them to participate in the national dialogue.

We know what works—access to early childhood education, increased wages for parents, SNAP benefits, WIC benefits, safe and affordable housing. We have all the infrastructure it takes—why can't we get this done? Our efforts focused on poverty are as chaotic and vulnerable as Barbie's basement with the floating plastic bags, wires, and electrical outlets.

This is a national emergency, and yet, what is each of us doing to deal with it? What do we do every second that goes by while too many young children in this country are striving to make seven hundred more neural connections? Each second that goes by is an opportunity to break the cycle of poverty.

The film *A Place at the Table* is a true reflection of hunger in America. The well-known adage "we can judge a society based on how it treats its children" should be a warning to us all.

ↄ

Mariana Chilton, PhD, MPH, is an associate professor of public health at the Drexel University School of Public Health. She founded and directs the Center for Hunger-Free Communities. She is also the founder of Witnesses to Hunger, which works to increase women's participation in the national dialogue on hunger and poverty. Dr. Chilton carries out research with Children's HealthWatch to study the health impacts of food insecurity among young children age zero to four. Her work investigates the health impacts of nutritional well-being, public assistance participation, housing instability, and employment. She has testified before the US House of Representatives and the House and Senate Agriculture Committees to inform policy decisions regarding child nutrition. Dr. Chilton received her PhD from the University of Pennsylvania, her master of public health in epidemiology from the University of Oklahoma, and her bachelor of arts from Harvard University. Her awards include the Manna Nourish Award, the Young Professional Award in Maternal and Child Health from the American Public Health Association, the *Philadelphia Business Journal* "40 Under 40" Young Professional Award, and the National Lindback Award for Teaching Excellence.

Angel's Story

FOOD RESEARCH ACTION CENTER

To understand how families end up in the unhappy situation of skimping on food so as to pay rent, visit with a father like Angel. Angel, who is shy about sharing his last name, lives in Washington, DC, with his wife and two daughters. He and his wife are legal residents and their children are US citizens. Angel moved to the United States from El Salvador about twenty-five years ago, and he speaks English well enough to get by, but not well enough to land a high-skill professional job. He is a hard worker and a devoted family man, and the best job he can find is one stocking shelves and taking inventory thirty-five hours a week at a local grocery store. He wants to work more hours, but his employer keeps him at just under full-time.

Angel earns about $1,400 a month and spends $1,000 of that on his high rent. That leaves $400 a month for groceries for his family of four, clothing for his two girls, bus transportation, electricity, and other necessities.

Angel says that he knows cheaper rent would take some of the pressure off the family budget. However, rents are high in the city, and he doesn't know how to drive. That rules out a move to a more affordable home in the suburbs. More important, Angel wants to stay in the family's current neighborhood because he says it is good for his two daughters. His older daughter's elementary school, which she loves, is walking distance from home. His younger daughter will join her sister at the same school in about a year's time. Angel believes that the most important thing for his children is stability. To give his daughters that, the family continues to spend a prohibitive amount on rent and spends very little on food. For years the family has lived on a diet of eggs, rice, and beans. Angel could barely afford a few of the discounted vegetables offered at the grocery store where he works.

Things improved greatly for the family once Angel started visiting a counselor, named Carlos Merchan, at a local health clinic. Merchan works with low-income men and helps them become better fathers, providers, and family men. Merchan says that Angel, like many of the fathers he works with, was extremely anxious about the scarcity of food in the home. Most of the men Merchan works with hold low-wage jobs and don't earn enough to fully support a household. "They worry constantly about bringing in enough money to take care of their family's needs," says Merchan. "When they can't pay for it all, they feel like they've failed as men."

Angel, he observed, was so anxiety-ridden about food for his family that he couldn't move forward with any other area of his life. "You can't talk to a father about child development and the importance of reading to your child when that father is worried about having enough food in the house," says Merchan. "You have to help the family take care of the basics first." Merchan helped Angel apply for food stamps, and the family was accepted into the program. Angel talked about the difference that food stamps make in the life of his family: "I feel so good every time I open the refrigerator. There's meat, fish, and vegetables. There's fruit that the girls like—strawberries and grapes—and there's vegetables like broccoli and carrots." When asked what the family is now eating for dinner, Angel took a long, satisfied breath and described each meal with great affection and pleasure: "Ahhhh! We now have carne asada, fish fillets, and chicken breast! We have salad, too, and vegetables. All I can say is, 'Thanks be to God and to the government for food stamps!'"

Carlos Merchan says that SNAP benefits give families who live with great uncertainty in their lives some basic measure of security: "So much is uncertain in their lives. Will they still have their job tomorrow? Will they be able to afford a hospital visit if somebody gets hurt or sick? What will they do if the rent goes up? With food stamps, these families can count on one certain thing—they will have enough food for the kids." Merchan says that once families feel secure that one of their basic needs has been met, they can move forward with other parts of their lives. For example, now that Angel isn't as worried about food, he is starting to focus on a new project—learning how to drive. If Angel learns to drive, he might be better able to take on side jobs to help bring in more income. "Food stamps help families get some of their confidence back," says Merchan. "They feel more confident that things might get better in the future."

Food assistance like SNAP is critical because, like Angel and his family, millions of households simply don't have enough money for food. A recent report by FRAC called "A Tightening Squeeze" finds that the median household's spending on food, when measured against the cost of a diet for a low-income family, fell from 2000 to 2010. The report cites some factors that may be driving this unhappy statistic: stagnant or declining wages, rising housing prices, and food inflation. The trends for the median low-income household and the median black or Hispanic household were especially of concern: all three kinds of household spent a monthly amount on food that was not adequate to support decent nutrition and health, even as defined by the government's inadequate definition of the amount of food needed for an emergency diet.

When families, senior citizens, single adults, and especially children suffer food deprivation, the health repercussions can be brutal. Young children are especially vulnerable, and women who skimp on the quality and quantity of their meals throughout their pregnancies have higher rates of low-birth-weight babies, one of the most important factors linked to negative impacts on child development. Children who are hungry are more likely to act up in school, more likely to be absent or tardy, and more likely to repeat a grade.

So many Americans move in and out of joblessness or poverty that the SNAP safety net helps a surprisingly large part of the population. Professor Mark Rank of Washington University has estimated, based on a longitudinal analysis, that half of all children in the United States receive SNAP benefits at some time by age twenty, often for just a few months, and that half of all adults do so at some time between the ages of twenty and sixty-five. In short, the Supplemental Nutrition Assistance Program, which helps buffer vulnerable Americans from the creeping, insidious damage that malnourishment and hunger can wreak on their health, has helped a remarkable number of people over the years.

CHAPTER 2

Local Leaders

Colorado

BOB WILSON AND LESLIE NICHOLS

FROM *A PLACE AT THE TABLE*

The problem that we run into in small towns is that the income level has gone down, the jobs are minimal, and the second-and third-generation people are having to leave the area to find work.

—Bob Wilson, pastor, Plateau Valley
Assembly Church of God, Collbran, Colorado

Hunger definitely impacts my classroom. I have had students come to me upset, and it's definitely a huge issue in our small community.

—Leslie Nichols, teacher,
Plateau Valley School, Collbran, Colorado

I struggle a lot, and most of the time it's because my stomach is really hurting. Sometimes when I look at my teacher, I vision her as a banana, and everybody in the class is like apples and oranges, and then, I'm like, "Oh great."

—Rosie Carey, student,
Plateau Valley School, Collbran, Colorado

Collbran, Colorado, is a small town of about a thousand people, 98 percent white. It lies east of Grand Junction at the end of a small cattle ranching valley. In 1999 Pastor Bob Wilson opened a local soup kitchen. Leslie Nichols teaches fourth- and fifth-grade multi-age students.

YOU WANT TO DO WHAT?

Pastor Bob Wilson

"You want to do what?" That was my initial response to some of my church members who asked about starting a local food bank at our church, Plateau Valley Assembly of God Church in Collbran, Colorado. My questions were many. Is there a need? Can we afford it? How will it work? Little did I know what God had in store for our community.

After some discussion with church and community members in March 1999, we discovered that Feeding America is the largest national dispenser of food products to food banks, and they directed us to the regional Food Bank of the Rockies in Denver and the Western Slope Food Bank of the Rockies in Grand Junction, forty miles away. We quickly became a partner agency of the WSFB of the Rockies. The application process was quite simple, as was the inspection of our church facility, which would house the food bank. The process took only a matter of days, and we were soon up and running.

In 1999, our initial year, we distributed 27,000 pounds of food to our community; growing every year, we distributed 240,000 pounds in 2011. Did our community have a need? The numbers speak for themselves. We saw a substantial increase in need due to the economic downturn around 2009.

In 2011 our food bank was used 2,035 times total, which represents 322 different families—about 10 percent of our Plateau Valley community. The food bank serves on average about forty families per week— although we may be helping more because some families who use our food bank make meals for other families besides themselves.

Volunteers from the community are eager to participate. On average, ten community members help at the food bank each month, but one person volunteers fifteen hours each week. A typical Friday night at the Plateau Valley Assembly of God Church Food Bank resembles controlled chaos. You can find people in line up to two hours before distribution begins. Often families attend together and visit with neighbors while waiting for their turn to go through the food bank. Some items have to be limited, but we find that if you say, "Take what you want," people will take less, as they know they can come back and get more next week.

In addition to the food bank, we have started a backpack program for children whose families do not visit the food bank but whose children were lacking in healthy food for the weekend. Today we send out approximately seventy backpacks filled with a weekend's worth of kid-friendly food. We also have an after-school program, Kids' Time, which includes homework help, snacks, playtime, and Bible stories. Currently Kids' Time serves an average of twenty-one children each day. As Christmas approaches, kids can earn "Kid's Bucks" by helping clean up, doing their homework, or helping another child with homework.

"Why do we do all this?" you may ask. The answer is simple: it is what churches should do, and that is why we do it. We do this for the right to tell people about Jesus, not through our words but through our actions. Jesus fed the multitudes. He used food to get people's attention. It is a way to display God's way of taking care of people. It is a kind of outreach; letting people know that we care . . . that God cares. It is important to understand that you, too, can do this. It is the right thing to do.

MAKING A DIFFERENCE, EVEN THOUGH IT'S NOT PERFECT

Leslie Nichols

Half of Plateau Valley School's three hundred students are on free or reduced-rate lunches, and 10 percent, as fourth- and fifth-grade teacher Leslie Nichols puts it, "are in really tough situations." Once a week for the last five years, she has filled up twenty to thirty bags of groceries collected by Pastor Bob from the food bank. Now the number is double what it was three years ago. She's not a regular churchgoer, but she knew, as she says, "that was my purpose. I had an opportunity to make a difference."

Leslie grew up in a small town in southern Iowa in the 1980s. Her father was a park ranger who took other jobs to boost the family budget, but sometimes it was not enough. Growing up, she experienced the stigma of being on the receiving end of government assistance.

"I was one of those kids who was hungry . . . it was difficult. . . . I could see how difficult it was for my mother when she would return from the food bank. It was embarrassing. . . . I remember I was in second grade . . . and just opening the refrigerator for the first time in my life and going, Wow, I'm one of those kids, you know, you see on TV. There were two carrots in the bottom of the crisper, and I just remembered thinking, *What are we going to do?*"

Leslie didn't do all that well in school, and she "lived under this umbrella of feeling inferior to others. . . . It messes with you. It's just always there."

She tries to know the schedules of the families she's helping so she can just drop off the bags while they're out. "I know that they're thankful because it's gone when I come back." And she knows she's not always delivering the most nutritious food. The bags typically contain peanut butter, soups, and a lot of snacks.

"Sometimes, I will admit, I do feel a little bit guilty bringing them food bags, because it's starch, it's a lot of carbohydrates, it's lots of sugars and other chemicals."

She tries to stop the kids from eating the snacks at school. "It's hard—I'm trying to help them eat more with one hand, and often trying to stop them eating with the other. In a perfect world, you would want it to be as well balanced as you could make it, but the reality is, you get what you can, and giving something is certainly more than nothing, and so you just kind of find a little bit of, I guess, reassurance in knowing that you are making a difference even though it's not perfect."

Family Breakfast—At School

FOOD RESEARCH AND ACTION CENTER

Alsup Elementary in Commerce City, just north of Denver, Colorado, is a community with pockets of deep poverty where children experience hunger and malnourishment. It's home to a growing number of working-poor families and a fast-growing youth population: the number of children under eighteen jumped to 16,000 in 2010, from 7,000 in 2000. Eighty-six percent of the children in the school district are eligible for free or reduced-price school meals. The number of households receiving SNAP benefits in the county encompassing Commerce City has sky-rocketed since 2007. Over 10 percent of children in the school district are homeless. And many children are coming to school hungry.

The principal of Alsup Elementary School, Teresa Benallo, says, "In every one of our classrooms—and we have twenty-six classes in all—there are several kids who are coming to school hungry. It seems to happen a lot in our kindergarten classrooms." Alsup Elementary serves breakfast in the classroom. This is a special type of federally funded school breakfast: it's offered free to all, and it's built into the regular school day, rather than being served in the cafeteria before class begins.

When Alsup Elementary started breakfast in the classroom, Teresa Benallo noticed that her students stopped getting into fights and stopped acting out in the mornings. Benallo says the reason is simple: The children feel cared for. "School breakfast gives our kids that 'family at the table time' that some may not get at home. If you walk into our classrooms, the feeling is, 'Okay, we're all coming together to enjoy our meal.' It's quiet and focused, and kids are snacking on their yogurts and cereal bars." Benallo says that the breakfast sets a positive tone for the rest of the

academic morning and students are more focused on learning. What Benallo has observed in her classrooms, researchers have found in their data:
Children who take part in a school breakfast program that's available to
all kids show improvements in school attendance and punctuality and decreased anxiety, hyperactivity, and depression. Research also shows that
low-income children who eat school breakfast have a better overall diet
than those who eat breakfast elsewhere or skip breakfast.

School breakfast and lunch also help prevent childhood obesity, a condition that is linked to adult-onset diabetes and chronic high blood pressure. Children who eat school breakfast and lunch are more likely to
consume fruit, vegetables, and milk at breakfast and lunch and are less
likely to have nutritional inadequacies. Research also shows that girls who
live in homes that are not food-secure and who eat school breakfast and
lunch are less likely to be overweight than girls who live in such homes
but who don't eat the school meals.

This particular advantage of the program is critical for communities
like Commerce City, where many children are overweight or obese. The
reasons why many of this community's children are hungry and obese
are manifold. Low-income families may only have access to cheaper,
starchy food, and it may be all they can afford. Families often don't have
many options as to where they can buy food; the county that encom-
passes Commerce City has eleven food desert census tracts, according
to federal data. The built environment in parts of Commerce City also
conspires against children and families who want to get outside and walk,
skate, bike, or do other outdoor activities. Several highways and four-
lane corridors cut through town, making it difficult, and even danger-
ous, to walk to certain parks and public sites. Many streets have narrow
sidewalks, while other streets have no sidewalks at all. Some streets aren't
even paved.

Teresa Benallo says another reason so many children are overweight or
obese is that they are eating calorie-packed junk food. The school breakfast and lunch programs help interrupt these unhealthy habits, she says, by
demonstrating to students that there is a healthier and more delicious
way to eat. Many of the lunches that Alsup Elementary serves are home-
made and include lean beef taquitos, salad, baked potatoes flavored with
rosemary, and macaroni and cheese mixed with squash.

The lunches served at Alsup Elementary are a snapshot of the fresher, healthier meals to come when all schools across the country embrace and follow the new federal nutritional standards. Some school districts are a few steps ahead and have already transformed their school kitchens into places where meals made with fresh produce, whole grains, and home-made sauces are cooked up on a daily basis. Other school districts are just starting to try out such meals. As school cafeterias move toward health-ier, more appealing meals, more and more children and teenagers will start getting in line for school breakfast and school lunch.

CHAPTER 3

The Grocery Gap

Finding Healthy Food in America

ALLISON KARPYN AND **SARAH TREUHAFT**

FROM *A PLACE AT THE TABLE*

We have about three grocery stores in Jonestown, Mississippi, but it's hard getting some of the things, like when you want fruit, no store sells fruit. Chips and ice cream and cakes, they have that here. They have lots and lots of stuff like that here. And that's why I go to Clarksdale sometimes for grocery shopping, or Batesville, about a forty-five-minute drive. For those that don't have transportation, it's hard. Maybe one store will have a few bananas. They have vegetables, but it's in the can. I love fresh vegetables and fruits. It's very frustrating they don't have it here.

—Ree Harris, Jonestown, Mississippi,
mother of four boys who works as a short-order cook

There's this thing called a food desert. So out in the county you have these mom-and-pop shops, and they don't have fruits and vegetables. There are several issues. . . . The big eighteen-wheelers deliver to Wal-Mart and Kroger and these other chains, but they don't go through the back roads. . . . You know, they're off the beaten path . . . they don't fit the business model, maximum delivery, minimum cost. And so we're consuming what's available to us.

—*Dr. Alfio Rausa,*
Mississippi State Department of Health

Access to healthy foods is a challenge for many Americans, but especially those living in low-income neighborhoods, communities of color, or rural areas. A 2009 US Department of Agriculture study found that 23.5 million people do not have a supermarket within a mile of their home. Low-income zip codes have 25 percent fewer chain supermarkets and 1.3 times as many convenience stores compared to middle-income zip codes. Predominantly black zip codes have about half the number of chain supermarkets compared to predominantly white zip codes, and predominantly Latino areas have only one-third as many. In rural areas the issues that give rise to the so-called food deserts are low population density, longer distances between retailers, and the rapid rise of super-centers and their impact on other food retailers. In the Mississippi Delta, over 70 percent of households eligible to receive food stamps need to travel more than thirty miles to reach a large grocery store or supermarket. Jonestown, Mississippi, with a population of around 2,000 people, 96 percent of whom are African American, is in the northwestern part of the state that has the highest rate of food insecurity in the nation. Mississippi also has the highest rate of obesity. Allison Karpyn, director of research evaluation at the Food Trust in Philadelphia, and Sarah Treuhaft, associate director of PolicyLink in Oakland, California, explore the rise and prevalence of food deserts.

An apple a day? It might depend on where you live.

The United States produces about 10 billion pounds of apples each year, yet many Americans can't buy an apple in their neighborhood. In thousands of communities across the country—particularly low-income communities, communities of color, and rural communities—it is virtually impossible for residents to follow government guidelines for eating well because there are no decent grocery stores selling fresh, nutritious food. The same places are often bombarded by an overwhelming variety of fast-food restaurants and convenience stores selling high-fat, high-sugar, processed foods.

Consider these examples:

More than 30,000 people live in West Oakland, California, but there is not a single supermarket within its eight square miles. What the community does have in abundance is liquor stores. Fifty-three of them to be exact.[1]

In the Germantown neighborhood of Quincy, a Boston suburb, 3,200 residents must travel eight miles to reach a supermarket.[2]

In rural Kansas, nearly ninety small-town grocery stores have closed in the wake of the Great Recession, leaving many residents without a store within ten or even twenty-five miles.[3]

In 2009 the US Department of Agriculture tallied up the number of communities across the country facing similar situations. They found that 23 million people did not have a supermarket within a mile of their homes and that 13.6 million people lived in 6,529 "food desert" communities that were both low-income and lacking in sufficient access to a supermarket or large grocery store (i.e., a store with annual sales of $2 million or more). They found that food deserts existed in every state in the continental United States and in all types of communities—from large and small cities to older suburbs and rural areas.[4]

This isn't simply a matter of convenience—food deserts represent a public health emergency. People living in neighborhoods without good sources of healthy foods have a harder time eating a nutritious diet. In turn, they suffer from higher levels of obesity and other diet-related illnesses. Obesity is now the leading cause of death in the United States. If current trends continue, one in every three Americans will have diabetes in 2050.[5]

And the most vulnerable children face the greatest risks. Children from low-income families are twice as likely to be overweight as those from higher-income families, and black and Latino children are about twice as likely to be obese compared with white children. (Obesity rates in these groups are 20 percent, 24 percent, and 12 percent, respectively.[6])

Because of these poor health conditions, babies born today in the United States are likely to live shorter lives than their parents—an unprecedented slide backward.

What happened? How did things get this way? What are the consequences? And what can be done about it? This chapter tells the story of America's grocery gap. It is based on our organizations' experiences working to improve access to healthy food in communities across the country, as well as our collaborative research, including our review of more than 130 studies of the grocery gap and its impacts on health conducted over the past two decades.

For many years, residents in the communities abandoned by supermarkets have organized to bring stores back, often with very little success. But recently there have been signs of change. Communities are developing new solutions to the grocery gap challenge, and their innovations are gaining momentum. A new cooperative grocery store with fresh affordable produce from nearby farms opened in West Oakland in 2009 after five years of planning. A mobile market is now bringing fresh produce to Germantown.

Efforts to open new grocery stores are under way in rural Kansas. Many of these initiatives have been spawned with assistance from the "fresh food financing" programs of partnerships between governments, investors, and community organizations that have been formed with the mission to bring healthy food into underserved communities. These partnerships are based on a successful Pennsylvania program that has become a national model.

WHERE DID ALL THE STORES GO?

I grew up near Frank School, a treasure trove of neighborhood stores. There were at least six small grocery stores within a few blocks, most of which were owned by Italian families, and all were great. There was Fasulo's, Travanty's, Capelli's, Pacetti's, Pasqualli's, and on and on up and down Twenty-Second Avenue and Fifty-Sixth Street.[7]

—*John Collins, Kenosha, Wisconsin, resident*

If you go to one of the communities identified as a food desert on the USDA's map and talk to longtime residents about their grocery store situation, you are likely to hear that it was not always so bad. Until about sixty years ago, most neighborhoods were home to a mix of independent "mom-and-pop" grocery stores, butchers, fish markets, and vegetable stands. But this picture changed dramatically after World War II. John Collins's town of Kenosha, for example, had 126 groceries in 1950, but only 60 by 1970, and 37 by 1980.[8]

Both the postwar wave of urban decline and suburban growth—helped by housing, transportation, and banking policies—and the major shifts taking place in the grocery industry contributed to the changing neighborhood grocery landscape.

In the 1960s and 1970s, white middle-class families left urban centers in droves to move to the suburbs, reacting both to the push of urban decline and the pull of good, government-backed mortgages and new suburban homes with yards. Supermarkets and other businesses followed them. Between 1968 and 1984, for example, Safeway closed six hundred of its inner-city stores.[9]

Without new investment and residents, urban neighborhoods declined precipitously, becoming more and more isolated, and decline was especially pronounced in urban communities of color, which were "redlined" from receiving bank loans and investment until the practice was outlawed in 1970. City officials' failed revitalization schemes often made the situation worse rather than better. Urban neighborhoods also became more racially segregated, since the suburbs were not initially open to African Americans and other people of color.

During the same postwar time period, the grocery industry continued to change from being primarily made up of small, independently owned grocers to being dominated by large supermarket chains. Food retailing is a notoriously competitive business, and beginning around 1920, grocers began shifting from small full-service stores to larger self-service stores to increase their profits. The first supermarket, King Cullen, opened in Queens, New York, in 1930, and with it arrived a new business model based on the volume of sales instead of the price of goods.[10] The model took off—during the 1950s alone, supermarkets doubled their share of the food retail market from 35 to 70 percent[11]—and it particularly flourished in the suburbs.

Land was abundant and cheap, and suburbanites owned cars, so they could drive to do their shopping. Stores grew larger and larger, averaging 45,000 square feet by 2000.[12]

Once the supermarket business model had suburbanized, it became extremely hard to go back into dense urban neighborhoods or spread-out rural areas. Development costs were higher in urban areas because land was expensive and cities had more regulations. Labor costs were also higher because, with fewer residents owning cars, customers were accustomed to making frequent, smaller shopping trips, which led to longer lines but lower per customer receipts.

Misinformation—and sometimes a lack of information—about market opportunities also played a role.[13]

Without nearby supermarkets—or the transportation to get to more distant ones—residents became captive markets for a limited number of small stores offering lower-quality goods at higher prices and with less variety. Myser Keels, who led a coalition that brought a supermarket to West Fresno, explains:

> We want choices. Some poor people use public transportation, and they don't haul all the groceries they need on the bus. And if they call a cab, the fare alone can put them in the hole. . . . It's just a tragedy that we don't have a decent shopping center in our area.

WHO DID THEY LEAVE BEHIND?

The grocery gap phenomenon is widespread across the country, and where it shows up is predictable rather than random. The story of the grocery gap is a chapter in the larger story about inequality in America. It is about how some neighborhoods provide many opportunities for their residents to live healthy and productive lives, while others seem to conspire against good health and economic success. And it is about how policies and business decisions play a role in shaping life opportunities.

Dozens of studies by academic researchers as well as community organizations have documented that fewer supermarkets or other stores selling affordable, high-quality, nutritious food are located in poor communities, communities of color, and rural communities. According to a national study by public health researchers at the University of Michigan, low-income neighborhoods have half as many supermarkets as wealthy neighborhoods, and predominantly black neighborhoods have four times fewer supermarkets than predominantly white neighborhoods.[14] A study by the New Mexico Food and Agriculture Policy Council found that the same market basket of groceries costs $85 for rural residents and $55 for urban residents.[15]

Some researchers have gone beyond using supermarkets as an indicator of access to healthy food and have surveyed the selection, quality, and prices of food sold in neighborhood markets. They find that the stores in low-income communities and communities of color are less likely to stock healthy foods, they offer lower-quality items, and they have higher prices compared to stores in communities that are higher-income or predominantly white.

Dr. Manuel Franco's research on Baltimore's neighborhood food availability provides an example. His team of Johns Hopkins University researchers surveyed 226 stores across 159 Baltimore neighborhoods for availability of healthy foods. They found that nearly half of the stores in low-income neighborhoods had low availability of healthy foods, and that Baltimore's black residents were about five times more likely to live in a neighborhood with low healthy food availability compared to the city's white residents (24 percent compared to 5 percent). Their in-store surveys showed that even the supermarkets in low-income and African American communities offered fewer healthy foods than the supermarkets in other communities.[16]

These sort of detailed studies begin to paint a clearer picture of the reality of the grocery gap, but they still don't explain what it is like to live in a place where the most basic and fundamental goods cannot be found. For that, one must speak with actual food desert residents. And when you do, you hear a lot of things that run counter to everyday mythology about the habits and behaviors of poor people.

A few years ago, PolicyLink partnered with Michigan State University to research the challenges to increasing access to healthy food in Detroit and Oakland and the policy opportunities in doing so. To understand resident perspectives about food, we spoke with more than 150 residents in supermarket-poor neighborhoods, including African Americans, Mexican and Vietnamese immigrants, youth, and elders. They told us that they cooked most of their meals at home (with the exception of the youth), that they wanted to improve their diets, and that they wanted convenient access to fresh, affordable, high-quality ingredients to prepare healthier meals at home. Almost all of them were dissatisfied with their food shopping options and felt that not being easily able to find the food they wanted in their neighborhood markets was inequitable and unjust.

Many knew that there were better options in nearby neighborhoods. A Detroit resident who drove through the suburbs every day to get to work described how "the grapes aren't as big, the cherries aren't as red" in the stores in the city compared to the suburbs. An African American woman living in West Oakland explained: "Yes, there's a difference in the stores in our area compared to the stores in Montclair or somewhere else [in the Oakland Hills]. You know, the vegetables are great up there, everything is so beautiful. And you come down, I think we get ours last off the truck."[17]

HEALTHY FOOD = HEALTHY PEOPLE

The lack of healthy food is not only unjust; it has serious health consequences.

Decades of public health research have shown that neighborhood environments influence the health of residents. Examining forty-five years' worth of life expectancy and other data, the Alameda County Public Health Department found that someone who is black and born in West Oakland is five times more likely to be hospitalized for diabetes and twice as likely to die of heart disease, and can expect to live fifteen fewer years than a white person born in the Oakland Hills.[18]

A burgeoning subfield of research looks more specifically at the "food environment": how the presence or absence of stores selling healthy foods or an overabundance of unhealthy foods affects resident health. How does this happen? Without nearby access to healthy ingredients, people have a harder time meeting recommended dietary guidelines for good health, such as eating fruits and vegetables and lowering their fat intake. In New York's East Harlem neighborhood, four out of every ten residents surveyed said that they did not follow the recommended dietary guidelines because the necessary foods were less available and more expensive in their neighborhood stores.[19]

Data analyses of the eating habits of people living in areas without supermarkets prove this point. A study of adults in North Carolina, Baltimore, and New York City found that those with no supermarkets within a mile of their homes were between 25 and 46 percent less likely to eat a healthy diet than the people with the most supermarkets near home.[20] Another found that adults living in rural Mississippi counties without large supermarkets were 23 percent less likely to consume the recommended amounts of fruits and vegetables compared to those living in counties with supermarkets.[21]

On the flip side, study after study has shown that greater access to supermarkets or healthy foods in neighborhood stores corresponds with healthier eating. One very well-respected study found that for every additional supermarket in a neighborhood, produce consumption increases 32 percent among African Americans and 11 percent among whites.[22] A survey of produce availability in New Orleans's small neighborhood stores found that for each additional meter of shelf space devoted to fresh vegetables, nearby residents eat an additional 0.35 servings per day.[23]

In addition to making it possible—and even more likely—that residents will eat healthy diets, greater availability of healthy foods corresponds with better health outcomes, including lower levels of obesity or overweight, diabetes, and cardiovascular disease.

Adults living in neighborhoods with supermarkets or with supermarkets and grocery stores have the lowest rates of obesity and overweight.[24] And analyses of California and New York find that people who live in neighborhoods where fresh food markets outweigh convenience stores and fast-food restaurants have lower rates of obesity.[25]

All of this research suggests that making affordable, healthy foods more available to underserved residents will lead them to make healthier choices about what to eat and result, ultimately, in better health for them.

HEALTHY FOOD = HEALTHY COMMUNITIES

Beyond the benefits to individual health, grocery stores and other fresh food markets contribute to the overall health of neighborhoods and local economies and can catalyze revitalization and investment in distressed neighborhoods.

Grocery stores and supermarkets are known to be economic "anchors," meaning that not only do they supply significant numbers of local jobs (averaging one hundred to two hundred per supermarket) but they generate additional economic activity in the area. Think about a grocery store located in a shopping center: your main trip might be to the grocery store, but if a hardware store and a toy store are right next to the grocery store, you may stop there as well. Smaller groceries, cooperatives, and farmers' markets can also generate foot traffic for other small neighborhood businesses. Farmers' markets and public markets are also important public spaces where social and educational activities often take place.

When communities don't have grocery stores, their residents must drive, take the bus, or catch rides to stores located in other neighborhoods. In addition to the inconvenience and added transportation expense, a lack of grocery stores also leads to what economic development experts call "leakage": residents spend their money outside of their neighborhood and their dollars do not support local businesses and local jobs.

Brahm Ahmadi, who has been working to start a full-service grocery store in West Oakland, talks about these lost economic opportunities a lot. He estimates that $6 to $7 of every $10 that West Oakland residents spend on food is spent outside the neighborhood's small stores—adding up to $35 million to $45 million in annual leakage.[26]

According to the Food Marketing Institute, the average supermarket has about $25 million in sales annually.[27] Ahmadi's market research suggests that multiple grocery stores could thrive in West Oakland.

The presence of a high-quality grocery store is also a staple of a good neighborhood—and the absence of one is a symbol of distress. When new markets open in long underserved neighborhoods, they can change the perception that the neighborhood is not a good place to do business. They can also bolster neighborhood housing values and create value for low-income homeowners. A study of the impact of new supermarkets on neighborhood housing values in Philadelphia found that the value of houses located between a quarter-mile and a half-mile from the new store increased by 4 to 7 percent after the store opened.[28]

WHAT'S BEING DONE TO BRING STORES BACK?

As soon as supermarkets disappeared, residents began organizing to bring them back, but it was often a fruitless effort. As Lucinda Hudson, long-time activist and neighborhood association president in Philadelphia describes the situation: "For three decades, we pushed and cried and prayed for a supermarket. . . . No businesses would open here."

Now the tide is beginning to turn. Policymakers, public health agencies, foundations, and community groups have begun to recognize that addressing the grocery gap can improve physical and economic health in the most vulnerable communities. Beginning to see the business opportunities in underserved communities, grocers are adapting their practices to meet the needs of a more diverse customer base. And a supportive policy and financing model—the Pennsylvania Fresh Food Financing Initiative (FFFI)—has emerged that can help overcome the biggest impediment to opening new grocery stores in food desert communities: the lack of start-up funding.

Thanks to that model, Lucinda Hudson's neighborhood finally got a supermarket in 2008 when Jeffrey Brown opened the eleventh store in his regional Brown's ShopRite chain in her Parkside neighborhood. Today that store is doing just as well as any of the suburban stores in the chain and selling just as much produce—busting the myth that a supermarket couldn't survive in the neighborhood, as well as the myth that its residents wouldn't buy produce if they had the opportunity to do so. Brown says he couldn't have opened the store without the program's assistance.

The Pennsylvania Fresh Food Financing Initiative is an innovative public-private partnership that helps entrepreneurs develop grocery stores, farmers' markets, and other food retail options in underserved low-income neighborhoods by providing them with onetime loans and grants. It officially began in 2004, but the seeds for the initiative were sown in 2001 after a task force formed to explore ways of expanding access to affordable, nutritious food in areas with high childhood obesity rates and low supermarket penetration recommended a statewide initiative to fund fresh food retail development. State representative Dwight Evans championed this recommendation, and with the support of other key legislators, the Pennsylvania General Assembly appropriated $30 million in economic stimulus dollars over three years to create the Fresh Food Financing Initiative (FFFI). A community development financial intermediary, the Reinvestment Fund, matched $30 million in state economic stimulus dollars with more than three times that amount in private capital, building a pool of funds to support food retail development in underserved communities throughout the state.

The results are impressive: eighty-eight new or improved grocery stores and other healthy food retailers in Pennsylvania's underserved low-income and working-class cities and rural areas, 5,000 full- and part-time jobs created or retained, and more than 400,000 residents with improved access to nutritious food. The Pennsylvania FFFI has supported many different types of fresh food markets, including grocery stores, corner stores, co-ops, and farmers' markets. It has been lauded by the US Centers for Disease Control and Prevention, the National Conference of State Legislatures, and the National Governors Association as an innovative model for improving public health.

Recognizing FFFI as a model that could be adapted to fit their own needs, California, Illinois, and New York State, as well as the city of New Orleans, have launched their own fresh food financing efforts. Many more states—Arizona, Colorado, Georgia, Illinois, Louisiana, New Jersey, Maryland, Massachusetts, Minnesota, Mississippi, Nebraska, Tennessee, and Texas—are developing programs to provide start-up funding for new food ventures.

And in 2010 the federal government took the model nationwide by launching the Healthy Food Financing Initiative (HFFI). Like the Pennsylvania program, HFFI is a public-private partnership that seeks to expand access to nutritious foods and create jobs by helping food retailers open or expand in underserved urban, suburban, and rural communities. It is a partnership between the Department of Agriculture, the Treasury Department, and the Department of Health and Human Services.[29] Since its launch, $77 million has been allocated for HFFI and projects improving access to healthy food, and the president's proposed budget for 2013 includes an additional $285 million for the program. HFFI has won wide support from diverse groups, including community developers, civil rights activists, public health experts, children's advocates, and the National Grocers Association.

Fresh food financing initiatives are a policy idea whose time has come, and there is tremendous momentum at the local, state, and national levels to establish these funding pools and other policies to support retail development in underserved communities. But the scale of the problem still dwarfs the scale of the solution. Much more start-up funding is needed to truly spur the innovation in business models needed to eliminate all 6,529 food deserts. Other policy strategies are also needed to address the grocery gap. For example, at the local level, zoning and land use plans and policies should encourage fresh food retail as well as food production in underserved areas. And at the national level, the Farm Bill was up for reauthorization in 2012, and it should support programs, including HFFI, that bring nutritious food into food desert neighborhoods.

CONCLUSION: MUCH MORE THAN A STORE

A grocery store doesn't just bring food to a neighborhood, it can create an environment of possibility that spills over into the entire community.

—*Jeff Brown, CEO of Brown's ShopRite supermarkets*

Sometimes a grocery store does much more in a community than sell food: Sometimes it actually changes lives. The store that opened in Parkside brought about three hundred jobs to the neighborhood. But there is more. Brown did not just hire residents—he hired residents who were having the hardest time finding work, including forty people who were formerly incarcerated. Brown partnered with two area nonprofits to run a job training program targeted to veterans, formerly incarcerated residents, and women seeking independence from public assistance.

Brown has done other things to link the store to the community. Before opening the store, his team met with community groups, neighborhood associations, and church groups to find out what they wanted the store to carry. As a result, the store stocks a variety of halal products (food and other products permissible under Islamic law) used by the neighborhood's large Muslim population and African food staples to meet the needs of its West African residents. The store is also made available as a meeting space for community groups—for free.

Parkside's success is truly a "win-win-win"—for Brown as a business owner, for the community in terms of having its grocery needs met, and for the community's most vulnerable residents who are now in good, stable jobs. Not every grocer is like Jeff Brown, and not every store is like ShopRite. But with winning programs such as the Fresh Food Financing Initiative in place, many more can be.

⁓

Allison Karpyn is director of research and evaluation at the Food Trust in Philadelphia. She also works as an adjunct professor at Drexel University, Thomas Jefferson University, and the University of Pennsylvania.

Sarah Treuhaft is an associate director at PolicyLink in Oakland, California. She is an urban planner who works with local and national partners on research and action projects to create more opportunity-rich communities.

CHAPTER 4

A Top Chef Goes to Washington

TOM COLICCHIO

FROM *A PLACE AT THE TABLE*

Probably six or seven hundred chefs here are really committed to helping this problem that we have with childhood obesity and hunger. . . . Let's fund school programs at a spending level that significantly raises the quality and variety of what schools can afford. . . . The dollars haven't changed since 1973. We need to get better, nutritious foods in school, and the only way to do that is by increasing the amount of the reimbursement.

> —*Tom Colicchio, producer of the popular TV program* Top Chef, *giving evidence to a House of Representatives committee hearing on school lunches, 2010*

Senator, I think it's important to focus on what the cost of inactivity might be. And as you well know, Senator, from your experience, you fund your priorities.

> —*Tom Vilsack, secretary of agriculture, giving evidence to the same committee, 2010*

Every five years, Congress reauthorizes the Child Nutrition Act, which determines funding and guidelines for school meals. In June 2010, Rep. George Miller, a Democrat of California who was chairman of the House

Committee on Education and Labor, opened a session to discuss new leg-
islation to "address critical health and economic needs in this country."

Among the experts called was Secretary of Agriculture Tom Vilsack,
who told the committee, "A country as strong, as rich, as powerful as
ours—and yet we have youngsters who are hungry. It's one of the reasons
why Harry Truman, in 1946, established the school lunch program, because
he recognized that a country was only as strong as its youth." Also testify-
ing before the committee was Tom Colicchio, an award-winning chef, the
producer of Bravo's Top Chef, *an executive producer of* A Place at the
Table, *and a longtime campaigner to eliminate hunger among kids in*
America. Recently, he challenged his colleagues to cook the most nutri-
tious school lunch on the federal budget of $2.68 per child. Colicchio, who
was appearing before Congress for the first time, told about his work on
Top Chef *and his upbringing in a family of Italian Americans in Elizabeth,*
New Jersey. Here is his testimony.

Ladies and Gentlemen of the Education and Labor Committee:

I am here today to express my support for the Improving Nutrition for America's Children Act sponsored by Chairman Miller
and to urge you and your fellow representatives to do everything
in your power to find the funds to push this crucial piece of legislation through.

I'm wearing a few different hats at this hearing today: First off, there
is my public one; as host and judge of a popular television program
[*Top Chef*], I find myself in the slightly surreal position of being able
to comment on issues of importance to me to a public willing to listen. I've decided to use this to the advantage of the millions of American children who rely on school, preschool, after-school, and summer
feeding programs for adequate nutrition, who don't have lobbyists
with deep pockets at their disposal advocating on their behalf.

I'm also before you as a chef. Once upon a time my job wasn't public at all—we stayed in the kitchen cooking, and then early the next

morning we trolled the farmers' stalls and fish markets to choose the day's food. Nobody gave a hoot what we had to say, just what we sent out on the plate. Today that's changed a bit, and chefs are frequently called upon to cook at fund-raisers for food pantries and food-based charities to help meet the needs of those who struggle with hunger. As a group, we chefs have never been more active and never raised more money than we do now, and yet studies show that more people are hungry or food-insecure in this country today than at any other time in history. It's frustrating, and has spurred me to ask . . . *why?*

I'm here, too, as a business owner. At my restaurants, I have dozens of employees working long hours, often more than one shift. I understand how urgently many of them need to know that their kids are receiving healthy nutrition at the schools and day care centers where they spend a big part of each day. It is hard enough to make a living in today's economy; no working parent should also worry whether their child has had enough to eat. I am encouraged that Chairman Miller's bill allows for additional meals for children who are in day care longer than eight hours, as so many are, or spending time in after-school settings. In addition, Chairman Miller's bill makes important strides to ensure that low-income kids don't go hungry during the summer months when school is out.

I'm here before you as a father to seventeen-year-old Dante and eleven-month-old Luka. My kids, like kids everywhere, are more than happy to slurp down junk food and empty calories—pizza, sodas, candy, and deep-fried anything. But the fact that they would eat this whenever doesn't give me permission to shrug my shoulders and say, "Well, that's what they want!" It's my job as a parent to make sure they have a variety of real, nutritious foods served to them at every meal so that they grow into robust, healthy kids capable of meeting their full potential in life. And yet, I hear people say, "We'd like to improve school lunch, but all the kids want to eat are pizzas and burgers. If we give them good food, they won't eat it."

Come on, people! We're the adults. It's up to us to do better. My kids would also happily live in front of the Xbox and never take another shower as long as they live. Not gonna happen. When I give them healthy, delicious food, they eat it, with gusto. On a recent *Top Chef* episode, we challenged our contestants to prepare healthy, nutritious lunch for schoolchildren here in DC that was also delicious. What do you know? The kids ate it, happily, and they asked for seconds and thirds.

I'm also here before you as the son of a "lunch lady." My mother, Beverly Colicchio, worked for decades as a cafeteria supervisor in Elizabeth, New Jersey, where I was born. Elizabeth is not a wealthy town, and at the high school where she worked, almost 70 percent of the students qualified for free or reduced-price breakfast and lunch. My mother told us that often the meals she served those kids were the only food they got all day. It was upsetting to her that the budgetary constraints imposed by low federal reimbursements meant that the schools couldn't afford much in the way of fresh fruits and vegetables, whole grains, legumes, and high-quality proteins. The cheapest food, contracted out to the lowest bidder, was usually what was on the menu, and the kids who ate it didn't have the option of refusing. On a diet that may have met nutritional guidelines without being truly healthy and whole, we expect our kids to learn, behave, socialize appropriately, and develop into healthy teens and adults, and we are quick to label and punish them when they don't. Without regular exposure to real food—made from whole ingredients in a variety of textures, shapes, and colors—these children never develop a preference for healthy food and thus perpetuate the cycle of poor nutrition that can lead to a lifetime of costly and debilitating health problems like obesity and diabetes, not to mention their lost potential as active, healthy citizens. Schools today are forced to supplement their meager budgets with vending machines that supply empty calories from soft drinks and junk food. I ask you: How many of you here today would be content to let the bulk of your children's daily calories come from soda, chips, or branded fast food? And yet, we are sitting by and allowing that to happen for families who are struggling and relying on us to do better. As thinking adults, as fellow parents, this is an egregious abdication of our responsibility toward kids, and if it is at all within our means to fix it—and I believe it is—then I urge you now to make it right.

Let's fund school lunches and breakfasts at a spending level that significantly raises the quality and variety of what schools can afford and get rid of the junk food in vending machines once and for all. Let's fund healthy snacks and meals in day care centers and after-school programs. Let's expand access by broadening area eligibility requirements for summer feeding programs and expanding direct certification to eliminate redundant paperwork for families and schools.

There can be no better investment—no better stimulus to our economy—than feeding this nation's children healthily and well. If we give the kids in this country delicious and nutritious food, we will instill in them a lifetime preference for healthy eating that will translate into vast savings in health care costs down the line. Providing the building blocks for millions of kids to grow and develop as they should will mean a population of robust and productive adults and a more competitive America. Malnourished kids aren't capable of vision and ideas, and without that we are relegating this great nation to a future of mediocrity and poor health. I think we can do better, and I urge you today to get behind Chairman Miller's bill and make it happen.

Thank you.

The bipartisan House bill, which called for an increase of $8 billion over ten years, passed, but when it was taken up by the Senate, the increase was cut almost in half—to $4.5 billion. The Senate version, known as the Healthy, Hunger-Free Kids Act, was passed by the House and signed into law by President Barack Obama in December 2010.

Anti-hunger groups praised the key provisions of the new act, which broad-ened the after-school meal program to cover all fifty states (previously it cov-ered only thirteen) and generally improved access to—and the quality of—school meals. But they were disappointed that, despite their heavy lobbying, the extra $4.5 billion had come from cuts in the Food Stamp Program, where costs were rising. They pointed out that this was the second time Congress had raided funds from the Food Stamp Program in 2010, the first time being to fund states to pay teachers' salaries and Medicaid benefits. The overall result was a 10 percent cut in food stamp benefits. Anti-hunger groups vowed to fight the cut.

CHAPTER 5

Money Where Our Mouths Are

KEN COOK

FROM *A PLACE AT THE TABLE*

In the 1930s into the 1950s, and even a little bit beyond that, I think you could make the case that it really was family farmers who were mostly benefiting from these [federal] programs, but as the agricultural sector became more concentrated in terms of ownership of the land resources, more and more of these operations came to resemble agribusiness and not family farming.

—Ken Cook, president and cofounder of the
Environmental Working Group

We are spending $20 billion a year on agriculture subsidies for the wrong foods; $20 billion would go a very long way to promoting a healthy, educated population, starting with kids.

—Marion Nestle, professor of nutrition, food studies, and
public health at New York University

In 2012 Congress debated the new Farm Bill. House Republicans pressed hard to continue generous subsidies for the agriculture industry and, at the same time, make drastic cuts to the bill's funding of food stamps for the poor. Here, Ken Cook, whose Environmental Working Group (EWG) is a longtime watchdog of the Farm Bill, traces its evolution from the Great Depression to the present.

"If you had a dollar, where would you put it?" asked Tom Vilsack with the confidence of a politician who knows exactly how Washington works—or more precisely, how it would be working henceforth in the Obama era.

It was March 2009, the early, heady days of the new administration, in which Mr. Vilsack served as the freshly confirmed secretary of agriculture. The topic at hand: the first budget the White House submitted to a new, overwhelmingly Democratic, and presumably like-minded, Congress.

"Would you give it to a child for more nutritious eating?" the secretary rhetorically inquired. "Or would you give it in a direct payment [farm subsidy] to a high-income operation?"

The president's budget had, of course, answered his questions: it proposed cutting billions in farm subsidies, targeting reductions to the largest, most prosperous farms in the country, which had in most cases been receiving them for decades. The savings would help boost spending for programs aimed at feeding and improving nutrition for low-income kids.

The entire proposition amounted to something of a no-brainer in those times—or so Secretary Vilsack more than implied.

It was hard to argue with him. After all, while the rest of the economy spiraled downward into the then-unknown depths of the Great Recession, the farm economy was booming by any measure. As unemployment in the rest of the economy lurched up above a sickening 10 percent, crop prices and farm incomes were regularly setting new all-time highs. Residential real estate values vanished in the pop of the Wall Street bubble, leaving millions of homeowners underwater on their mortgages and triggering a surge of personal bankruptcies and foreclosures. Down on the farm, land prices shot upward in double digits, setting record prices year after year and leaving farm balance sheets healthier than they'd ever been. Car companies on the brink of insolvency desperately sought federal bailouts, and long-established car dealerships shut their doors. Farm equipment companies, meanwhile, couldn't keep up with demand, and their dealers could scarcely keep a tractor or combine on their lots.

Most tellingly, as the general economy rotted and sagged, the rolls of the last remaining federal welfare assistance programs, the Supplemental Nutrition Assistance Program (SNAP, formerly known as "food stamps") ballooned. Enrollment eventually surpassed 49 million people—one in seven Americans, half of them kids, now tragically qualified under the program's brutal means test. How brutal? If, as a family of three, you earn more than about $24,000, you're generally too well off for SNAP. So dire was the situation that a few months later, when the stimulus legislation passed, it contained a significant, multibillion-dollar boost in spending to bolster the assistance offered under SNAP.

By comparison, roughly $5 billion in direct farm subsidy payments wastefully kept flowing from the treasury to the very farms that were enjoying the most favorable economic conditions in American history. Over 60 percent of that taxpayer money went to the top 10 percent of beneficiaries (and as usual, 60 percent of farmers received no subsidies at all).

So, faced with the choice Tom Vilsack posed at the start of the Obama administration, where did America end up putting that dollar? Hungry kids or the biggest, most profitable farms in the country?

⸙

Taxpayers shelled out more than a quarter of a trillion dollars for various federal farm subsidies between 1995 and 2010. But to characterize this staggering sum as a big government bailout or welfare would be manifestly unfair—to bailouts and welfare.

Bailouts, after all, are short-term loans. Whether the beneficiaries are car companies or banks too big to fail, taxpayers usually get their money back in a few years—with a dollop of interest paid on top.

Welfare recipients are subjected to stringent means testing. Both a time limit on benefits and work or training requirements are commonly imposed on able-bodied applicants. In return, beneficiaries collect modest government benefits that are more or less the same for everyone in the program.

With crop subsidies and crop insurance, it's none of the above.

Those hundreds of billions of dollars weren't emergency loans; they were cash payments made directly to individuals from Uncle Sam.

As for means testing, in the world of farm subsidies you're disqualified if your adjusted gross nonfarm income tops $500,000 (almost ten times the average income for U.S. households) or your adjusted gross farm income exceeds $750,000. By "adjusted" is meant income after all deductions, and even then you can still qualify for commodity loan programs that often result in cash payments anyway (if the farmer defaults on the loan). The subsidized crop insurance program, in which taxpayers cover 60 percent of the farmer's annual policy premium on average, has an altogether different income threshold. Bill Gates could qualify.

What about the time limit on farm subsidy benefits? The limit is whichever comes first: forever, or the government money runs out. The work requirement has its nuances: for some subsidies you need not farm at all, while for others someone has to, it just doesn't have to be you. Owning all or part of the operation from afar will suffice, even if you never get your boots dirty. To be clear, the US Department of Agriculture has cracked down on one nagging problem with absentee owners in recent years: the USDA assures Congress that almost none of the subsidies paid to dead farmers are improper.

And does everyone receive more or less the same amount from the government, as is the case with SNAP (whose average monthly household benefit is under $300)? Not at all. Crop subsidies are paid on a per-bushel or per-pound basis. Technically, several programs have limits of $40,000 per person per year. But the rules are so malleable, and so weakly enforced, that big farms face essentially no barriers to absorbing federal money on each and every bushel of grain or soybeans, or every bale of cotton, they grow. As a consequence, the vast bulk of federal farm subsidies concentrate in the hands of a relative few, very large farming operations growing five favored crops: corn, wheat, rice, cotton, and soybeans.

We know this to be the case because my organization, Environmental Working Group, began filing a series of Freedom of Information Act (FOIA) requests in the early 1990s that enabled us to publish the amount of money each farm subsidy recipient collected between 1995 and 2010 in a massive online database (at http://farm.ewg.org).

The top farm subsidy recipients have collected tens of millions of dollars (leaving aside co-ops, some of whose larger farm operations have collected millions individually). The top 10 percent of federal crop subsidy beneficiaries hauled in 76 percent of the money over that period, averaging $447,000. The top 1 percent (about 28,000 agribusiness operations) received 26 percent of the money, about $1.5 million apiece on average, at a total, mind-numbing cost to taxpayers of $42.7 billion.

So deeply rooted and routine have these payments become that nowadays most recipients can't be bothered cashing paper checks. The USDA electronically zaps the funds directly into their checking accounts year after year, the way many of us auto-pay our mortgages. The comparison is made even more apt by one well-documented effect of subsidies: the income stream boosts the value of the land to which the subsidies are attached, by some estimates as much as 20 percent. Of course, when we pay our mortgage, we're building equity in our property. When we pay farm subsidies, we're building equity in someone else's.

From a program that began in the Great Depression as a desperate and, in my view, noble effort to provide emergency aid to millions of farm families who had a shot at earning a decent living on the land, farm subsidies have strayed over the last eighty years to become a largely dysfunctional entitlement. Farm supports most notably enrich a small group of very big, expanding, and well-heeled landowners who now control a good share of the country's land. For most of their history, farm subsidies helped farmers weather their own success. Crop producers adopted yield-boosting technologies apace, which made them ever more efficient at maximizing their output. They chronically overshot demand for their corn, wheat, cotton, and other commodities, and prices and incomes regularly plummeted as a result. The government stepped in with a variety of tools over the decades: we've tried direct cash payments, loans, production controls, export subsidies, storage payments, and a whole range of instruments through which Washington bought surplus food to help clear the market, then gave it away—as with the original Food Stamp Program (which is now a cash benefit) and the ongoing Food for Peace foreign aid program (which would deliver a lot more and cost a lot less if the aid was provided in cash to support farmers in the afflicted regions instead of as American corn, wheat, and rice shipped on US vessels).

Today students of farm subsidies consider the system downright elegant by comparison to its ancestral forms. That's a clear sign we've been studying them far too long. By any detached and sober appraisal, farm supports remain a sui generis contraption that might have sprung from the fevered antigovernment fantasies of Tea Party cynics if Congress hadn't actually cobbled it together first.

With the passage of the 2007 energy bill and the 2008 farm bill, Congress managed to devise an interlocking maze of subsidies that, taken together, force taxpayers to spend billions of dollars no matter what the condition of the farm economy. First off are the "direct payments" that go out to farmers and landowners even if crop prices and farm profits are setting record highs—and most such records have been set in the past few years—or even if the recipient plants no crop at all. Direct payments have averaged around $5 billion per year since 2005.

Next are the "countercyclical payments" made when crop prices fall below a level set in law by Congress. These payments have declined from about $4 billion in 2005 to $200 million in 2010 because crop prices have been higher than average over those years. "Market-loss" payments comprise another layer of crop subsidy that slows to a trickle when prices are robust but can gush from the treasury by the billions when prices dip. The last time that happened (just a few years back), farm subsidy costs topped $20 billion in one year.

The taxpayer cost of yet another subsidy subsystem, the federal crop insurance program, mushroomed from $2.7 billion in 2005 to more than $10 billion in 2010, precisely because prices were high. As crop prices increase, so do the government's premium subsidies, as well as the subsidies it pays to crop insurance companies for administrative and operating costs. And since taxpayers also pay a portion of crop insurance claims, the costs we incur for any crop losses climb when crops are more valuable.

Even after the bitterly contested 2010 Affordable Care Act's reforms eventually take effect, most crops will fairly be said to have better, and certainly more affordable, "health" coverage than many people in this country—and for crops it is more or less single-payer coverage at that (the single payer being you, the taxpayer). Taxpayer-subsidized crop insurance is available to farmers if their crop is eligible for coverage in their area, and it provides, at no cost, 50 percent catastrophic coverage to farmers. (Most farmers opt for a higher level of coverage, which is subsidized but not free, so the average premium subsidy is 60 percent.) Over one hundred crops are covered, but in 2008 just four crops—corn, cotton, soybeans, and wheat—accounted for more than two-thirds of the total acres enrolled in crop insurance and for the vast majority of subsidies through the commodity programs.

Small wonder that since 1995 America's crop insurance program has cost taxpayers $45 billion. Nor was it a surprise that by 2011, as the subsidy lobby retreated from direct payments, which went from embarrassing to indefensible during the prolonged commodity boom, a new, shamelessly avaricious idea took their place. Commodity groups proposed federally subsidized "shallow loss" revenue insurance, a program that would lock in, at taxpayer expense, as much as 95 percent of the business income crop farmers enjoyed during the recent record-setting years. It is the culmination of a trend that has seen "crop insurance" morph into revenue insurance, which these days accounts for over 80 percent of the taxpayer-subsidized policies. The plan was to pay for this breathtakingly generous new entitlement by siphoning off some of the funds that would be saved by the "reform" of ending direct payments, which actually had been scheduled to end in 2002.

While the rest of the country has been caught up in populist anger over government spending, the farm subsidy lobby has had considerable luck launching big government programs that would be unthinkable in other sectors of the economy. Let's put it this way: if you believe the federal government has an important role to play in the nation's economic life, admit it, you're a liberal. You're just not as liberal as the average Republican member of the House Agriculture Committee.

〜

As the farm policy debate raged throughout 2007 and 2008, corn growers made a point of saying that the farm legislation they were focused on would not be coming out of congressional agriculture committees at all, but from the energy committees. Sure enough, the 2007 energy bill featured exactly the kind of top-down, government-picks-a-winner mandate that conservatives of every stripe routinely decry. By 2015, the law decreed, Americans would have to put 15 billion gallons of corn ethanol in their gas tanks annually, a scheme designed to absorb as much as 40 percent of the country's corn crop, keeping prices strong. Accompanying tax bribes—I mean, breaks—were extended to gasoline blenders to defray the cost of adding that ethanol to gasoline, at a price tag of about $5 billion a year (about what we've spent on direct payments).

Since not even those government props have been sufficient to keep ethanol profitable, the ethanol lobbyists have been laying siege to Capitol Hill and the White House to ratchet up the mix of ethanol in gasoline by 50 percent, from 10 percent to 15 percent ethanol. In early 2012, they succeeded. Next will come a demand to expand the 15 billion gallon annual corn ethanol mandate to 20 billion gallons or more. The corn ethanol lobby has also sought a federal version of subsidies that some state legislatures have already been talked into providing: money for the equipment changes that will enable gas stations to pump higher ethanol blends—up to 80 percent ethanol. Not even the gas stations want that subsidy.

One thing government farm subsidies have reliably produced, other than ingratitude and a sense of entitlement among their recipients, is a demand for more subsidies. Commodity crop agriculture, for decades now a virtual ward of the federal government, offers fresh proof of that maxim each year. The ensemble of ethanol subsidies and the proposed new scheme for "shallow loss" revenue insurance are but the latest examples; many other handout proposals are in the offing as Congress takes up the next farm bill.

Noticeably, by 2011, Congress had lost a good deal of its enthusiasm for ethanol—the special interest that had long had its way with politicians of both parties on the Hill. The $5 billion ethanol tax credit for gasoline blenders expired, for instance, despite an all-out campaign on the part of corn and ethanol interests to extend it that was voted down in the Senate. Erstwhile congressional champions of corn ethanol as the hoped-for "bridge to the next generation of advanced biofuels" finally began to ask pointed questions about promises made during the 2007 energy bill negotiations—namely, that corn ethanol gradually would give way to fuels made from algae, switchgrass, and other supposedly sustainable feed stocks. (It didn't help the ethanol lobby's case when, in a lapse from the industry's "bridge" story line, a prominent official with the corn growers was caught deriding biofuel alternatives as "unicorn" fantasies.) Legislative riders to appropriations bills registered strong congressional opposition to subsidies for ethanol-friendly gas pumps, cotton subsidies, and payments to millionaire farmers. Direct payments were pronounced "dead" whenever Congress took up the next farm bill.

Taken together, if subsidies as we've known them for generations haven't hit a wall, they have at least hit some speed bumps.

When Tom Vilsack came to town in 2009 to serve under Barack Obama, he had the audacity to hope that Washington would see the sense in withholding scarce taxpayer money from some of the country's most profitable farmers, who, without our help, and while the rest of the economy was in the tank, were getting wealthier by the day. He further assumed that the country would devote some of the savings to help the recession-swollen ranks of poor and poorly nourished kids, many of whom live in households where hunger is part of life's routine and for whom the only reliable (if less than healthy) meal each day is the subsidized lunch they receive at school.

The early signs were promising. The American Recovery and Reinvestment Act of 2009, otherwise known as the stimulus bill, increased SNAP funding by $20 billion, mostly by increasing benefits, and added another $300 million to help state governments cope with the program's swelling enrollment. Most economists saw that investment as the single most effective quick boost to the economy in the entire stimulus bill, as at-risk families immediately send their newly increased benefits ricocheting through the food system.

However, the massive SNAP investment in the stimulus bill did not represent the kind of trade-off that Secretary Vilsack described. Vilsack's choice of where to put a dollar was more directly offered a year later, when Congress took up the renewal of the national school lunch program. To most experts, it is the ideal place to intervene in the food system to produce better results for America's health and fairer, more efficient support for American agriculture—in particular, for farmers who grow the fruits and vegetables all of us should be eating more of, especially our kids.

And talk about a crisis. Consider all the attention paid in recent years, from the White House to Wal-Mart, to the need to reduce the damage that the American diet is doing to our spreading girth and diminishing health. Heart disease is on the rise, diabetes is epidemic, and diet-related cancers are prime targets for preventive health care.

Most disturbing of all, America's kids are increasingly both overweight and malnourished. Children in low-income households have a very good chance of being both hungry and obese. These are precisely the people who would benefit from reform of the national school lunch program, which operates in more than 100,000 schools and provides free or low-cost meals to more than 30 million children every day. We had a remarkable opportunity to intervene as a society and get our kids hooked from the start on healthy food and healthy eating when the school lunch program was up for review in Congress in 2010. But a successful intervention was going to cost money—billions of dollars more per year than we've been spending so that we could serve kids lunches with more fruits, vegetables, and other healthy fare.

A mountain of research shows that the country would have saved many more billions than we invested, because healthy school lunches reduce the lifetime medical costs of diet-related illness and boost the economic productivity that comes with a healthier workforce. En route to those long-term gains, we'd have kids who are happier and perform better in school—especially poor kids, many of whom simply would not get nearly enough to eat without school lunch.

So what happened? Congress did pass a new school lunch law, and that law did make some laudable improvements. But funding for the legislation was woefully far short of what was needed to fix school lunch. President Obama, aided by the star power advocacy of first lady Michelle Obama, had proposed adding $1 billion per year to the program—a sum considered minimal to the task at hand by experts in child nutrition.

As the Senate considered the measure, the Obama administration had a clear opportunity to propose a boost to school lunch money for poor, hungry kids that would be paid for by cuts to farm subsidies—in particular, the disgraced $5 billion direct payment program that was showering money on a white-hot farm economy. My organization published analyses showing that modest cuts to direct payments (confined to the biggest recipients) and crop insurance could have provided the $1 billion that President Obama sought and more. Bolder cuts would have yielded an even better outcome for kids, the economy, and taxpayers.

Neither Mr. Vilsack nor anyone else in the Obama administration said a word.

In the end, the school lunch bill that Congress sent to the president's desk authorized less than half the increase he requested. And guess how the legislature of the richest country on Earth found the money to pay for that embarrassingly small investment in our children and our future?

By cutting into the funds that had been added just a year before to SNAP. Thankfully, budgetary sleight of hand largely preserved the benefits, but the program was undermined all the same.

It was as if Secretary Vilsack had asked, "If you had a dollar, where would you put it? Would you give it to a child for more nutritious eating? Or would you give it . . . to a child for more nutritious eating?"

The critical question here is not where the Obama administration was during this fight. They were where political machines can always be found: in a backroom counting votes. The real question is: where was the food movement?

Where were the legions of passionate locavores when local kids had a shot at tasting local greens from a school salad bar? Where were the armies of disgruntled parents who had a chance to speak out on behalf of a plate half covered in fruits and vegetables, as the USDA recommends, instead of a ladleful of oversalted slop from the lunchroom steam table? Where were the critics of industrial agriculture and factory farms when the freezer truck backed up to the grade school cafeteria loaded with chicken nuggets, tater tots, mystery meat, surplus cheese, and chocolate milk?

The lesson here is painfully simple. If "civilians" (as in taxpayers) don't stand up in politically significant numbers to demand different priorities, the farm subsidy lobby and other vested interests will maintain their iron grip on spending for programs that those in the food movement don't support. At the same time, the entrenched lobbies will slash or block investments in healthy eating and conservation and nutrition assistance.

Not nearly enough of us are ringing the phones, firing off emails, or darkening the doorsteps of politicians who, left to their own devices, as we've seen, will readily conclude that America can't afford to feed kids better at school—poor kids in particular—beyond a bit of money scraped together out of another program that feeds those same poor kids at home.

We face the same disconnect between the broadly shared values within the food movement and our ability to give political voice and power to those values in the looming federal budget fights. What is at risk? Federal nutrition assistance programs for low-income Americans, international food aid, food safety enforcement, an array of programs that support local food initiatives, conservation of land and water, the survival of small and medium-size family farms . . . just about any policy or program you could think of that is in support of the "good food movement" is on the chopping block.

If you were to interview any food shopper, whether they were strolling through a farmers' market or a supermarket, or if you surveyed the leaders of any of the hundreds of public interest organizations working to reform our food system, I'm betting they would agree with every one of the following values—and probably many more.

> No child should go to bed hungry or poorly nourished, at home or around the world.
>
> We should be safe from food-borne illness, we should be able to know where our food comes from, and we have a right to know what's in it.
>
> Our food and diets should be a source of health and well-being, not ill health and disease.
>
> The food economy should be one of opportunity, and its workers should be fairly compensated.
>
> Farm animals should be treated humanely.
>
> Agriculture should regenerate and protect the environment, not degrade it.
>
> Fresh, local, affordable food should increasingly be a commonplace, not a novelty, in American agriculture.

In order for the food movement to find the political voice we still clearly lack, we have to find ways to work together on the many values that unite us. Until we do, Mr. Vilsack's principled choice—hungry kids or big-time farm operators—will be one of those "hypothetical questions" politicians in Washington are always telling us they refuse to answer.

Which is exactly why those are their favorite questions of all.

Ken Cook is president and cofounder of the Environmental Working Group (EWG), a public-interest research and advocacy organization that uses the power of information to protect human health and the environment. The author of dozens of articles, opinion pieces, and reports on environmental, public health, and agricultural topics, including Mulch, a blog about food and agriculture policy, Cook is regularly listed as one of Washington's top lobbyists by *The Hill* (the Capitol Hill newspaper). Cook was named the "Ultimate Green Game Changer" by the Huffington Post in 2010, and in 2011 he was listed as one of the "Seven Most Powerful Foodies in the World" by journalist and food movement icon Michael Pollan. Cook is a frequent source of environmental perspective and commentary in national print and broadcast media. Regularly quoted by the *New York Times,* the *Washington Post,* the *San Francisco Chronicle,* and other papers, Cook has also made frequent appearances on the *News Hour with Jim Lehrer,* CBS's *60 Minutes,* National Public Radio, and the evening newscasts of ABC, NBC, CBS, and CNN, among other programs. Cook earned BA (history), BS (agriculture), and MS (soil science) degrees from the University of Missouri–Columbia. He is a board member of the Organic Center and the Amazon Conservation Team. Cook lives with his wife, Deb Callahan, and their son in San Anselmo, California.

CHAPTER 6

Food Stamps

Once We Had It Right[1]

GUS SCHUMACHER, MICHEL NISCHAN, AND DANIEL BOWMAN SIMON

FROM *A PLACE AT THE TABLE*

There are people who are living on that food stamp allocation and you really can't. For us, it was an exercise that ended in a week. For millions of other people in this country, that's their way of life; every day is a struggle, just to eat.

—*US Rep. James McGovern of Massachusetts,*
who lived on food stamps for a week

The intent of the original 1939 Food Stamp Plan was to provide help to those in need so that they could purchase "surplus" agricultural products (pears, butter, cheese, milk, potatoes, snap beans, whole wheat flour, for example) that the secretary of agriculture wanted to support. The program, originally backed across the political spectrum, shifted over the years from one forged by common sense to one that primarily benefits already subsidized commodity crops and the processed foods derived from these crops. Gus Schumaker, Michel Nischan, and Daniel Bowman Simon trace the history of America's first line of defense against hunger.

The original 1939 Food Stamp Plan was guided by common sense. The approach was: since we have an agricultural surplus and it is imperative to help farmers get by, we might as well make sure that surplus gets to the families who are hungry. It was the perfect combination of good intentions and good sense, or empathy and economics. But something went badly wrong. Today, no one knows exactly which foods those who receive food stamps buy with their government assistance, but what little data is available suggests that much of it goes to buying artificially cheap, highly processed prepared foods such as instant rice, instant noodles, hamburger-pasta meals without the hamburger (meat is expensive), and bagged snacks to quiet hungry children from morning to night.

In the intense debate over whether SNAP programs make for healthier diets, some want to stop food stamp recipients from buying foods and beverages of minimum or no nutritional value—foods that lead to obesity. Those in opposition argue that consumer freedom is paramount, that such modifications to the program punish low-income people, and that more effective ways to address obesity are available. In short, the government shouldn't act as "food police," even if the funding for the program is coming from government coffers.

We decided to look at the early history of the Food Stamp Plan. Why was it called "food stamps"? Why was this plan supported by liberals and conservatives alike? Why, over time, did conservatives and liberals join together in sometimes selfless acts of bipartisanship when it came to the well-being of our nation's disadvantaged families and farmers? Why did the system shift from what seemed to be one forged by common sense to one that primarily benefits already subsidized commodity crops and processed-food companies? Finally, how might we now find ways to recapture some of that original common sense to benefit American farmers, the American economy, and American citizens living at or below the poverty level?

⚮

Under the headline "$1.50 in Food for Dollar," an article in the *Washington Post* on March 14, 1939, explained the new food stamp program. For each dollar of orange stamps purchased, an unemployed person would get an additional 50 cents in blue stamps. Orange stamps were good for any grocery items, except drugs, liquor, and items consumed on the premises. Blue stamps would buy only surplus foods—dairy products, eggs, citrus fruits, prunes, fresh vegetables.

The first healthy-food incentive program was born. And the government had a say in what could be purchased with food stamps. On September 26, 1939, the *New York Times* announced the list of approved foods for blue stamp purchase. It included butter, eggs, raisins, apples, pork lard, dried prunes, onions, except green onions; dry beans, fresh pears, wheat flour and whole wheat flour, and cornmeal. Fresh snap beans were designated as surplus for October 1 through October 31.

In December 1939, the USDA's Milo Perkins, coordinator of the Food Stamp Plan, told farmers the new Food Stamp Plan would improve farm income as well as the public health. "For fresh fruits and vegetables there is a tremendous potential market."[2] He envisioned that people with limited economic means, given purchasing power, would buy "trainload after trainload of citrus, tomatoes, cabbage, peaches and other fruits and vegetables."[3] The government, Perkins said, was "interested in the Stamp Plan as a means of helping local producers in the area around which the program is in effect."

By May 1941, First Lady Eleanor Roosevelt, vacationing in Maine, reported in her popular syndicated "My Day" column that ten Maine cities and towns already had the Food Stamp Plan in operation. "In the near future, 125,000 needy people in Maine will have the opportunity to increase their food consumption through the use of the free blue surplus stamps," she wrote. "This is an important step in long range national defense. Our nutrition problems have been great and we are only just beginning to understand that the Government must assist people from the economic and educational standpoint, in order that we may remedy some of the defects which we now know exist in the feeding of our children."[4]

And what better program to see that children were appropriately fed? Throughout this early Food Stamp Plan, truly fresh produce was the aim. In July 1941, at the height of the growing season in many states, all fresh vegetables were placed on the surplus list while canned and frozen vegetables were excluded. At the same time, according to an article in the *Herald Statesman* (of Yonkers, New York) from August 8, 1941, "soft drinks, such as ginger ale, root beer, sarsaparilla, pop, and all artificial mineral water, whether carbonated or not," were removed from the Plan. Retail food merchants were warned not to sell those items for either orange stamps or blue stamps. However, natural fruit juices, "such as grapefruit, orange, grape or prune," were not considered "soft drinks" and could still be sold for orange stamps.

Newspaper accounts from that era do not reveal any public or political kerfuffle over the removal of soft drinks from the list of items that food stamps could buy. As reported in the *Atlanta Constitution*, according to a nationwide poll conducted by George Gallup himself in November 1939, the majority of Americans—rich and poor, Republican and Democrat— overwhelmingly supported the Food Stamp Plan. The poll asked: "The Government has tried out a Food Stamp Plan which lets people on relief buy certain surplus farm products below their regular selling price. The Government makes up the difference to the merchant. Do you approve or disapprove?" Approvals outweighed disapprovals 70 percent to 30 percent. It appeared the Food Stamp Plan was a good idea because it helped solve multiple problems at once.

During World War II, crop surpluses became crop scarcities and unemployment dwindled. Consequently, the first Food Stamp Plan came to an end in March 1943. All seemed well, but as Janet Poppendieck pointed out in her book *Breadlines Knee-Deep in Wheat*, "the truly unemployable needed food assistance more than ever as food prices rose sharply under the pressure of wartime scarcities."[5]

However, it was not until the late 1950s, with the coupling of hunger and agricultural surplus, that food stamps were again politically viable. As a senator, John F. Kennedy was a sponsor of food stamp legislation. Congress passed a law in 1959 allowing the USDA to resume food stamp benefits, but it was not until Kennedy was sworn in as president that real food stamp momentum resumed.

In his first official act as president, on January 21, 1961, Kennedy issued Executive Order 10914, entitled "Providing for an Expanded Program of Food Distribution to Needy Families." The order explained that "the variety of foods currently being made available [to needy families] through commodity distribution programs is limited and its nutritional content inadequate."[6]

Based on this executive order, using Section 32[7] funds, the Food Stamp Program pilot began in Paynesville, West Virginia, in May 1961 and shortly thereafter in seven other locations across the country.

Early research in two pilot areas showed more than 85 percent of food stamps were exchanged for animal products and fruits and vegetables.[8] Looking at particular expenditures, the study found that in Detroit in September-October 1961, participants in the Food Stamp Program purchased 11.4 pounds of fruits and vegetables weekly, whereas eligible non-participants only purchased 8.28 pounds of fruits and vegetables weekly.[9]

According to a USDA website, by January 1964, the successful pilot program had expanded from eight areas to forty-three areas in twenty-two states, serving 380,000 participants.[10]

THE GREAT SOCIETY AND
THE FOOD STAMP ACT OF 1964

Future food stamp legislation under President Johnson's Great Society produced the Food Stamp Act of 1964 "to permit those households in economic need to receive a greater share of the Nation's food abundance." The House version of the bill initially defined "eligible foods" as "any food or food product for human consumption except alcoholic beverages, tobacco, and foods identified as being imported from foreign sources."[11] The bill was then amended to also exclude from purchase "soft drinks, luxury foods, and luxury frozen foods, as defined by the Secretary." The House passed that version of the bill on April 8, 1964.

But then lawmakers made a key change: the Senate removed the exclusion of soft drinks (as well as luxury foods), saying those restrictions presented an "insurmountable administrative problem"—they were too difficult to impose. The Senate cited studies showing that: "Food stamp households [in the Kennedy pilot] concentrated their purchases on good basic foods. For example, fruit and vegetable consumption was largely accounted for by seasonally abundant fresh items; potatoes, greens, tomatoes, cabbage, apples, and assorted citrus fruits." In other words, excluding soft drinks was both unwieldy and unnecessary—food stamp recipients were already buying good basic foods on their own.

Still, Illinois senator Paul H. Douglas, a leading liberal Democrat who had chaired President Kennedy's Task Force on Depressed Areas, was ill at ease. He was worried that the food stamp benefits would be used for items other than "good basic foods" and on the Senate floor made an impassioned plea to exclude carbonated soft drinks from the food stamp legislation. He warned that if soft drinks were included, "this will be used as propaganda against an otherwise splendid and much needed measure." He explained that soft drinks "have no nutritional value—none at all. They are poor alternatives for milk or chocolate milk. Actually, they are bad for kids, rather than good for them." Douglas's proposed amendment to prohibit the use of stamps for sodas was rejected in the bill passed by the Senate on June 30. After the bill went to conference, President Johnson signed the Food Stamp Act into law on August 31, 1964.

FROM 1964 TO THE PRESENT DAY

The stage was set for a debate on nutrition—just as the link between the consumption of inexpensive, highly processed foods with obesity (along with obesity-related diseases) was beginning to appear. There was also a broader awareness of serious issues of poverty in America's underserved urban and rural communities.

One evening in 1968, Sen. George McGovern watched the first major documentary on hunger in America, *Hunger: U.S.A.*, produced by CBS. The documentary featured a young boy who told a reporter he was "ashamed" because he could not afford to buy lunch at school as he watched paying students eat. "It was not that little boy who should feel ashamed," McGovern said, "it was I, a US senator living in comfort, who should be ashamed that there were hungry people—young and old—in my own beloved country."[12] The very next day, Senator McGovern introduced a resolution to create the Select Committee on Nutrition and Human Needs, known as the Senate Hunger Committee.

The time was right to properly address hunger, as the Food Stamp Program remained popular among both Republican and Democratic citizens. In a 1969 Gallup poll, McGovern's welfare proposal, which would provide food stamps for all families living in extreme poverty (incomes less than $20 per week), received a bipartisan stamp of approval by the American people. Nearly seven in ten (68 percent) interviewed in a late March survey favored the idea, with majority support coming from rank-and-file Republicans and Democrats and persons at every economic level.

Three decades had passed and the program was still as popular as ever, but in spite of popular support, McGovern's Senate Hunger Committee faced serious challenges as some politicians joined to portray food stamps as the poster child for federal waste, fraud, and abuse.[13] Despite the opposition's best efforts, the committee successfully pushed on. The key to success was McGovern's closest ally, Kansas Republican senator Bob Dole. Once fierce political enemies, they had become good friends through their work on the Hunger Committee. The two worked tirelessly to craft the Food Stamp Act of 1977.[14] The remarkable difference between this act and the 1964 legislation was that it eliminated a purchase requirement. Participants no longer needed to buy a portion of their food stamps to receive the benefits.

Around the same time, the elimination of the food stamp restriction to the purchase of surplus agricultural products began to show negative impacts on the health of those who so heavily relied on the benefits. In April 1975, the American Enterprise Institute released a report, "Food Stamps and Nutrition," concluding that, "overall, the Food Stamp Program has failed to serve its twin objectives of improving nutrition access for the poor and supplementing agricultural incomes despite the tremendous growth in funding over the past decade."[15]

The report's principal author, economist Kenneth Clarkson, concluded that, although money was entering the economy, "the majority of the food dollars spent at retail (62 percent) goes to transportation, processing, and wholesale and retail handling. . . . Little of the dollar gets to farmers—and that which does benefits mainly those farmers who are already well off."[16]

Also in the report, economist Yale Brozen wrote about the program's failure to meet its other original intent, support for family farmers: "As to the second objective of the Food Stamp Program, supplementation of the income of poor farmers, Food Stamps fail, as miserably here as they do at eliminating malnutrition."[17]

As Senator Douglas had done before him, Senator Dole recognized the need for a major change in the Food Stamp Program to improve recipients' diets. In an August 31, 1975, op-ed in the *Los Angeles Times,* he reminded readers: "The program's reason for being presumably is the nutritional enhancement of poor people's diets." Senator Dole cited the American Enterprise Institute report that found, as Senator Douglas had predicted in the 1964 hearings, "vast increases in soft drink purchases and other foods of low nutritional value by program beneficiaries. In a survey conducted in Fayette County, Pennsylvania, the nutritional level of Food Stamp users actually declined because the families bought fewer milk products, eggs and grains, and more sweets and fatty foods." To drive the point home, Dole warned, "If these findings should prove generally applicable, they clearly would indict the program."

Despite growing awareness of the connection between obesity and lack of access to healthier foods, and despite release of significant studies and countless recommendations over the ensuing decades, Congress could not find its way to change the food content of the Food Stamp Program. The only major changes were administrative, shifting from paper food stamps to electronic benefit transfer (EBT) cards and renaming the program "SNAP" (Supplemental Nutrition Assistance Program).

In less than half a century, the Food Stamp Program had morphed from a commonsense program that blended the traditional American benevolence—lending a firm hand to those in need—to a program that was pumping nearly $70 billion into the American economy in sparse $4.45 per person daily increments. Most of those billions end up in the hands of the major food processing and food distribution corporations, with limited impact on smaller American farmers. From a benefit that was broadly viewed in both 1939 and 1969 by the American public as good and worthwhile, the program was, for political reasons, painted as the epitome of welfare abuse. Ironically, growing numbers of the general public, riled by inflammatory campaign statements, began blaming the poor for the program's high cost and low benefits.

Also, what had been seen as an effective market-support program favoring the consumption of "good, wholesome foods" while benefiting fruit, vegetable, and livestock farmers has largely turned into a double subsidy for large-scale conventional crops, funded by the American taxpayer. Cereal and oilseed crops are subsidized once in direct payments to large-scale farmers and then again by purchases made by SNAP recipients.

American fruit and vegetable farmers receive minimal funding support from the federal government. So, the farmers who produce fruits and vegetables, the very foods originally designated for market support by the blue stamp benefit in the Food Stamp Plan of 1939–1943, have been boxed out of both sides of the economic equation. This is especially ironic since the updated "USDA Dietary Guidelines for Americans, 2010" advise Americans to "make half your plate fruit and vegetables."[18]

THE BIRTH OF WIC

These changes to food stamps, and the double subsidies they created, opened the door for recipients to shift their purchases from good basic foods toward items such as sugar-laden soft drinks, carbohydrate-laden minute meals, and low-nutrient chips and snack foods. Major soft drink and convenience food companies significantly increased their marketing budgets to capitalize on the new opportunity, resulting in explosive growth of sales and consumption. The price of these "occasional foods" dropped while the cost of good basic foods rose. The disparity left families with the conundrum of being able to afford only the foods they previously indulged in as occasional treats.

Concerned doctors began to see the negative health impacts as more mothers and their young children arrived at clinics with health issues related to lack of access to affordable healthy food. These doctors were especially concerned with the health of pregnant mothers and infants and toddlers in their critical developmental years. Studies regarding the health impacts of dietary choices were just beginning, but these doctors were so moved by the evidence before their eyes that they needed no clinical motivation. In 1968, concerned Atlanta doctors established a USDA Food Commissary next to their health clinic, stocked with USDA commodity foods.

Experimental programs were launched in Chicago, Illinois, and Bibb County, Georgia, in 1970. On April 5, 1970, in an *Atlanta Daily World* article titled "Free Food Program for Babies, Mothers," Georgia state welfare director Bill Burson proclaimed: "We are proud to be part of an experimental program which proposes better health for the nation's children. At the test stage, it [offers] immediate help to mothers and babies in Bibb County and, if successful and practical, the national program developed from it will have far-reaching effects for the nation's children."

In Baltimore, Dr. David Paige of Johns Hopkins University organized a food voucher program for mothers and young children at his clinic. Building on Dr. Paige's model, in 1972 Sen. Hubert Humphrey sponsored legislation for a Special Supplemental Food Program for Women and Children as a two-year pilot program.[19] Unfortunately, the USDA took little action on Senator Humphrey's new program until a federal court mandated that the USDA implement the congressionally authorized program, to be known as WIC, for Women, Infants, and Children.

The first authorized WIC pilot site finally opened in Pineville, Kentucky, in 1974, and by the end of 1974, the pilot program was operating in forty-five states. In 1975, WIC was established as a permanent program with statutory emphasis "to provide supplemental nutritious food as an adjunct to good health during such critical times of growth and development in order to prevent the occurrence of health problems."[20] The program was organized as additional and supplementary to food stamps.

In effect, an entirely new program had to be created, deployed, administrated, and funded in part due to the voids created by shifting the Food Stamp Program away from its initial focus on purchase of more healthy basic agricultural products. The original WIC program was not without its shortcomings, as it focused largely on liquid milk, infant formula, and instant baby food. Fresh fruits and vegetables were overlooked.

EXPANDING FRESH FRUIT AND VEGETABLE OPTIONS FOR LOW-INCOME RECIPIENTS

In 1986, recognizing the lack of a provision concerning fresh fruits and vegetables in the WIC program, the Massachusetts Department of Food and Agriculture organized a $17,000 pilot program to provide vouchers for summer and fall fruits and vegetables to WIC families. These vouchers could only be spent at local farmers' markets in the state. Other states quickly followed, including Iowa, Connecticut, and New York. In 1992, Cong. Chet Atkins (Massachusetts) and Sen. John Kerry (Massachusetts) created and managed legislative passage of the first congressionally mandated WIC Farmers' Market Nutrition Program, now operating in forty-five states. Although voucher amounts are a meager $20 to $30 per WIC participant annually, an estimated 2.2 million WIC participants benefit each year, with $22 million invested with 17,363 farmers at 3,645 farmers' markets nationwide.[21]

In 1989, Massachusetts created a Senior Farmers' Market Nutrition Program for low-income seniors, modeled on the successful WIC program. In 2000, the USDA used authorities under its Commodity Credit Corporation to provide one-year funding nationally for the Senior Farmers' Market Nutrition Program (SFMNP). To sustain the program, Cong. John Baldacci (Maine) initiated funding in the Farm Bill that year. Reauthorized in 2008, this popular program benefits 809,000 low-income seniors and nearly 19,000 small farmers at 2,200 farmers' markets.[22]

の

The USDA recognized the success of these farmers' markets nutrition-incentive programs. With numerous studies indicating that people need to consume significant amounts of fruits and vegetables daily to achieve optimal nutrition, the WIC Cash Vegetable Voucher Program was implemented in 2007. The investment of $700 million annually to increase consumption of fruits and vegetables appears significant, but it is thinly spread among one million mothers and seven million infants and children, for an average annual benefit of $97 per person. With nearly tenfold that amount spent on highly processed convenience foods—the only affordable food choices available through the current form of SNAP—WIC cash vegetable vouchers seem destined to provide limited impact.

Hidden in plain sight, the result of all this becomes apparent in the cost to the American economy of diet-related, diet-preventable diseases, such as complications from obesity and type 2 diabetes. These two conditions cost the American public close to $250 billion annually.

It appears suspect to invest nearly $70 billion annually in SNAP benefits that cause a portion of those $250 billion in diet-related medical costs. And one can imagine that had the list of authorized foods in the original 1939–1943 Food Stamp Plan, such as beans, apples, and all fresh vegetables, not been expanded to include and indeed favor nutrient-poor foods in 1964, the need for a supplementary WIC program might have never arisen, and health care costs would undoubtedly be lower.

FOOD ASSISTANCE AND THE ECONOMY

While much attention is paid to the costs of both food assistance programs, there has been limited discussion with regard to their impact on the US economy. But indeed, these tens of billions of dollars yield a significant impact. While figures on exactly how much of which products are being purchased using SNAP benefits are not collected by the USDA from retailers, there are studies that indicate the program's significant economic impact.

A USDA report, "The Business Case for Increasing Food Stamp Participation," published in 2002 during the George W. Bush administration, found that every $1.00 in SNAP benefits generated $1.84.[23] A 2010 revision to the 2002 report lowered that figure to $1.79 for every dollar spent. In an independent study, Moody's Economy.com found that every SNAP dollar spent generates $1.73 in real GDP increase, positing that "expanding Food Stamps . . . is the most effective way to prime the economy's pump."[24] The argument is clear that the program creates positive economic impact.

Economists are beginning to study the economic impacts of purchasing locally produced goods. While conclusive studies have yet to be published, one might assume that if $1.00 in SNAP benefit spent creates $1.73 in GDP when spent in the global food distribution system, the same dollar will likely create more economic "bang" in the local economy if spent on products grown in the state where the benefit is distributed. It is also important to understand that small and midsize farms are small businesses. With the intense focus of both political parties on the important role of small businesses in spurring meaningful economic recovery, such an approach makes tremendous sense.

President George W. Bush was a proponent of improved access to the SNAP program. Troubled that only half of eligible recipients were actually participating in the program in key states such as California, he instructed the USDA to improve access and established the Office for Strategic Partnership and Outreach in 2007 in an effort to close the gap.

California is at the top of the list where state and local political leaders tend to consider SNAP a blatant example of waste, fraud, and abuse. SNAP sign-up for eligible California recipients is estimated at 50 percent, leaving 50 percent of its vulnerable citizens uncovered.[25] The resulting loss to California's troubled economy is an estimated $4 billion in direct SNAP spending. When applying the stimulus match of the USDA and Moody's studies, the negative economic impact on California in the name of "fraud protection" nears $7 billion. Imagine what the impact would be if enrollment increased and the resulting benefits were spent on the agricultural products of California.

BACK TO THE FUTURE

We often wish we could turn back the hands of time when we have either made a questionable decision or realize we might have decided differently if we were fully aware of the decision's impacts. In the case of the Food Stamp Program, we actually have an opportunity to do just that. There is intense interest in revitalizing the US economy, resisting the shipment of jobs and revenues overseas as a result of globalization. Retooling a program that once pumped real money directly into the US agricultural economy, into the pockets of farmers who grew foods that people cooked and ate, might be just what the doctor ordered.

Specialty crop production (fruits and vegetables) creates more economic value (jobs, equipment, and infrastructure support) than cereal and seed crop agriculture. A 2010 Leopold Center study found that by converting Midwest conventional crop production to fruit and vegetable production at a level to meet the existing demand for those products, the Midwest would benefit from a $1 billion increase in related economic activity.[26] Along the same lines, if Maine had the opportunity to rely on the existing SNAP and WIC funding in the state, it is certain that economic activity would increase.

Today, we have the tools to finance and establish the food-related businesses necessary to convert back toward a more regionalized food system that supports and encourages specialty crops and other viable food production in the region. A number of financial sponsors are willing to underwrite these investments. Private grants and financing in the form of program-related investments and mission-related investments, along with other instruments from financial institutions that focus on the triple bottom line (or people, planet, profit), can complement the low-interest US Treasury loans through community development finance institutions ($5 billion annually) in rebuilding seriously underserved urban and rural communities.

We have an opportunity to correct some of our earlier mistakes. To prove the concept, several nonprofit organizations, private funders, and some municipal, state, and federal leaders have been supporting programs that offer incentives for healthy foods, directing existing federal food as-sistance dollars toward locally grown agricultural products. The programs have been enthusiastically embraced by food assistance recipients, market managers, farmers, funders, and citizens alike. It seems like following the original intent of the Food Stamp Plan is a promising concept.

In further exploring how these incentives might be scaled to benefit local economies within the states, there is an opportunity to restore to our farmers and our disadvantaged citizens their unalienable rights of "Life, Liberty, and the pursuit of Happiness." Hyperbole? Maybe not. In truth, life is richer when people have access to a healthful, meaningful diet. Lib-erty is realized when all people have real choices of what they can feed their families. Happiness is the joy of being able to afford fresh, locally grown foods, cooking them as a family, and sharing a good secure life together.

⚬

Gus Schumacher is executive vice president of Wholesome Wave and formerly commissioner of the Massachusetts Department of Food and Agriculture. He served earlier as a senior agricultural project lender at the World Bank and later served as the USDA's undersecretary of farm and foreign agricultural services.

Michel Nischan is founder, CEO, and president of Wholesome Wave. A James Beard Award–winning chef, restaurateur, and author, Nischan has spent his career working toward restoring local, sustainable food systems and the cultures they support. He was recently elected a lifetime Ashoka Fellow and serves on the board of trustees for the James Beard Foundation and the Rodale Institute and as an advisory board member for the Center for Health and the Global Environment at Harvard Medical School.

Daniel Bowman Simon is the founder of SNAPgardens.org, which raises awareness that SNAP (food stamp) benefits can be used to purchase food-producing plants and seeds and strives to facilitate successful gardening. During the election cycle of 2008, he founded TheWhoFarm, a nonpar-tisan advocacy campaign for an organic farm on the White House lawn.

Seeds of Plenty— From Food Stamps

DANIEL BOWMAN SIMON

Since 1973, the Food Stamp Program has allowed participants to buy garden vegetable seeds and plants with their benefits. But the option has been languishing dormant, virtually unknown to participants and administrators alike. In proposing the option as an amendment almost forty years ago, Sen. James Allen of Alabama explained on the Senate floor the multiple reasons it made practical sense: "The recipients of food stamps would thus be able to use their own initiative to produce fruits and vegetables needed to provide variety and nutritional value for their diet. The amendment would allow the food stamp recipient to purchase with his food stamps seeds and plants for the purpose of growing food for consumption by himself and his household. It would allow a person to buy $1 or $2 worth of seed or vegetable plants and possibly have available a plot of land and be able to raise $50 or $100 worth of food for himself and his family. It would encourage industry on the part of the food stamp recipient and it would be at no cost to the Federal Government." The Agriculture Committee chair Eugene Talmadge added, "The amendment does have considerable appeal. If someone can buy some seeds and produce more food, he could perhaps get more value with those food stamps than by trading them in the store." The amendment passed on a voice vote.

Fast-forward to 2008. As a garden advocate, I was approached by a woman at a farmers' market. She told me that she used her food stamp benefits to grow a garden, but that she didn't know anyone else doing the same, that most people didn't even know it was possible. She asked me to spread the word. I took on her challenge with a fighting spirit, founding SNAP Gardens in 2011. Farmers' markets and food stamp offices all over the country now display SNAP Gardens posters and are working to make gardening a viable and smart choice for all.

⌒

Daniel Bowman Simon has been spreading the SNAP Gardens message with lectures, appearances at farmers' markets, and through his website, SNAPgardens.org.

CHAPTER 7

Today's "Eat More" Environment

The Role of the Food Industry[1]

MARION NESTLE

FROM *A PLACE AT THE TABLE*

We subsidize the basic ingredients in processed foods. We do not subsidize fruits, vegetables, and whole grains because the producers tend to be small producers. They don't have the kind of political clout that the big commodity producers of corn and soybeans and wheat that gets processed do.

—Marion Nestle

If you look at what has happened to the relative price of fresh fruits and vegetables, it's gone up by 40 percent since 1980 when the obesity epidemic began. In contrast, the relative price of processed foods has gone down by about 40 percent. So, if you only have a limited amount of money to spend, you're going to spend it on the cheapest calories you can get, and that's going to be processed foods. This has to do with our farm policy and what we subsidize and what we don't.

—Marion Nestle

Marion Nestle is the acclaimed monitor, investigator, and critic of America's food industry. In her blog at www.foodpolitics.com, she regularly chastises the industry for its heavy-handed exploitation of America's underclass. It's not just being confused by good fats and bad fats, good and low carbs. It's also the bewildering number—320,000—of different food products and the $34 billion the food industry spends on advertising mostly cheap snack foods and sodas. What gets lost in the decision over what to buy is the all-important calorie count, the daily intake, which, for Americans, has steadily gone up—from 3,200 in 1970 to 3,900 today. An increase of one hundred of those calories came between 2001 and 2002.

She has written several books about the diet wars and food safety, including Food Politics: How the Food Industry Influences Nutrition and Health *(Berkeley: University of California Press, 2002). In her latest book,* Why Calories Count: From Science to Politics *(Berkeley: University of California Press, 2012), Nestle collaborated with Malden Nesheim, Professor Emeritus of Nutritional Science at Cornell University, to explore how the food industry created the "eat more" environment that has led to the obesity epidemic.*

Weight gain, as we keep saying, is caused by eating more, moving less, or doing both. Rates of overweight and obesity began to rise sharply in the United States in the early 1980s. Did Americans start becoming less active at that time? Did they begin to eat more? Or, as is widely believed, did both things happen simultaneously? Let's take a look.

TREND: CALORIES EXPENDED IN PHYSICAL ACTIVITY

Practically anyone you ask will tell you that people in general and kids in particular are less active now than they were in recent decades. Kids hardly ever take physical education classes, walk or ride bicycles to school, or play spontaneous sports. If enrolled in organized sports, they spend more time hanging around than running around. You cannot tear them away from computers, video games, or other sedentary online entertainment. On this basis, some researchers insist that declining levels of phys-

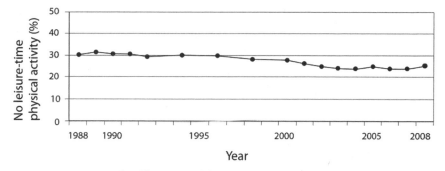

Figure 17 Rates of self-reported leisure-time inactivity, 1988–2008. If inactivity is declining slightly, activity levels must be increasing slightly. *Source:* CDC, "Physical Activity Statistics," available at: www.cdc.gov /nccdphp/dnpa/physical/stats/ (updated February 2, 2010).

ical activity—not eating more calories—must be the chief cause of today's obesity crisis.[2]

We wish we had compelling reasons to believe this idea to be correct, but we do not. If anything, research shows the opposite. Studies indicate a slight *increase* in physical activity since the early 1980s. Even research based on self-reports, which tend to exaggerate the most healthful practices, finds practically no change in calorie expenditures since 1980. The Centers for Disease Control and Prevention, for example, conducts periodic surveys of physical activity levels based on self-reports. These show a slight increase in reported activity levels from 1990 to 1998. The CDC also asks questions about leisure-time sedentary behavior. The responses indicate a slight decline in inactivity from 1988 to 2008, as shown in Figure 17.[3]

Additional CDC surveys record small increases in physical activity among men and women from 2001 to 2005. But other investigators report slight decreases in activity and slight increases in inactivity among ninth- and tenth-grade boys and among both black and white girls between the ages of nine and nineteen. The studies that found such results used different methods, age groups, and time periods and are not easily compared. To try to make sense of the conflicting data, Australian investigators reviewed every study they could find on levels of physical activity, but observed that almost none had collected baseline data on childhood activity from the earlier years. Without a baseline, they could not identify a trend.

They noted, however, that today's declining rates of active transport (walking, cycling), school physical education, and organized sports constitute what they call an "activity-toxic" environment for kids. Kids want to be active but are constrained by school policies and curricula, parental concerns about safety and convenience, and the almost universal lack of sidewalks, bike paths, and safe places to play.[4]

Years ago kids were watching television and reading comic books. Are they really less active now? Without better data, we cannot agree that declining physical activity is the more important cause of rising rates of overweight, especially because most data are self-reported. We did find one longitudinal study that measured baseline calorie intake and expenditure with doubly labeled water. Baseline total energy intake and resting energy expenditure predicted subsequent obesity, but energy expenditure from physical activity did not.[5] Overall, the available evidence points to calorie intake as a more important cause of obesity than calorie output.

TREND: CALORIE INTAKE

Studies of calorie intake are much less ambiguous. For them, we have baseline data. Compared to studies dating back to the early 1970s, recent studies show a clear increase in calorie intake, as shown in Table 21.

These figures require some interpretation. They were obtained from self-reports of one-day diet recalls, cover different age groups, may not represent average daily intake, and undoubtedly underreport calories. Taking the results at face value, men in recent years reported eating about two hundred more calories per day than men in 1971–1974. For women, the increase for the same time period has been more than three hundred calories a day. Since 2000, reported calorie intake has declined somewhat, possibly as a result of extending the age range of participants (older people eat less). But whatever the exact number, calorie intakes seem to have increased.[6] Why? To answer this question, let's look at concurrent changes in the food environment.

CALORIES IN THE FOOD ENVIRONMENT

Since the early 1980s, the US food environment has changed in ways that encourage eating in more places at more times of day in larger portions.[7]

Table 21 Trends in Self-Reported Calorie Intake, 1971–2008, Per Capita Per Day

Year	Men	Women
1971–1974	2,450	1,540
1976–1980	2,440	1,520
1988–1994	2,670	1,800
1999–2000	2,620	1,880
2001–2002	2,620	1,845
2003–2004	2,610	1,850
2005–2006	2,640	1,785
2007–2008	2,510	1,770

Sources: 1971–2000 figures are from National Health and Nutrition Examination Surveys (NHANES) of people ages twenty to seventy-four (CDC, "Trends in Intake of Energy and Macronutrients—United States, 1971–2000," *Morbidity and Mortality Weekly Report* 53 [2004]: 80–82); 2001–2008 figures come from *What We Eat in America* surveys of people ages twenty to seventy-four and older (USDA, Agricultural Research Service, data tables from *What We Eat in America*, NHANES 2007–2008, revised August 2010, available at: www.ars.usda.gov/Services/docs.htm?docid=18349).

Note: Calories rounded off to the nearest 5.

We attribute these changes to food industry responses to a sharp increase in the number of calories available in the food supply. For more than seventy years, from the early 1900s to the early 1980s, the US food supply provided an average of about 3,200 calories per person per day, with a variation of plus or minus 200 calories. But by 2000, the available calories had increased to 3,900 per person per day, in parallel with rising rates of obesity. We illustrate these trends in Figure 18.

Although calories in the food supply have increased by 700 per person per day since 1980 or so, the constituent proportions of protein (11 percent of calories), fat (41 percent), and carbohydrate (48 percent) show no evident change during that period. The mix of sources within those categories also did not change, except for the replacement of some fats from meat and dairy products with those from liquid oils. Calories from proteins, fats, and carbohydrates increased in direct proportion to total calories.[8]

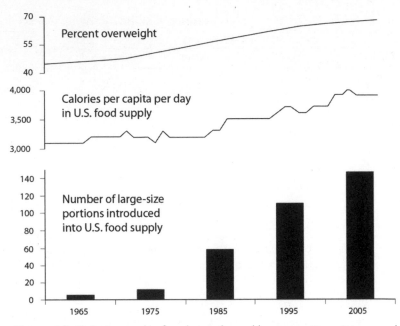

Figure 18 Calories in the food supply and large portions increased in tandem with rates of obesity from 1960 to 2005: trends in over-weight (top panel), calories in the food supply per capita per day (middle panel), and the introduction of larger food portions (bot-tom panel). Figure courtesy of Dr. Lisa Young.

Nevertheless, the kinds of foods that deliver many of the calories to American diets are a matter of considerable concern. The National Health and Nutrition Examination Survey (NHANES) collects data on dietary intake that can be used to identify the foods that are leading sources of calories in American diets. Table 22 summarizes data from the 2005–2006 NHANES. The leading contributors are desserts (grain-based and dairy), sodas, pizza, chips, and burgers. Chicken appears as the number-three source, no doubt because the category includes fried chicken and McNuggets. These are largely foods of low nutrient density and high calorie density—junk foods. Worse, the top *three* food sources of calories for children ages two to eighteen are grain-based desserts (138 calories per day), pizza (136 calories), and sodas and energy and sports drinks (118 calories). Together these three food sources contribute one-fourth of a child's daily calorie intake. NHANES figures are national av-erages; some children obtain even more of their calories from such foods.[9]

Table 22 Top Fifteen Sources of Calories in US Diets, Ages Two and Older

Rank	Calorie Source	Calories per Day from That Source
1	Grain-based desserts (cakes, cookies, pies, doughnuts)	138
2	Yeast breads	129
3	Chicken and chicken mixed dishes	121
4	Sodas, energy and sports drinks, sweetened waters	114
5	Pizza	98
6	Alcoholic beverages	82
7	Pasta and pasta dishes	81
8	Tortillas, burritos, tacos, nachos	80
9	Beef and beef mixed dishes	64
10	Dairy desserts (ice cream, sherbet, pudding)	62
11	Chips: potato, corn, other	56
12	Burgers	53
13	Reduced-fat milk	51
14	Cheese	49
15	Ready-to-eat cereals	49

Source: USDA, Center for Nutrition Policy and Promotion, "Dietary Guidelines for Americans, 2010," available at: www.cnpp.usda.gov/DietaryGuidelines.htm.

Sugary drinks are of special concern. A later analysis of NHANES data from 2005 to 2008 reports that boys ages twelve to nineteen consume nearly 300 calories a day from sugary drinks alone, and that 5 percent of the US population consumes nearly 570 calories a day from such drinks. These contain sugars but no or few nutrients and are as low in nutrient density as you can get.[10]

The Causes

Why more calories became available is a matter of some conjecture. One frequently cited cause is the influx of women into the workforce, creating demands for convenience. But before blaming women for causing obesity, consider the labor statistics. These suggest that while women in the workforce—and longer working hours—may be contributing factors, the timing isn't quite right. By the early 1980s, half of working-age women had already entered the workforce, and from 1981 to 2007 the percentage only increased from 52 to 60 percent.[11] In any case, women can hardly be blamed for the food industry's creation of high-calorie, low-nutri-ent-density convenience foods. We think the evidence points more strongly to two other causes: agricultural policies and the advent of the "shareholder value" movement, which changed the way Wall Street evaluates publicly traded corporations.

Agricultural Policies. In 1973 and 1977, Congress passed laws that reversed long-standing farm policies aimed at protecting prices by controlling production. These policies paid farmers to set aside acres, but that changed when Earl Butz, a former dean of agriculture at Purdue, became USDA secretary and reportedly urged them to plant "fencerow to fencerow." Whether Butz really said this or not—no source has ever been found for the statement—the new policies encouraged farmers to plant as much as they possibly could. Food production increased, and so did calories in the food supply. The addition of seven hundred calories a day per capita made the food industry even more competitive. Food companies now had to find new ways to sell products in an environment that offered a vast excess of calories over the needs of the population. Even if, as the USDA maintains, Americans waste a third of available calories, the food supply is still highly overabundant.[12]

The "Shareholder Value" Movement. The onset of a movement to force corporations to produce more immediate and higher returns on investment especially increased competitive pressures on food companies. The movement's start is attributed to a speech given by Jack Welch, then head of General Electric, in 1981. Corporations, Welch said, owed more to their shareholders. His company would now focus on producing faster growth and higher profit margins and returns to investors. The movement caught on quickly, and Wall Street soon began to press companies to report not only profit but also increased *growth* on a quarterly basis. Food companies were having enough trouble producing profits in an overabundant food economy. Now they had to demonstrate profit growth every ninety days.[13]

The Consequences

Competitive pressures forced food companies to consolidate, become larger, and seek new markets and ways to expand sales in existing markets. The collateral result was a changed society. Today, in contrast to the early 1980s, it is socially acceptable to eat in more places, more frequently, and in larger amounts, and for children to regularly consume fast foods, snacks, and sodas—changes that singly and together promote higher calorie intakes. Here we highlight just a few of the ways in which the altered food environment promotes overeating.[14]

Foods Away from Home. An abundance of food creates a cheap food supply, making it less expensive for people to eat foods prepared outside the home. Beginning in the late 1970s, spending on away-from-home foods rose from about one-third of total food expenditures to about one-half. The proportion of calories obtained from away-from-home foods rose from less than 20 to more than 30 percent, with much of the increase coming from fast food. Among children, the percentage of daily energy eaten away from home increased from 23 to 34 percent. According to an analysis of national food consumption surveys, children get more of their daily calories from fast-food outlets than they do from schools, and fast food is the largest contributor to the calories they consume outside the home. USDA economists say that the average meal eaten away from home by adults adds 134 calories to daily intakes, and one meal a week eaten at a restaurant can account for a two-pound annual weight gain.[15]

New Products. The low cost of basic food commodities has encouraged food companies to make new forms of tasty packaged food products. Manufacturers introduce nearly 20,000 new products into the food supply each year, nearly half of them candies, gums, snacks, and sodas. The habitual consumption of such foods is associated with long-term increases in calorie intake and body weight, and 40 percent of the calories in the diets of children and adolescents are reported to derive from high-calorie sweets and snack foods.[16]

Larger Portions. Once food became relatively cheap, restaurants, fast-food chains, and major food companies could offer foods and beverages in larger sizes to attract customers. Larger portions have more calories. They also encourage people to eat more and to underestimate the number of calories in their food by larger percentages. The increase in portion sizes is sufficient to explain rising levels of obesity (see Figure 18).[17]

Ubiquity. We like to ask the question: when did it become acceptable to eat in bookstores? Today snack foods are sold in 96 percent of pharmacies, 94 percent of gasoline stations, 22 percent of furniture stores, and 16 percent of apparel stores. Research shows that if food is at hand, people will eat it.[18]

Frequency. Nibbling may seem like a good idea, but the more times a day people eat junk foods, the more calories they are likely to consume. It now seems normal to snack and drink sodas throughout the day. Surveys find that children eat an average of three snacks per day, most of them high-calorie desserts, junk foods, and sweetened beverages of poor nutritional quality.[19]

Proximity. The mere location of fast-food restaurants near schools has been shown to promote fast-food consumption as well as overweight, even when corrected for community characteristics. Cornell professor Brian Wansink and his colleagues have demonstrated the calorie-promoting effects of having food close at hand. The closer the candy dish, the more candy consumed. The mere presence of vending machines encourages kids to buy high-calorie foods, which explains why health advocates would like to see vending machines removed from schools.[20]

Low Prices. Adam Drewnowski and his team at the University of Washington have shown that on a per-calorie basis, junk foods are cheaper than healthier foods. They estimate that following federal dietary advice to increase intake of fruits and vegetables would raise one's food costs by several hundred dollars a year. If fruits and vegetables appear more expensive than junk foods, it's because they are. The Consumer Price Index indicates an increase of about 40 percent in the relative cost of fruits and vegetables since the early 1980s, whereas the indexed price of desserts, snack foods, and sodas has declined by 20 to 30 percent. Lower prices encourage people to eat more. Higher prices discourage food purchases.[21] For example, as part of its contribution to obesity prevention, Coca-Cola now offers drinks in 7.5-ounce cans, but prices them higher than 12-ounce sodas. As a retailing executive once explained to us, if customers want smaller portions, they ought to be willing to pay for them.

Marketing Health. The food industry spends billions of dollars a year to encourage people to buy its products, but foods marketed as "healthy" particularly encourage greater calorie intake. Professor Wansink's experiments show that people eat more calories from snack foods labeled low-fat, no trans fat, or organic. Most people, he says, are "blissfully unaware" of how the food environment influences what they eat. People take in excessive calories "not because of hunger but because of family and friends, packages and plates, names and numbers, labels and lights, colors and candles, shapes and smells. . . . The list is almost as endless as it's invisible."[22]

Invisible to consumers, yes, but not to food marketers. The result of constant exposure to today's "eat more" food environment, as David Kessler explains in *The End of Overeating*, has been to drive people to desire high-calorie foods and to become "conditioned overeaters."[23] The power of this food environment to promote greater calorie intake is so great that even educated eaters have trouble dealing with it. If you as an educated eater have trouble managing "eat more" pressures, it is because it is virtually impossible for individuals to judge the number of calories they are eating.

⌒

Dr. Marion Nestle is the Paulette Goddard Professor of Nutrition, Food Studies, and Public Health at New York University. Her other books include *Safe Food: Bacteria, Biotechnology, and Bioterrorism* (Berkeley:

University of California Press, 2003) and *What to Eat* (New York: Farrar, Straus & Giroux/North Point Press, 2006). She is co-editor (with Beth Dixon) of *Taking Sides: Clashing Views on Controversial Issues in Food and Nutrition* (New York: McGraw-Hill/Dushkin, 2004) and author of *Pet Food Politics: Chihuahua in the Coal Mine* (Berkeley: University of California Press, 2008). She also edited the 1988 *Surgeon General's Report on Nutrition and Health.*

CHAPTER 8

The New Hidden Persuaders

The Digital World of Food Marketing to Children and Teens[1]

JENNIFER L. HARRIS

FROM *A PLACE AT THE TABLE*

These [agricultural] subsidies made products very cheap and therefore made it profitable for the food industry to invest in the infrastructure for processing those products into packaged goods that we see on every counter in every corner store, in every vending machine, and that are really ubiquitous now all around us.

—Janet Poppendieck, professor emerita of sociology at Hunter College, City University of New York, and one of the nation's leading writers about hunger in America

As the production of junk food increases, so do the efforts of the food industry to sell these products to children. Food companies have found creative and sophisticated new ways to advertise their products to children and teens. For years they have advertised on children's television shows and used promotions and licensed characters on product packages and kids' meals—tactics that all parents recognize. But today, writes Jennifer L. Harris, director of marketing initiatives at the Rudd Center for Food Policy and Obesity at Yale University, companies bombard young people with advertising messages in the digital media where children now spend most of their time, interacting with their peers, out of sight of their parents. Many of these newer techniques are designed specifically to take advantage of the unique developmental needs of children and teens. They also circumvent limitations on unfair child-targeted advertising practices that only apply to television advertising. As the child obesity epidemic spreads, accompanied by increasing concern from doctors and the public health community, the food industry has taken some voluntary actions to limit the types of foods advertised in children's media, but these actions barely scratch the surface of food marketing to young people.[2]

As every parent knows, kids spend a lot of time online. The most comprehensive analysis of young people's media use was conducted by the Kaiser Family Foundation in 2009.[3] This report showed that eleven- to fourteen-year-olds (aka "tweens") spent the most time online of any age group—one hour and forty-six minutes every day (see Table 8.1). Teens spent somewhat less time online (one hour and thirty-nine minutes) and children (eight- to ten-years-old) spent forty-six minutes online on average. Across all three age groups, social networking, playing games, and watching videos were the top three online activities; however, the amount of time spent on each activity changed with age. Children spent the most time playing games—one-third of their online time. Children spent some time, but not much, social networking and watching videos. Playing games online peaked among tweens, and then dropped for teens. Tweens and teens also watched sixteen minutes of online videos per day or more. However, tweens and teens spent approximately one-quarter of their time online engaged in social networking.

In 2006 one analysis showed that food companies spent more than $75 million on marketing on company websites, in online ads, by word of mouth, and in other digital marketing specifically targeted to children and teens.[4] One-third of this money was used to market sodas; sugary cereal and snack food marketers also targeted children and teens extensively online.

Researchers found that the food companies' early digital marketing efforts targeted to children were full of branded characters, attention-

Table 8.1 Time Spent on Computer (hours:minutes)[5]

Activity	Children (8–10 years)	Tweens (11–14 years)	Teens (15–18 years)
Social networking	0:05	0:29	0:26
Games	0:17	0:19	0:14
Video websites	0:08	0:18	0:16
Instant messaging	0:03	0:14	0:14
Other websites	0:07	0:10	0:13
E-mail	0:02	0:07	0:06
All other	0:04	0:10	0:11
Total	0:46	1:46	1:39

grabbing animation, and colorful text and images.[6] They contained numerous features designed to engage children with the brands for long periods of time, such as games, movie promotions, music, and coloring pages. Many websites even provided children with features that enabled them to interact with the brand when they were not on the websites, including screen-saver and ring-tone downloads and greeting cards and other messages to send to friends.

Much has changed since this original research. In 2009 young people were also spending up to twenty-one minutes per day instant-messaging and using email.[7] More recently, those activities have been replaced by social media, primarily Facebook. Food marketers have kept up with this trend.

Many companies now have comprehensive social media marketing strategies that get kids to promote foods and beverages to each other, especially through Facebook and YouTube. And today young people's media use is changing again: mobile media is the newest digital marketing frontier. In 2011 more than 37 percent of social media occurred on mobile devices, such as smartphones and tablets.[8] Playing downloaded game apps and viewing videos are also popular activities on these devices. As of 2011, a few food and beverage companies had taken the lead in designing mobile marketing programs and apps that now allow them to interact with kids 24/7.

At the Rudd Center for Food Policy and Obesity over the past three years, we have documented food company marketing practices targeted to children and teens, and we often have been simultaneously amazed and appalled by the creativity, technological sophistication, and audacity of the companies that communicate with children on the Internet. We also have learned that it is difficult for parents to keep up with their children's use of digital media; most are unaware of how much food marketing occurs in these media and the manipulative tactics used to target their children. The following sections describe the digital techniques commonly used to market foods and beverages to children and teens and discuss how companies' quest to engage young people where they spend so much time can damage their health.[9]

"HEY KIDS: THIS IS ADVERTISING!"

Nearly every food brand that markets its product directly to children also maintains a website designed for children. Companies often place a disclaimer, "Hey kids: This is advertising!" on the home page to "warn" children that the website contains advertising. Instead of acting as a deterrent, this message signals a fun and engaging place, full of games, virtual worlds, and other clever interactive activities.

At first glance, these websites appear to be safe, child-appropriate places for children to spend their time (as General Mills informs parents on the home page of its child-targeted websites). However, these sites are in fact advertising—and a form of advertising that child development experts believe is nearly impossible for children to resist. In addition, virtually all the foods that companies promote on these sites are products that children should consume rarely or not at all; sugary cereals, fast food, and candy are featured on the most popular sites.[10]

For our reports documenting the marketing practices targeted to youth by cereal, fast-food, and sugary drink companies, our colleagues at Berkeley Media Studies Group analyzed the content of thousands of pages on child-targeted websites. Virtually every page contained some type of advertising, ranging from brand logos and pictures of the products to "webisodes," which are basically longer-length commercials. The most common element on food companies' child-targeted websites was "advergames," or online games that incorporate branded messages within the games. We conducted an analysis of food company websites frequently visited by children and adolescents in 2009 and found that 38 percent contained advergames.[11] We could find just one website, a section of the site of the Dole Food Company, that contained advergames to promote healthy foods, such as fruits and vegetables.

Advergames literally encourage children to play with their food. For example, in a game called "Fruity Cheerios Bumper Boats," the game characters ride inside boats made out of Fruity Cheerios and try to bump other players away. In "Out on a Limb," children catch falling Pop-Tarts characters in a toaster and avoid falling coconuts. In the "Oreo Double Stuff Race," children's characters must untwist an Oreo cookie, lick off the icing, and dunk the two pieces in a glass of milk faster than their opponents.

The most sophisticated sites are virtual worlds that invite children to create an avatar and have their own adventures inside this branded world. For example, in Millsberry (General Mills's virtual world to promote its children's cereals—a site that no longer exists), children create avatars who explore the city, build a house, use "Millsbucks" to buy stuff, including General Mills's products, and communicate with other Millsberry "citizens" (i.e., other visitors who have created their own avatars).[12] Both McDonald's and Burger King also host virtual worlds for children, McWorld.com and ClubBK.com. ClubBK.com, which resembles a children's video game, encourages children to explore the site to discover new features and collect "crowns." The home page even features a leaderboard; currently it boasts that "lilchez" has earned almost 4 million crowns.

Advergames and virtual worlds are not the only features of these sites. They contain an amazing variety of fun and cool features designed to engage children with the brands. For example, at ReesesPuffs.com, children create their own songs and download them to their computers. At HappyMeal.com, children can upload their own picture, insert Ronald McDonald into the picture, pick a frame, add a message, and send it to a friend. On another McDonald's site, www.Ronald.com, Ronald McDonald teaches very young children about letters and numbers. Ironically, this site targets preschoolers who cannot yet read but includes the disclaimer, "Hey Kids: This is Advertising!" in tiny type at the top.

Many of these child-targeted websites are extremely popular. In 2009 approximately 1.2 million children (six- to eleven-year-olds) went to food company websites that contained advergames and visited an average of thirty-five pages each month.[13] The most popular site was Millsberry.com, which averaged 284,000 unique child visitors each month. McDonald's hosted thirteen different websites, which attracted 365,000 unique child visitors in total per month, including HappyMeal.com with 189,000 visitors and McWorld.com with 101,000 child visitors. Millsberry.com and ToppsTown.com were the most engaging sites, with children and teens visiting the sites for more than one hour per month. Young visitors to Millsberry.com averaged three visits per month, spent 21 minutes on the site each time, and visited 101 pages. Young people visited ToppsTown.com on average 3.4 times per month for almost 22 minutes each time.

THE PUBLIC HEALTH CONCERN

In the same way that companies use product placements to incorporate brands into movies and television shows, food companies use games and other fun activities on their websites to disguise this persuasive intent. Food companies know that advertising is more effective when viewers do not think of it as advertising and automatically tune it out. Yet on websites they are specifically targeting children who are poorly equipped to defend against any type of advertising, especially advertising in the form of fun and games.

On television, the Children's Advertising Review Unit (CARU), an advertising industry self-regulatory body, specifically prohibits the incorporation of advertising messages inside children's television shows.[14] Their concern is that children do not have the cognitive ability to identify advertising that is embedded within entertainment. Yet there are no self-imposed restrictions on advertising to children on the Internet. On television, the Federal Communications Commission (FCC) imposes a limit of ten and a half to twelve minutes of advertising per thirty minutes of children's programming.[15] However, there are no such limits on the Internet. As discussed, the average child spends as much as twenty-one straight minutes immersed in advertising content on some food company websites.

Moreover, there is increasing evidence that advertising to children on the Internet can increase consumption of unhealthy foods. The Internet allows companies to integrate incentives for purchasing the product within the games and other website features. For example, at Postopia.com (now PebblesPlay.com), children are encouraged to ask their parents to buy Post Fruity and Cocoa Pebbles cereals to get a code on the package that gives them extra advantages in the games. Similarly, special codes on McDonald's Happy Meals boxes allow children to get special offers in McWorld.com, such as "a virtual mPet for your mPal." Tailored to a somewhat older audience, Coca-Cola's MyCokeRewards.com features 424 pages full of rewards to redeem by collecting codes from underneath bottle caps. This site averaged 42,000 unique child visitors and 129,000 teen visitors every month in 2010.[16]

In an experiment we conducted on the effects of playing advergames, children who played games for Pop-Tarts and Oreos consumed more junk food and fewer fruits and vegetables during a snack afterward (compared with playing online games that were not food-related).[17] Children who played advergames from Dole that promoted healthy eating ate more fruits and vegetables, but even those games did not get many of the children to eat less junk food. An interesting finding was that the effects of the unhealthy advergames were stronger for children who regularly played these games; it appears that this influence could increase the more time children spend playing them. Other researchers also have found that playing advergames increases children's preferences for the food brands that are advertised.[18]

Marketing to children on these websites can be especially powerful because children choose to visit these websites and they actively participate in the advertising, unlike television ads, which are selected for them and viewed passively. It's like the student who picks up a new concept more quickly by doing a hands-on project than by listening to the teacher in class. Children who "learn" about brands by interacting with them on these websites are likely to absorb and retain this information more thoroughly. And what children learn through these websites is that the unhealthy foods and beverages they promote are fun and cool, and consuming them has many rewards with no negative consequences.

Companies have learned that associating their products with positive emotions and continually reminding children of these associations creates strong emotional ties to the products in children's minds.[19] These positive associations not only lead children to pester their parents to buy the products but also create loyal customers for their brands once children are old enough to make their own purchasing decisions. In the words of one market research firm, "We are showing that the initial connection and affinity to a brand is made on an emotional level—and that when purchase decision time comes nearer, the young consumer is looking for affirmation for the emotional choice they have already solidified."[20]

Perhaps the most disturbing feature of food company websites is that they directly communicate with children behind parents' backs. In fact, many features of child-targeted websites appear to be designed specifically to bypass parents' scrutiny. With few exceptions, children do not need their parents' permission to access food company websites, even though many require children to create a user ID and password and store children's names, birth dates, preferences, and past activity.[21] These sites effectively bypass regulations established by the Children's Online Privacy and Protection Act (COPPA) because they do not maintain email or other contact information for the children.

Another sneaky feature of many of these sites is that they use children to advertise to their friends. For example, at TrixWorld.com, children can send a "secret fruitalicious coded message." The child provides the email address and name of a friend, best friend, brother, sister, or relative (the child indicates which one). Similarly, ReesesPuffs.com asks kids to "tell your friends" by entering the child's name and email address and the name and email address of a friend. The friend then receives an email saying, "Hey [friend's name], [child's name] wants you to check out REESESPUFFS.COM. Take a look!" Finally, companies advertise their child-targeted websites on other websites that children frequent. Parents may believe that educational children's websites (such as CoolMath-Games.com and FunSchool.com) or sites for television stations that do not accept food advertising (such as Disney.com or NickJr.com) are relatively commercial-free. However, millions of impressions for banner ads appear on these sites. These banner ads usually include attention-grabbing Flash animation, often include a fun activity or game embedded within the ad itself, and always provide a direct link to the company's child-targeted website.

So what do parents know about these websites? We've learned that they actually know a lot about how food companies advertise to children on television and about the tricks that companies use to get children to nag their parents for products in the supermarket, such as popular cartoon characters like Dora the Explorer or promotions like "Win a Wii" on product packages.[22] However, advertising to children on the Internet is not something that parents readily understand; these tactics did not exist when today's parents were young. For example, one-third of parents in one study did not know whether their children played advergames, and many had never heard of advergames (even when their children told us they played them). During focus groups with parents, most were appalled and outraged when we showed them examples of some of the popular child-targeted food company websites.

Some companies appear to have somewhat curtailed these practices. In the early research on digital food marketing to children, Kellogg's FunKTown was highlighted as the largest and most elaborate child-targeted advergame site, but the site no longer exists.[23] At the end of 2010, General Mills discontinued its extremely popular Millsberry.com website. However, Kellogg and General Mills continue to maintain smaller websites to promote individual child-targeted brands, such as www.ReesesPuffs.com, www.TrixWorld.com, and www.FrootLoops.com. In addition, Kellogg's Frosted Flakes cereal now has its own Facebook page and Apple Jacks has an iPhone app for one of the games featured on its website. Clearly, these companies have not stopped targeting children through digital media; in fact, they have adapted their message to the new media.

"LIKE" US ON FACEBOOK!

Since we started tracking food marketing to children, the use of social media to market foods and beverages has exploded. In 2009, eleven of the twelve largest fast-food restaurants maintained Facebook accounts, and by 2010 all had active Twitter accounts.[24] In 2010 there were at least thirty-three Facebook accounts for sugary drinks and twenty-three Twitter accounts.[25] On YouTube as well, eleven of the top fast-food restaurants and twenty-five sugary drink brands maintained their own channels.

Forrester Research predicts that companies will triple their spending on social media marketing in the next five years.[26]

Even the advertising community has not been able to keep up with this new form of marketing. Although the companies collect substantial amounts of information about their own Facebook fans and YouTube channel viewers and subscribers, reliable data are not yet available to monitor these media from the outside. However, we do know that young people frequently visit social media sites, especially Facebook and YouTube.

From October to December 2011, 63 percent of twelve- to seventeen-year-olds visited Facebook on average more than once per day and spent thirteen minutes there each time.[27] Of note, Facebook's terms of service do not technically allow children under age thirteen, but children simply enter a different birth year to join. *Consumer Reports* and Pew have studied this issue and found that in 2011 five million Facebook users were younger than thirteen[28] and that 37 percent of ten- to twelve-year-olds had a Facebook account in 2010.[29] From October to December 2011, comScore reports, 15.5 percent of six- to eleven-year-olds visited Facebook on average four times per month and the number of child visitors increased by 55 percent from December the previous year.[30] Both children and teens are also frequent Internet video viewers. According to Nielsen, they respectively account for 8 percent and 15 percent of all online video watching.[31] From October to December 2011, 58 percent of teens and 16 percent of children visited YouTube, and teens visited on average twenty-one times per month for fifteen minutes each time.[32]

We also know that many company-sponsored social media pages are extremely popular with young people. One study found that 29 percent of teens had added at least one brand as a Facebook "friend."[33] Food products are among the most popular brands on Facebook. As of September 2011, Coca-Cola was the most popular brand of any type, with 34 million fans, and Starbucks was number three with 25 million fans.[34] Also in the top twenty brands on Facebook were Oreos (number 4), Red Bull (number 5), Skittles (number 8), Pringles (number 11), Ferrero Rocher (number 14), Monster Energy (number 15), and Nutella (number 16). All these pages had more than 10 million fans.

On YouTube, Starbuck's video channel had five million views and Domino's had three million in 2010.[35] In 2011 Red Bull's video channel had an incredible 158 million views, Coca-Cola's had 23 million, and Monster Energy's had 11 million.[36] One children's cereal, General Mills's Golden Grahams, even has its own YouTube channel, with 43 videos and almost 300,000 views.[37] In its 2010 annual report, Kellogg Company boasted about its Pop-Tarts social media campaign, which featured "nearly 3 million Facebook fans and a YouTube channel that gets more than 40,000 views each day."[38]

ENLISTING YOUNG "BRAND AMBASSADORS"

The characteristics of social media that make them so attractive to advertisers that want to reach young people are the same characteristics that make them a significant concern for the public health community. With social media, advertisers no longer direct their messages at consumers. Instead, consumers direct the companies' messages to their peers, often adding their own photos and endorsements to the mix. This form of marketing has many names: viral, word-of-mouth, peer-to-peer. Especially for older children and teens whose most important developmental need is to create their own identities, separate from their parents, these brand endorsements by peers become extremely influential. And companies take advantage of this vulnerability. Coca-Cola's vice president of global advertising strategy described its target audience for a new Coca-Cola Music marketing campaign: "Teens are the most demanding target audience. . . . They demand to interact and participate with brands and be a part of the conversation. This program has been designed with that understanding and to enable teens to view, participate and share the content and experiences."[39]

Our research on fast-food and sugary drink marketing reveals many common practices that companies use to foster personal relationships with their brands and encourage young people to advertise to each other.[40] On Facebook, for example, "The Coca-Cola Facebook Page is a collection of your stories showing how people from around the world have helped make Coke into what it is today." When Facebook members go to Facebook.com/coca-cola (or any other brand's Facebook page), they can "like" it and become a "fan" of Coke; Coke will then be featured on their own Facebook pages. Fans also can post comments and pictures to Coke's "wall," and these posts will appear on the "news feeds" sent to their Facebook friends.

The most common features on brand Facebook pages are designed to encourage fans to interact with the brand repeatedly and spread the word to their friends. Contests are frequently featured, often with pictures of the winners. For example, Dunkin' Donuts has featured a "fan-of-the-week" sweepstakes, and Sobe has run a similar "Lizard-of-the-week" contest. Polls and voting are also popular. Fast-food companies often ask fans to pick their favorite menu items and pizza toppings and provide advice on how to improve the menu. On sugary drink pages, fans are invited to vote for Monster Energy's "2010 Camping World Truck Series Most Popular Driver," the next Boston basketball court for Red Bull to refurbish, and the newest Mountain Dew flavor ("FanDEWmonium"). Food-brand Facebook pages also often feature photo albums and videos from fans, many of them showing the fan with the brand product.

Outbound links to brand websites, blogs, Twitter and Flickr pages, loyalty programs, and sweepstakes pages are also common. In addition, food company sites increasingly incorporate product purchase features. For example, on Pizza Hut's page, fans can "order from Pizza Hut without ever leaving Facebook!" and Coke fans can download an app that they can use to design their own flavor and that also directs them to Coke's "Freestyle" machines to purchase their custom flavors.

YouTube channels for fast-food and sugary drink brands provide essentially longer-length commercials for the products that viewers spread virally to their friends. Red Bull's channel hosted 363 different videos, mostly featuring its athlete and sporting event sponsorships, which accumulated more than 40 million views. Its most-viewed video was eight minutes long and featured stunts by street trials rider Danny MacAskill. Gatorade's ninety-second 2010 Super Bowl commercial received more than 900,000 views, one Domino's video promoting its "Pizza Turnaround" received 1.2 million views, and a Starbucks video featuring hip-hop artist MC Yogi generated almost one million views.

We expect that social media will continue to increase in importance as a marketing tool for food companies to reach young people as teens and even children continue to spend large amounts of time on social media. We also expect companies' social media marketing to evolve as new social media platforms become hot. Recently, companies have begun to add Tumblr to their lists of social media marketing tools. Use of this new site has skyrocketed, especially with eighteen- to twenty-four-year-olds. As with Facebook, its popularity will probably soon trickle down to teen users.

THE DEVELOPING WORLD OF MOBILE MEDIA

As the use of smartphones, tablets like the iPad, and other mobile devices explodes, social media is also moving to these mobile platforms. In 2010, 75 percent of teens owned a cell phone,[41] and 49 percent accessed the Internet on their phone.[42] Just about anything that can be accessed on the Internet with a computer is now available on mobile devices. Companies view mobile marketing as an enormous opportunity. Interactive marketing is no longer limited to the confines of the home or laptop; marketers can now reach consumers anywhere at any time.

In 2011 spending on mobile media marketing surpassed spending on social media and email marketing, and Forrester Research predicts that companies will increase their spending on mobile marketing another five-fold in the next five years.[43] Mobile devices allow companies to provide consumers with marketing messages—special deals, entertaining content, peer endorsements—at the actual time they make their purchase decision in the store or restaurant.

Marketing via social media and games is especially suited to mobile devices. All major social media sites, including Facebook, Twitter, and YouTube, have websites accessible through mobile media. In 2011 videos accounted for half of all mobile traffic.[44] Teens make up 19 percent of the mobile video audience and watch more than seven hours per month, compared with just over four hours for the general population.[45] According to comScore, 46 percent of teens with mobile Internet access visited social media sites in the past month. In addition, 42 percent of teens played games on their mobile phones in the past month, and teens are more likely to play games than other mobile phone users, but much less likely to notice in-game advertising.[46]

The food companies adapted early to mobile marketing. In 2009 we found that eight of the top twelve fast-food restaurants ran banner advertising on mobile websites, and this number increased steadily throughout the year.[47] In 2010 we found mobile banner ads for Amp and Red Bull energy drinks, as well as Coca-Cola Classic, Fanta, Mountain Dew, Pepsi, Sprite, and Sunkist.[48] Compared to banner advertising on the Internet, these ads were relatively simple; however, the majority advertised special deals or other promotions that the viewer could participate in immediately, such as "Play Coca-Cola on SCVNGR at the mall. Unlock secret rewards," "Wanta be the 4th Fantana? Click here," or "Por solo un $1" (with a picture of a Coca-Cola fountain drink from McDonald's).

Food and beverage companies have also pioneered branded mobile applications. In 2009 eight fast-food restaurants had mobile applications. Most of them featured restaurant locators, but others enabled users to order via their smartphone. For example, Pizza Hut's mobile application allowed users to add toppings to a virtual pizza on the screen or order chicken wings by adding sauce and chicken to a virtual bowl and coating the wings by shaking the phone. Pizza Hut boasts that its app was downloaded more than two million times and generated more than $7 million in sales in the first year.[49] Dunkin' Donuts also promoted a "Dunkin' Run" app that allowed users to coordinate with friends who also had the app to consolidate an order and present it to the cashier at the restaurant.

Advergames have also made their way to smartphones. Coca-Cola and Red Bull lead the way with fun, interactive, downloadable mobile game applications. The Coca-Cola game apps include: "Magic Coke Bottle," in which users, as with a Magic 8-Ball toy, shake the phone for an answer; "Spin the Coke," which allows users to integrate their friends' Facebook profile photos into a "spin the bottle" game; and "ZOOZbeat Sprite," which is available by texting a code from underneath the cap of Sprite bottles. This app works by "shaking, tilting or tapping the iPhone screen to create and combine rhythmic and melodic tracks that can be uploaded to ZOOZbeat.com for listening and sharing in .mp3 format with friends via Facebook and Twitter." Red Bull also has three iPhone game apps, such as "Red Bull Racing Challenge," for which 25 to 41 percent of downloads are made by teens.[50] Of note, the American Academy of Pediatrics has recommended that no one under age eighteen ever consume energy drinks, including Red Bull.[51]

In a disturbing new development, Kellogg's introduced an Apple Jacks iPhone game app in 2011 that was clearly targeted to children: "The race to the bowl is on! Play as Apple or CinnaMon as you race through the frozen Ice Kingdom, collecting tasty Apple Jacks cereal pieces for extra race points."[52] Ironically, parents give cell phones to their children so that they can monitor their whereabouts when they are not at home, but parents now must worry about companies selling junk food and other tempting products to their children outside the home where they cannot monitor these activities.

ADDITIONAL CONCERNS FOR LOW-INCOME AND MINORITY YOUTH

Many in the public health community believe that marketing junk food to children and adolescents crosses the line, especially when that marketing targets low-income and minority youth.[53] Even more than higher-income and white youth, these young people face alarming rates of obesity, consume too much fast food and sugary drinks, and have limited access to healthy foods. Companies have the right to produce and sell junk food, but it is unethical to spend billions of dollars to convince young people that they have to have them when consuming these products can contribute to a lifetime of poor health and chronic disease.

Food and beverage companies do not appear to target low-income youth specifically; however, we have found numerous instances in our research of marketing that targets minority youth. For example, Reese's Puffs is the least nutritious children's cereal on the market, yet advertising for Reese's Puffs on television and the Internet predominantly features black children.[54] The food brands with the most advertising on Spanish-language television, radio, and Internet include McDonald's, Burger King, Domino's, Coca-Cola, M&Ms, and Snickers.[55] Black children and teens were ten times more likely to visit Sprite's website (SpriteStepOff.com) than all youth and three to four times more likely to visit numerous websites for McDonald's, Wendy's, Dunkin' Donuts, NOS Energy Drink, and Mountain Dew (GreenLabelSound.com). Coca-Cola in particular boasts about its efforts to reach "multicultural" youth. The company has identified black youth as a growth market because of their purchasing power and trendsetting,[56] and it predicts that 86 percent of its future sales growth will come from Hispanics, blacks, and Asians.[57]

Many parents are not aware of these newer digital marketing techniques and how much food advertising exists in the new media that their children spend so much time with. When we show them how food marketing to children and teens looks today, they, too, are outraged.[58] Food companies will change their marketing practices in the face of public pressure, and parents can demand that food companies stop undermining their efforts to create a healthy environment for their children.

〜

Jennifer L. Harris is director of marketing initiatives at the Rudd Center for Food Policy and Obesity at Yale University. She is responsible for identifying and coordinating research initiatives to understand and communicate the extent and impact of children's exposure to food advertising. Dr. Harris received her BA in political science from Northwestern University, her MBA in marketing from the Wharton School at the University of Pennsylvania, and her PhD in social psychology from Yale University. Before returning to graduate school, she worked for eighteen years as a vice president in marketing at American Express and ran a marketing consulting firm specializing in marketing strategy and new product and market development. Dr. Harris has written on the psychological and behavioral effects of advertising on children and adolescents and conducted research to quantify the amount and types of food marketing seen by young people and its impact on their health and diet.

CHAPTER 9

The ABCs of School Lunch

JANET POPPENDIECK

FROM *A PLACE AT THE TABLE*

What's served in the schools is very much a function of the kind of investment we've been willing to make.

—Janet Poppendieck, professor emerita of sociology at Hunter College, City University of New York, and author of Free for All: Fixing School Food in America

In 2011 America's public schools served more than 5.7 billion lunches, about two-thirds of them free or at greatly reduced prices, to children from low-income families. But the school lunch program is under attack on several fronts: for containing foods that contribute to the alarming rates of childhood obesity, for stigmatizing the "poor kids" who take the reduced-price meals; for allowing junk foods to be sold in schools to help pay for the official, federally supported lunches; and for not moving toward the ultimate reform: the free school lunch.

Here Janet Poppendieck, one of the nation's leading writers about hunger in America, puts forward the arguments for radical change. This essay is based on her field research in which she interviewed school food service personnel, advocates, and school administrators and was also a participant-observer in school cafeterias and kitchens.

School lunch is a hot topic. Rising rates of childhood obesity and type 2 diabetes have focused attention on our national diet as never before, and naturally people are discussing the $10 billion federal program that delivered more than 5.7 billion lunches last year. All across the nation, parents and their allies are organizing to demand healthier, fresher, and more appealing school food. Farm to Cafeteria programs that promote the use of locally grown produce are under way in more than nine thousand schools spread across all fifty states. Efforts to return to fresh "scratch" cooking, programs to engage children in producing and preparing food, attempts to integrate school food into the curriculum, crusades to increase the availability of vegetarian alternatives, and campaigns to reduce fat and salt in school meals are ubiquitous. Would-be reformers, however, are up against some formidable obstacles. There are some things they ought to know about school food in the twenty-first century if they are hoping to work effectively for change: the ABCs of school lunch.

First, a few basics. The National School Lunch Program (NSLP) was enacted in 1946 "as a measure of national security, to safeguard the health and well-being of the nation's children and to encourage the domestic consumption of nutritious agricultural commodities."[1] The federal government had first gotten involved in school lunches in the midst of the Great Depression when it set up work relief projects to staff cafeterias and donated surplus farm commodities removed from the market in price support operations. When the surpluses of labor and commodities dried up during World War II, the program was converted to a cash subsidy to help schools purchase food. A mounting concern about the impact of diet on the fitness of the nation's youth to serve in the armed forces, coupled with a determination to ensure that there would be outlets to absorb American farm surpluses after the war, induced Congress to give the program a permanent legislative basis in the National School Lunch Act.

In 2011 the NSLP served an average of 31.6 million lunches each school day. About two-thirds of those were served free or at sharply reduced prices to children from low-income families. Children qualify for free meals if their family income is at or below 130 percent of the federal poverty line or $24,817 per year for a mother and two kids. Those with incomes between 130 and 185 percent of the poverty line ($35,317 per year for a family of three) may purchase a lunch for a locally determined price not to exceed 40 cents. Students from families above that cutoff must pay a locally determined "full price." These standards are not adjusted for regional variations in the cost of living; students in real need may be relegated to the full-price category in high-cost-of-living areas. The US Department of Agriculture, which administers the program at the federal level, reimburses schools $2.77 for each lunch served free, $2.37 for each reduced-price lunch, and 26 cents for each misleadingly labeled "full-price" lunch. In addition, schools receive an entitlement to commodities based on the number of lunches they serve.[2] Both the reimbursements and the commodities are available only to meals that comply with the federal nutrition standards prescribed by the USDA and monitored by state educational agencies.

A IS FOR À LA CARTE

School lunch is not what it used to be. Walk into the lunchroom of nine out of ten American secondary schools or two-thirds of elementary schools and you will find the school cafeteria selling other foods in competition with the federally subsidized and nutritionally regulated school lunch. Some schools may sell just a few items, but in many schools you will find the school food service doing a brisk business in burgers, pizza, fries, nachos, cookies, pastries, sports drinks, and chips of all descriptions. This is an arrangement that comes fairly close to defeating the purpose of the National School Lunch Program. In the first place, it makes a mockery of the carefully wrought federal nutrition standards and the much-debated menu planning systems designed to produce balanced, nutritionally sound meals. School food service menu planners struggle to create lunches that will comply with a federal "meal pattern" designed to reflect the "Dietary Guidelines for Americans." But why should a student try an unfamiliar vegetable or acquire a taste for low-fat milk if her favorite snack foods are available across the room or next to the cashier?

The most recent Child Nutrition Reauthorization, the Healthy, Hunger-Free Kids Act of 2010, has given the secretary of agriculture, for the first time, the authority to set nutrition standards for so-called competitive foods: all foods sold in competition with the "reimbursable" school meal, as the official, nutritionally regulated and federally subsidized meal is commonly known in the trade. Competitive foods include food in vending machines, food sold in school stores and snack shops, food distributed in classrooms, food sold at school-sponsored fund-raisers (although exemptions may be applied to these), and food sold à la carte in the cafeteria. The USDA is hard at work on a "proposed rule," the first step in the federal rule-making process. The proposed rule will be followed by a comment period and then a final rule. Almost all observers and stakeholders are anticipating an intense battle between the snack food industry, on the one hand, and public health and parents' groups, on the other. A new study published in 2012 in the journal *Pediatrics* found that adolescents in states with strict competitive food laws may provide ammunition to the public health forces.[3] It is probable that any proposed rule will set limits on the calories, fat, saturated fat, salt, and added sugars that can be part of a serving and that it will eliminate some of the most egregious items.

Unless the new rules convince schools to do away with the competitive foods altogether, however, à la carte and other competitive foods will continue to undermine the National School Lunch Program, because à la carte service stigmatizes the federal lunch. Where à la carte lines are completely separate—a common situation in some areas of the country—it can lead to a form of segregation in the cafeteria: affluent youngsters in one area, poor students in another. In many California schools, à la carte items are sold at carts and windows that open onto outdoor eating areas. "Those who were provided with lunch . . . were the only ones who actually ate the school food. There was also a separate door for them to go to receive their lunch and they had to eat in the cafeteria because the school dishes and trays were not allowed outside. The system for free/reduced lunches made the students who received them stand out, it divided the high school," wrote a UC Santa Cruz student describing the lunch setup in his high school. The California situation is the extreme, a function of school architecture and climate as well as prevailing attitudes, but it is an extreme that highlights a common phenomenon in much of the country. Once you set up an à la carte line—a separate place that sells kids' favorite foods—the students with money will gravitate to that line to choose their meals and snacks unconstrained by federal meal patterns, and fairly soon the rumor will spread that only "poor kids" eat the "school lunch" (sometimes disparagingly referred to as "county food" or "welfare food"). Then, in a classic display of the self-fulfilling prophecy, affluent students, especially at the high school level, will avoid the regular line for fear that someone might think they are getting a free meal.

So, if à la carte sales undermine the nutritional integrity of school food and stigmatize the official meal, why do they exist? Why are food service directors competing with themselves in the school cafeteria? The short answer is money: the tyranny of the bottom line. Food service directors and school business officials firmly believe that à la carte sales subsidize the reimbursable lunch.

B IS FOR BOTTOM LINE

"We don't like it, but we have to sell à la carte to stay in the black," is the common refrain of school food service professionals.[4]

Schools sold a few à la carte items when I was a kid; you could buy milk or a piece of fruit or an ice cream bar to supplement the lunch you brought from home or to add to the reimbursable meal. The expansion of à la carte into a substantial business venture, however, arose in the wake of the Reagan-era cutbacks in domestic social spending. The Omnibus Budget Reconciliation Act of 1981, which came on top of significant child nutrition cuts in the last years of the Carter administration, reduced the federal subsidy for full-price meals by more than one-third, sharply cut the subsidy for reduced-price meals, restricted the federal commodity allocation, and added new requirements for documentation and reporting. The results included a steep decline in participation; the National School Lunch Program lost more than one-quarter of its paying customers in the period between 1979 and 1983.[5] Food service directors found themselves facing a financial disaster: fewer lunches sold, smaller reimbursements for each meal, fewer federal commodities, and expensive new accounting requirements. Local school districts were resistant to picking up the slack; declining enrollments and taxpayer revolts had reduced their revenues just as mounting pension and health care costs escalated the demands on their resources. Although local school systems had traditionally put money into school meals, hard-pressed school boards began to demand that school cafeterias "break even" and "operate like a business."

Many food service departments turned to à la carte sales and fast-food clones as a way to bring paying customers back into their cafeterias.

The other side of the break-even ledger—cutting costs—also accelerated the conversion of the school lunchroom into a fast-food emporium. Food service departments tried to reduce the cost per meal by replacing the fresh preparation of food on-site with bulk convenience foods. Many school cafeterias went from homemade meals to defrost-and-reheat entrées and even whole prepackaged and frozen meals reminiscent of TV dinners. Such changes not only allowed schools to reduce total labor hours but permitted the substitution of cheaper, less-skilled workers for employees with cooking skills. These workers were more easily replaced, less likely to make a career in food service, and less able to bargain for wages and health coverage. Schools reaped further financial savings by arranging schedules—"short hours"—that kept most workers below the threshold for benefits. School menu planners also found that they could reduce risk—the risk of food-borne illness and the risk of an expensive lawsuit—by transferring liability up the chain through the use of precooked and frozen items. And of course the cost-saving retreat to frozen pizza and frozen chicken nuggets meshed nicely with the business ideology—"Our children are our customers; we have to give them what they want."

Even with these cost-saving strategies, breaking even is a challenge in many school districts. The federal reimbursements are sufficient to cover the costs of producing the meals in some districts, but not in others, and with the exception of a two-cent-per-meal differential in favor of "severe need" districts, the reimbursement is a one-size-fits-all proposition, a crucial factor over which food service managers have no say. The adequacy of the reimbursement depends on local labor and food costs, the volume of meals served, and even the weather. An unusually large number of snow days, for example, with money going out to pay salaried staff and amortize equipment but no money coming in from sales and reimbursements, can convert a program from the black to the red. Districts set the price of "paid" meals locally, but too high a price, or too rapid a price increase, can easily deter participation.[6] Clearly, the break-even challenge facing school food managers varies depending on the percentage of students eligible for free and reduced-price meals and a host of other factors—whether the campus is "open" (students are permitted to leave the school at lunchtime) or "closed" (students are not allowed to leave the campus), whether a school store or snack shack is operated by some campus entity other than the food service (a student organization or the principal, for example), and the extent to which vending machines are available on campus.

Regardless of the availability of these alternatives, however, the level of participation in the reimbursable meal is the key to solvency. The higher the ADP (average daily participation), the larger the pool of fees and reimbursements over which to distribute fixed costs like administrative salaries and cafeteria electricity bills. The exhortation to "operate like a business" has been taken to heart by some districts in the form of "branding" the school cafeteria. A catchy name for the food service and a school logo and color scheme applied to everything from cafeteria workers' uniforms to paper cups and napkins are designed to entice students into eating the school meal. In an effort to boost participation, food service menu planners across the country have turned to the same fast-food clones that characterize the à la carte line: pizza, (baked) fries, nuggets, and patties—"carnival foods," as one critic put it. In short, selling food to children puts children—and behind them the billions of dollars' worth of food advertising aimed at children—in charge of the school food menu. The conversion of students into customers has gotten out of hand.

C IS FOR COMPLIANCE

No amount of hype about branding the cafeteria and kids as customers can change the underlying reality: school food is not really a business, and this is nowhere more evident than in the host of federal state and local regulations with which it must comply. Food service managers are subject to many of the same regulations with which their commercial counterparts must comply—health and safety regulations, employment practices regulations, environmental regulations—but the two sets of regulations that constrain them most are unique to school food: the nutrition requirements and the rules for managing the three-tier eligibility and reimbursement system.

For most of the past fifteen years, school meals have been required to meet two sets of nutrition standards. The first, established during World War II, reflected wartime concerns about getting enough food: the War Food Administration required school lunches that received donated commodities to provide one-third of the recommended dietary allowances (RDAs) for protein, calories, and a short list of vitamins and minerals. The standard of one-third of RDAs was transferred into the permanent program when the National School Lunch Act was passed in 1946. By the 1980s, however, health concerns had shifted from a focus on deficiency diseases to the perils of overconsumption; critics charged that school menus were high in fat and saturated fat and pointed out that the Department of Agriculture was not following its own dietary guidelines. Legislation passed in the mid-1990s required school meals to conform to the "Dietary Guidelines for Americans"—specifically to reduce fat to no more than 30 percent of total calories and saturated fat to 10 percent or less.

It turned out that reducing fat to 30 percent or less of calories while maintaining the minimum number of calories needed to supply one-third of the RDAs is no easy job. In short, if you reduce the fat, it is hard to meet the calorie minimums, at least within the financial constraints typically faced by school menus. The quickest, least expensive fix—and the one frequently recommended by state reviewers when they encountered a calorie deficit—was to add sugar! Sweetened, flavored milks became a staple of the cafeteria. An additional serving of vegetables, the element in which American diets are most glaringly deficient, would usually have filled the calorie gap, but it was beyond the financial reach of most schools.

The Healthy, Hunger-Free Kids Act of 2010 revised the nutrition standards for school meals based on recommendations developed by the Institute of Medicine. A range of calories for each age/grade grouping was substituted for the old calorie minimums, and the 30 percent of calories from fat regulation was scrapped. In short, the USDA has developed "meal patterns" that, if followed, will supply approximately one-third of the dietary reference intakes (DRIs), which have replaced the RDAs. Schools will no longer be routinely monitored for the long list of "target nutrients" but only for calories, saturated fat, trans fat, and sodium. The new meal patterns call for more fruits and vegetables than the old plan; specify a variety of vegetables, including weekly servings of deep green, red, and orange vegetables and legumes; and require the inclusion of whole grains. The new regulations have just been released, so schools will have some time to comply, including a very gradual phase-in of the stringent new sodium limits.

The nutrition standards, though a challenge, are a piece of cake compared to the task of managing the free/reduced-price/full-price structure. Applications must be distributed and retrieved; getting them back is often a time-consuming struggle. Once the applications are complete, schools are required to verify the information provided on a random sample equivalent to 3 percent of the applications submitted, a task they assert they are singularly ill equipped to complete. And once eligibility is established, each meal must be assigned to the proper reimbursement category. The labor costs of carrying out this federal mandate are substantial, but the penalties for mistakes are also significant. The state agencies that supervise school food programs conduct detailed audits at least once every three years and can withhold reimbursements for claims that cannot be substantiated. The rate of "erroneous payments" is extraordinarily high. About one in five students in a recent federal audit were certified inaccurately or erroneously denied benefits.[7]

In an effort to reduce errors, many school food service operations have invested in elaborate software that allows cashiers to identify each child's category with a combination of swipe card and picture ID. The swipe card tells the cashier which category of lunch should be claimed, and the picture, which appears on the computer screen, allows the cashier to make sure that the card is being used by the right child. Other schools have gone to finger imaging; "Kids don't forget their fingers," an exasperated cafeteria manager told me. Because the computer software allows parents to prepay for school meals, both school food service staff and advocates had hoped that this would reduce the stigma associated with free meals, but savvy children are foiling this intent by insisting on paying cash: "I have to have cash in my hand, Mom, or the kids will think I'm eating free." In schools where cash payment is not permitted, a whole new round of troubles has arisen as schools try to figure out what to do when a child arrives at the cashier with a lunch on the tray but insufficient funds in the account. Incidents in which such lunches were confiscated and discarded have generated controversy in numerous communities.

As onerous as they are, the costs to school systems of trying to comply with the three-tier eligibility system are not the highest price we pay for this "administrative absurdity." The biggest cost is the stigma that this system generates. Some schools go to great lengths to protect the privacy of the youngsters who are eligible for free and reduced-price meals, but in the lunchroom, too often, "everybody knows." And if students don't know precisely who is eating free or at a reduced rate, they know that someone is, that these categories exist. It is not much of a problem at the elementary level, but once students reach the socially sensitive junior high years, it provides a basis for "ranking," for hierarchies of prestige, and students who need the food begin to forgo the meal rather than be seen as "poor." The three-tier system deters some students in need from taking advantage of the meals that are prepared for them and burdens others with a sense of shame.

Further, the benefit structure in the program almost ensures that some children in need will be excluded from the free and reduced-price category and does so in a manner that breeds resentment. In most means-tested programs, benefits decline gradually as income rises. Having an income a few dollars over the cutoff makes you ineligible for a relatively small benefit—for years the minimum SNAP benefit was $10 a month. In school food, however, if your family is $5 over the cutoff for reduced-price meals, the loss is substantial. If the full price is $2.75 and you have three children in school, you are missing out on a benefit worth more than $1,400 per year. And while the $2.75 is a bargain and is kept below-market by the combination of the small cash subsidy and the commodities entitlement, it is still too high for many families whose incomes are above the 185 percent of poverty cutoff, particularly if they live in high-cost-of-living areas of the country.

THE ULTIMATE SCHOOL FOOD REFORM

It is time to change the way we pay for school food in the United States. Instead of selling food to students and then creating systems to identify and absorb the cost for those too poor to purchase it, we need to provide meals to all children as a regular part of the school day. This approach, called "universal free school meals"—or just "universal" among advocates—would have multiple advantages. First, it would reduce and eventually eliminate the stigma attached to eating school lunch. I say "eventually" because youngsters now in high school and junior high have already absorbed the idea that school lunch is for poor kids, and they are not likely to part with this idea overnight. But as middle-class parents come to realize that they do not need to give their children lunch money and that they are already paying through the tax system, eating school food will become the norm. Second, it will make wholesome school meals fully available to students who are now priced out—too affluent for the reduced-price category, but too financially strapped to pay the full price. Third, it will eliminate enormous quantities of costly paperwork and processing of applications and the complex and error-prone process of counting and claiming, freeing time and energy for education and reducing the true cost of providing healthy meals. Fourth, it will transform youngsters from "customers" back into "students." Schools will be able to offer a variety of healthy foods without playing to the tastes promoted by food manufacturers and advertisers. Fifth, it will permit the integration of school food with the curriculum; the cafeteria will reinforce rather than contradict what students are learning in health class, and it will become a place where cultures, geography, biology, and history can be explored. Finally, without the need for a cashier, the lunch line will move more quickly, leaving more time for children to eat and promoting a more civil atmosphere in the lunchroom. The Healthy, Hunger-Free Kids Act took modest steps in this direction, promoting the direct certification of children whose families receive benefits from the Supplemental Nutrition Assistance Program (SNAP) and Temporary Assistance for Needy Families (TANF), and authorizing pilot programs of "community eligibility" in which schools with large numbers of directly certified children could opt to feed all children free of charge, relying on a formula rather than individual applications to determine the federal reimbursements.

These innovations are important—not only to the children in the schools selected to participate but also as pilots of a more sensible approach to managing this system. But a bolder move to a federal universal funding scheme would truly enable school lunch to realize its potential contribution to the health and education of our children. There is, of course, "no such thing as a free lunch," but how we pay for it is a social choice that is ours to make. It is time to invest in the future and free the school lunch program to do its job.

໑

Janet Poppendieck is professor emerita of sociology at Hunter College, City University of New York, and senior research associate at the Center for New York City Food Policy at the City University of New York School of Public Health. She is the author of *Sweet Charity: Emergency Food and the End of Entitlement* (New York: Viking, 1998) and, most recently, *Free for All: Fixing School Food in America* (Berkeley: University of California Press, 2010). She can be contacted at janpop@verizon.net, and more information about her other books is available at www.janetpoppendieck.

PART II

FEEDING THE
HUNGRY

CHAPTER 10

Feeding America in Times of Change

MATT KNOTT

FROM *A PLACE AT THE TABLE*

In 1980, there were 200 food banks in this country. Today, there are over 40,000.

—Title card from **A Place at the Table**

And so we had a proliferation of emergency responses, soup kitchens, food pantries moving from literally a shelf in the cupboard of the pastor's office to an operation with regular hours. . . . We have basically created a secondary food system for the poor in this country.

—Janet Poppendieck, professor emerita
of sociology, Hunter College, New York

The "rediscovery" of hunger in America in the 1960s included the opening of the first food bank in Phoenix, Arizona. It brought together government-provided surplus food and leftovers from food manufacturers and super-markets and made it all available to the hungry at local distribution centers. Here Matt Knott, interim president and CEO of Feeding America, the nation's largest hunger relief organization, traces the history of the organization and explains what it does and what it hopes to achieve.

As the nation's leading domestic hunger relief organization, Feeding America provides food assistance through its national network of more than 200 member food banks and 61,000 local agencies, like food pantries, soup kitchens, and after-school programs. We provide nearly 3.3 billion pounds of food and grocery items to more than 37 million people in communities all across America.

Feeding America began in Phoenix, where John van Hengel, a retired businessman, had been volunteering at a St. Vincent de Paul soup kitchen and trying to build programs to find food to serve the hungry. He and a small team of volunteers began by picking citrus from private homes in an old milk truck and delivering it to inner-city missions. But the process was inefficient, and the needs of the community were greater than they were able to meet.

Van Hengel's inspiration came to him one day when he met a desperate mother who regularly rummaged through grocery store garbage bins to find food for her children. She suggested that there should be a place where, instead of being thrown out, discarded food could be stored for people like her to pick up, similar to the way banks "store" money for future use. With that idea, an industry was born.

Known as the "father of food-banking," van Hengel is credited with revolutionizing the charitable emergency food system. He began by soliciting donations of surplus food from local grocery stores, offering them a business solution for the cost of dumping food. In the late 1960s, he received a grant from St. Mary's Basilica in downtown Phoenix to purchase an abandoned building and convert it to a warehouse where donated goods could be inspected, sorted, and stored, and then distributed to smaller social service agencies in the community that were feeding people in need. Thus, van Hengel created the St. Mary's Food Bank, the first of its kind. In its first full year of operation, John and his volunteers distributed 275,000 pounds of food into the community.

In the years following van Hengel's establishment of the St. Mary's Food Bank, the operation grew and word of its success spread to other states. By 1977, food banks had been established in eighteen cities across the country. John van Hengel's work garnered support in the form of a $50,000 federal grant for St. Mary's Food Bank staff to teach officials in other western cities how to establish similar operations. In 1978 the federal government doubled the grant, allowing St. Mary's Food Bank to extend the food banking program into the South. In 1979 the organization began soliciting national food donations and formally incorporated the existing network of food banks as Second Harvest, a biblical reference that appealed to landowners and farmers to leave a "second harvest" for the poor.

Soon the organization became an efficient clearinghouse for large donations from national corporations and adopted uniform standards for storage capacity, quality control, and management. In 1982 the Community Service Administration, which had provided steady annual funding for Second Harvest, closed, and the Second Harvest network became a privately funded charitable organization. The number of food banks involved in Second Harvest continued to grow, as did the volume of donated food each year. In 2008 Second Harvest changed its name to Feeding America to better reflect the mission of the organization. Today Feeding America is the largest, most efficient domestic hunger relief organization in the country.

But ending hunger is not just about delivering food. It is about providing nutritious food that supports the health and well-being of the people we serve. People who struggle to get enough to eat typically find it equally as difficult to get the right kinds of food they need to stay healthy. To best serve them, the Feeding America network operates with farmers and produce growers, packagers, and shippers to secure fresh fruits and vegetables that would otherwise go to waste. With the help of partners in the produce industry, Feeding America provides more than 500 million pounds of fresh fruits and vegetables each year. In addition to being able to provide fresh produce, Feeding America food banks have increased their capacity to handle other fresh perishable foods such as dairy, meat, and fish by expanding the fleets of refrigerated trucks and vans that deliver these foods to their agencies safely over long distances. Last year nutritious foods such as fruits and vegetables, cereals, grains and pasta, meats, dairy, and 100 percent juices made up 78 percent of the total 3.3 billion pounds we distributed. The organization's goal is to increase that by providing an additional one million pounds of fresh fruits and vegetables annually by 2015.

In addition to food distribution, the Feeding America network operates programs that serve vulnerable populations; provides nutrition education and job skills training; connects people with government food assistance programs; raises public awareness of hunger; conducts research to understand and develop effective solutions to the problem; and advocates for public policies that protect low-income families. To support its efforts, Feeding America builds partnerships with hundreds of food manufacturers, corporations, foundations, individuals, and government and nonprofit agencies, as well as with companies across a variety of sectors such as financial, insurance, and investment, in order to secure funds and other resources that help our food banks build and expand programs that serve the great number of American families in need.

Prior to the 2008 recession, Feeding America food banks generally served individuals and families for whom making ends meet was a constant struggle. But in an uncertain economic environment, the landscape of hunger changes rapidly. Since the recession, the need for food assistance has changed dramatically. What was once thought to only be a problem for people in impoverished communities is now a problem for millions of people who once had stable jobs and secure retirements and considered themselves middle-class. People from all walks of life and all income levels are finding themselves in need of food assistance, many for the first time in their lives.

In 2010 Feeding America conducted the largest and most comprehensive of its quadrennial studies of domestic hunger, documenting the incidence and prevalence of hunger in the United States and the response of the emergency food assistance system, which includes public programs as well as the Feeding America network of food banks. That study, "Hunger in America 2010," found that since 2006 the number of people seeking help from Feeding America food banks and agencies has increased by a staggering 46 percent—a difference of more than 12 million people.

The findings were in line with the anecdotal experiences that Feeding America food banks had been reporting since 2007 about the alarming rate at which new families and individuals were becoming food pantry clients. High unemployment and underemployment had been forcing a growing number of people to seek food assistance from the Feeding America network. Our food pantries and kitchens were even reporting that people who had once been agency supporters or donors were returning as clients in need of help themselves. And often, the assets they had left made them ineligible for government programs, driving them to charities for food assistance.

The Feeding America food banks have witnessed a shift not only in the clientele they serve but also in the frequency with which clients are using food banks as a resource for food. The organization recently released a study that measured the frequency of Feeding America clients' use of our pantries. "Food Banks: Hunger's New Staple" shows that use of our food pantries has evolved from occasional emergency relief to a regular source of food for the people they serve.

In addition to studies that focus on the people served by the Feeding America network, the organization conducts annual research to identify and document exactly where hunger exists. Last year Feeding America completed the second of its annual "Map the Meal Gap" and "Map the Meal Gap: Child Food Insecurity" studies, which show that there are adults and children facing hunger in every county and congressional district in the country, even in the wealthiest. The overall hunger rates range from an estimated 5 percent of the people in Steele County, North Dakota, to 37 percent in Holmes County, Mississippi. But the rate for child hunger goes even higher—in Starr and Zavala Counties in Texas, where more than 45 percent of children are food-insecure. "Map the Meal Gap 2012" reveals the number of additional meals it would take to ensure that every man, woman, and child had enough to eat every day of the year. Food-insecure people report a food budget shortfall equal to approximately one week's worth of meals every month. This equates to an overall national food budget shortfall of at least $21.2 billion, or 8.4 billion additional meals, each year. By their own accounts, people who lack this "weeks' worth" of meals are trying to support themselves and be self-sufficient.

The problem is likely to get even harder for America's food-insecure families. Today we face a perfect storm of challenges that will have a potentially devastating effect on low-income families who face hunger, as well as on our network's ability to meet the needs of all people in need. High unemployment, increasing poverty, and the rising cost of fuel and food have driven sharp increases in the need for emergency food assistance. At the same time, the number of manufacturing donations and

USDA commodities distributed to food banks is decreasing—and our food banks are struggling to make up the difference. Funding for nutrition safety net programs is at risk of being cut as Congress works to reduce the federal deficit and balance the budget; such cuts would force families to dip further into their already meager food budgets to cover basic expenses and drive them to seek help from an already strained charitable food system.

But charities simply cannot end hunger alone. In this economy, millions of families are struggling and many will never fully recover. We at Feeding America know that we will be responding to this extraordinary need for food assistance for years to come. Only through thoughtful and strategic partnerships between the nonprofit, government, corporate, and philanthropic sectors will we be able to effectively fight hunger. Making sure that every person has enough food is critical to ensuring a prosperous future for our nation. Hunger undermines our communities, our educational system, our workforce, and our national security. It weakens our ability to thrive and compete in the global economy.

Hunger in America is a serious problem, yet one of the most easily solvable issues we face today. As John van Hengel once asked, "The poor we shall always have with us, but why the hungry?" The truth is that there is no reason why anyone should go hungry in America. The amount of food that goes uneaten in this country could feed every man, woman, and child if we could only bridge the gap between those who have too much and those who have too little. Until then, Feeding America continues to ensure that low-income families have enough to eat. We know that people cannot begin to think about their future if their biggest worry is how they'll feed their families today. When we give someone food, we take away that worry so that they can focus on doing well in school or finding a better job and ultimately building a better life for themselves and for their children.

∽

Matt Knott is interim president and CEO of Feeding America, and also chief operating officer, overseeing food sourcing, member relations, and planning.

CHAPTER 11

Faith and Food

DAVID BECKMANN AND SARAH NEWMAN

FROM *A PLACE AT THE TABLE*

We have tried a thousand points of light. We have tried it in spades, but with all of that expansion of private feeding, all of that effort, especially by the faith communities, we have not reduced hunger.

—David Beckmann, international anti-hunger campaigner through his organization Bread for the World

In Chapter 2, Pastor Bob Wilson asked the question: Why do churches and people of faith get involved in feeding the poor? His answer was because, for any person of faith, feeding the poor is the "right thing to do; it is what churches should do." These next two essays, by David Beckmann, head of Bread for the World, and Sarah Newman, the researcher on A Place at the Table, *explore further the link between faith and food. Beckmann's essay is taken from an interview with UrbanFaith.com news and religion editor Christine A. Scheller. It appeared at UrbanFaith on November, 2, 2010, the year Beckmann won the World Food Prize.*

THE EXODUS OF OUR TIME

David Beckmann

I grew up in a Christian home and my parents cared about people in need. My dad was really concerned about making democracy work. I was a student in the late 1960s . . . and being a young man at that time made me start asking questions about how we could get our country to address justice issues, [and] poverty issues especially. So that was really a turning point.

As I got into the policy and politics of poverty, it seemed to me that the underlying political will to do something about poverty was a lack of spiritual commitment. So for me, it has always made sense that it's God, politics, hunger, and poverty. . . .

What's most striking is that the world as a whole has made remarkable progress against hunger, poverty, and disease. I believe in God, and I see hundreds of millions of people who have escaped from poverty in places like Ethiopia, Bangladesh, and Brazil. That's why, for me, it makes sense that this is God moving in our history. And then I come back to the USA where we haven't made any progress against hunger and poverty since about 1973, and it informs, I think, the US situation. If Brazil and Bangladesh can reduce poverty, it's clear that we could do it in the US. We just haven't tried for a while.

In the '60s and early '70s, we had economic growth and we had a concerted effort under both [President] Johnson and [President] Nixon to reduce hunger and poverty and we cut poverty in half. So it's doable here too. . . . I think the fact that we work on world poverty and domestic poverty together makes it much clearer that our problem in this country is lack of commitment. . . .

[My new book] is written especially to people who are spiritually grounded in some way. I do think that when people realize that hundreds of millions of people have escaped from extreme poverty, if we think of that in religious terms, this is a great liberation; this is the Exodus of our time. It encourages us to think about our own country and think, "Well, let's get with the program." This is something God wants us to do. The second message of the book is that God is calling us to change the politics of hunger because the need is especially great right now. But the opportunities are also very clear. We can do a lot, but we can't food bank our way to the end of hunger. . . .

All of the food that we provide through food charities amounts to about 6 percent of the food that poor people get from federal food programs: food stamps and school lunches and so forth. What we do through charity is really important, but the churches and charities cannot fix this problem. We've got to get the government to provide leadership and we have clear opportunities right now. People are kind of wailing about the dysfunction of our politics, but in fact Congress and the president have done a lot for poor people over the last couple of years. . . . I just think God has put it on a plate in front of us. We can make changes.

[Our powerful democracy] sends a call to the faithful to get off the couch, right now. I hope we don't have one in three African American kids hungry ten years from now. There is no reason for that. Forget everything else. We know how to feed kids. . . . It's clear that there's an important leadership role to play in changing the politics of hunger. I think God is telling us to get with the program, but we really need the energetic leadership of African American people of faith.

WHERE SPIRITUALITY MEETS THE FRONT LINES OF HUNGER

Sarah Newman

Americans are a deeply religious people: 86 percent believe in God or a higher power, according to a 2010 study by the Pew Forum on Religion and Public Life. Across religions, food defines many customs and rituals that are both sacred and communal. For billions of people, eating isn't just a practice of nourishment but one of faith. And despite deep-seated historical and continuing religious conflicts, rituals and principles about food are more often similar among faiths than not.

So how can we tolerate an industrial food system out of sync with our faith traditions that leaves 49 million Americans hungry? More than one-third of all Americans are obese. They include rural and urban residents, children and elderly, all of whom are subsisting on unhealthy processed foods laden with salts and sugars. They are food-insecure and unable to access the sustainable food systems available to millions of other Americans at their supermarkets, local farmers' markets, and community-supported agriculture (CSA) programs.

But in the face of this food insecurity, ministers, priests, rabbis, imans, and lay practitioners, guided by their theological teachings and practices, are developing sustainable food systems that not only nourish but address poverty, health, and economic issues.

"The moral imperative of feeding the hungry is intrinsic to all major religions," says Jeremy Everett, a Baptist minister in Waco, Texas, who directs the Texas Hunger Initiative. He points to the Old Testament teachings that continue to be a guide for followers of the world's monotheistic traditions. In Deuteronomy 4:5, it is written, "There shall be no needy among you—since the Eternal your God will bless you in the land that the Eternal your God is giving you as a heredity portion—if only you heed the Eternal your God and take care to keep all this instruction that I enjoin upon you this day."

In Lancaster County, Pennsylvania, Dwain Lievengood is a Mennonite farmer who sells his produce at farmers' markets in Philadelphia. "Wealthy, poor, Democrat, Libertarian, Hindu, Jew—all end the day hungry if they've not eaten. I end the day short of my mission if I fail any person the opportunities to sustain their life by eating something healthy and healing," he says.

In Chicago, Rev. Al Sampson of Fernwood United Methodist Church has been setting up farmers' markets on the city's south side for three decades. Organizing is not new to Reverend Sampson. Nor is his connection to black farmers. In 1960, as a college student at Shaw University in Raleigh, North Carolina, he joined a lunch counter sit-in at a Woolworth's in Greensboro. He and his fellow activists were arrested, but didn't have money to post bail. So a local black farmer offered his land title for their bail. As Sampson says, "Black farmers were the backbone of the civil rights movement and the ones who were posting bail." This shaped his lifelong commitment to these farmers and to organizing as a civil rights activist through food justice.

Ordained by the Rev. Dr. Martin Luther King Jr., Sampson arrived in the early 1970s at Fernwood UMC, where he bridged the connection between Southern and Chicago African Americans through agriculture. Sampson's life has also been shaped by George Washington Carver, an African American scientist and botanist from the early twentieth century. Sampson's church has its own "Department of Agriculture": Sampson set up the George Washington Carver FARMS (Farmers Agribusiness Resource Management Systems) to work with black Southern farmers and co-ops in places like Alabama, Arkansas, and Mississippi to bring their produce to farmers' markets at Fernwood UMC and other churches on Chicago's south side, a neighborhood filled with hungry households. Sampson's weekly markets provide people in his community with access to healthy foods and help maintain a strong connection to their Southern heritage. Sampson believes he is helping people to "heal from the ground" through their access to fresh food.

Historically, he says, farm land has been a source of oppression, but today farm land is the key to addressing social inequalities—including poverty and hunger. He quotes Leviticus 23:22, which describes land as a tool of sustenance and equality: "And when you reap the harvest of your land, you shall not reap all the way to the edges of your field, or gather the gleanings of your harvest; you shall leave them for the poor and the stranger."

Also in Chicago, Angel Gutierrez, vice president of Community Development for the Catholic Charities of the Archdiocese of Chicago, provides meals for youngsters during the long summer vacation. Of the 12 million young Americans who are eligible for summer nutrition programs (meals that they normally receive during the school year through government-subsidized programs), several thousand participate in Gutierrez's program.

Last year Gutierrez joined up with more than thirty different denominational institutions to provide more than 311,000 meals to 20,000 children throughout the city. Like other religious leaders, Gutierrez says that his work is not just about making sure that these kids have food. He and his team are working to keep the kids safe, teach them job skills, give them job opportunities, reduce youth violence, and offer healthy foods and exercise.

It might sound like a lot to wrap up into a single meal, but Gutierrez and his team are inspired by the continuing expansion of their program, which is rooted in their Catholic faith. He says he is guided by the Beatitudes—"when I was hungry you fed me, when I was naked, you clothed me." Gutierrez believes that it is his responsibility to help end hunger. "We're talking about people having access to basic things. And it's our responsibility to say we need to lead." He understands the local economic benefits that his programs bring to the city. "Everything we do has an economic multiplier effect—feeding more kids, buying more food, and employing more folks."

Rabbi Harold Kravitz of MAZON: A Jewish Response to Hunger, believes that our current food system is a social injustice and that the religious response should not be charity programs but *tzedek* (justice). He points to the many civil rights movements that have used food as a bargaining tool in fighting injustice in society—Mahatma Gandhi's salt strike, a turning point in bringing down the British colonial government in India; Cesar Chavez's grape boycott to seek improved conditions for farmworkers in California; and Rev. Dr. Martin Luther King Jr.'s solidarity with sanitation workers.

In Los Angeles, Rabbi Noah Zvi Farkas of Valley Beth Shalom and Netiya in Los Angeles agrees. "Food is the ultimate social justice issue. This is not a political issue, but a human issue. That makes it the responsibility of religious leaders to address hunger, nutrition, and access."

Jeremy Everett is a third-generation Baptist preacher. As the head of the Texas Hunger Initiative (THI), based at Baylor University, he approaches hunger through the intersection of religion, politics, and culture, but with a Texas flavor. Everett's goal is "to ensure every Texan has access to three healthy meals seven days a week." He has established what he calls "food planning associations," working through faith and community institutions and politicians to implement substantial changes at the local level that increase participation in federal government welfare programs, like SNAP (food stamps). Principles of unity guide Everett. "It's important that we work across denominational lines. Baptists can't address it themselves and neither can the government. We all need to work together to do something to solve the problem in a holistic fashion."

In San Angelo, Texas, a city of 90,000 people with about 125 churches, Carol Rigby-Hiebert, a member of Southland Baptist Church, leads fifty religious institutions in the city. Her group works with Everett's THI on summer youth nutrition programs. Methodist, Baptist, Greek Orthodox, Catholic, and Presbyterian churches, plus a local interfaith group comprising Catholics, Muslims, and Jews, provide meals to children during July and August. In 2009, during the first summer program run solely by St. Paul's Presbyterian Church and the local boys' and girls' club, 9,000 meals were served. The following year, the program quickly expanded to eleven institutional sites and 11,000 meals. By 2011, Rigby-Hiebert and hundreds of other volunteers served 23,000 meals at thirteen sites, and they're expecting to have fifteen sites during the summer of 2012.

For Rigby-Hiebert, it's part of exploring how members can "live more by the mission that we are called to do by Jesus." Connecting to THI, she says, gave more direction and resources to the work that her group was already doing. Her efforts cross racial, ethnic, and religious boundaries and showcase the small city of San Angelo as a place "where people take care of each other." Her group is effective because what they are doing makes sense to its members, she says. It also provides an opportunity for her to connect the work to her faith: "Jesus's philosophy of action is what is expected of you if you're a follower. It is just what I see that I need to do."

Also working across religious traditions to address hunger is Kyle Ismail of Islamic Relief USA. "It's about relationship-building, socializing with one another, and acknowledging the dignity of other human beings." Islamic Relief USA supports local programs across the country, works with food pantries, recruits volunteers, and provides nutrition education and cooking classes. Ismail is reaching out across religious traditions to collaborate on programs in Chicago, Atlanta, Minneapolis, and Washington, DC. In Minneapolis, he works with the interfaith group Almaun—in Arabic, *Almaun* means "small acts of kindness." Almaun hands out meals as the first step in connecting people to bigger opportunities. The center also provides job training and help in paying bills and finding clothes. Ismail is guided by the Prophet Muhammad's teachings about feeding one's neighbor. "The person whose stomach is full while their neighbor is hungry is not a Muslim. This compassion is so fundamental. We want to find ways to embody that."

In the Bedford-Stuyvesant section of Brooklyn, New York, Rev. Dr. Melanie Samuels, an evangelical Christian, works in food programs in the local community. After fifteen years of living an affluent, quiet life in the suburbs, Samuels's life was transformed by a call from an ailing mother of four who couldn't feed her children. Samuels "realized there was a need beyond prayer." Guided by the biblical teaching that "faith without action is dead," Samuels drove sixty miles to New York City to deliver food and care for this woman. That was the beginning of the journey from her suburban life to Bedford-Stuyvesant, where she and her husband founded the evangelical Christian church Full Gospel Tabernacle of Faith and started to provide for people in the community spiritually and physically. What began in her church basement eventually grew into a large warehouse space as the Bed-Stuy Campaign Against Hunger.

But she often faced unexpected challenges. People left her church with bags of food, but some of them immediately threw out the unhealthy junk foods she was offering. "I thought I was doing a great job in helping them until I found out that I was contributing to poor health," she says. Samuels switched to healthy foods and expanded programs to offer cooking and nutrition classes for families, seniors, and children. The Bed-Stuy Campaign Against Hunger continues to grow—and now feeds more than 11,000 people a month.

Reverend Samuels believes that "giving back is part of who we are. It becomes really natural." In addition to addressing people's immediate hunger needs, she also helps people enroll in government services for which they are eligible (SNAP, legal assistance, Medicaid, and so on) and provides advice on the health problems that afflict the community, like obesity, high blood pressure, and heart disease. Her motto is: "Healthy families make great communities."

Away from the big cities, in the rural communities outside Philadelphia, the Amish and Mennonite farmers of Lancaster County make their own special connections with city-dwellers. The Philadelphia-based Food Trust operates a multitude of farmers' markets in underserved communities across the city and depends on many of the Lancaster County farmers. Despite the very different lives of the farmers and their customers, deep-rooted connections through their faith overcome their differences.

Dwain Lievengood, the Mennonite farmer, practices organic methods to raise vegetables and livestock. His relationship with his city customers is part of his religious practice. "I value my relationships with our customers in Philadelphia for more than the fact that they provide the cash that I need to remain in business. . . . The meal ingredients I provide to my customers are an act of ministry. A ministry promoting health and healing comes with a name, a family, a story, and journey that returns them one day to their Creator."

Farmers and consumers, living far apart, forge more than economic interdependence. John Shenk makes the weekly trip to west Philadelphia from Shenk's Berry Farm in Lancaster County. Describing farming done well as "an art form," Shenk thinks of his relationship with his customers as a cultural bridge. "Even though we are the ones bringing food to the city, it is by no means a one-way street."

Finally, back in Los Angeles, Rabbi Farkas of Valley Beth Shalom and Netiya, says that he meets the needs of others by working with Jews and Christians alike to grow food in the city for hungry people. He finds inspiration in the teachings in Isaiah 50, which is read every year on the Jewish holiday of atonement, Yom Kippur. God says that he "wants Jews not only to observe rituals, but to bring light in the world by feeding the hungry—living a life that is Godliness."

Collectively, religious leaders of all faiths are building sustainable food systems that empower individuals and local economies. As the Reverend Samuels of Brooklyn says, "It takes a whole village to feed the village."

In addition to leading Bread for the World, **David Beckmann** is a Lutheran minister and economist who worked at the World Bank. In America he has concentrated his work on hunger in the African American community and on federal policies that influence the issue of poverty. His latest book is *Exodus from Hunger: We Are Called to Change the Politics of Hunger* (Louisville, KY: Westminster John Knox Press, 2010).

Sarah Newman was the researcher on *A Place at the Table*. She lives in Los Angeles, where she is a food activist and member of Shitbl Minyan and shops at the La Cienga and Melrose Place farmers' markets. During the making of the film, she met many American religious leaders and lay workers involved in the fight against hunger.

CHAPTER 12

The Oregon Food Bank

SHARON THORNBERRY

FROM *A PLACE AT THE TABLE*

We have basically created a kind of secondary food system for the poor in this country.

> —*Janet Poppendieck, professor emerita of sociology,*
> *Hunter College, New York*

Sharon Thornberry grew up on farms in Iowa in the 1950s and learned a lot about communities and their relationship to food. Later, her family experienced food insecurity. In the early 1990s, she started to work for the Campaign to End Childhood Hunger led by the Oregon Food Bank (OFB). At that time the OFB, which had adopted as its mission "to eliminate hunger and its root causes," was the only statewide food bank in America. The OFB became one of the first food banks in the nation to undertake advocacy for low-income people and attack the root causes of hunger. In 1998—a time when Oregon was one of the most food-insecure states—Sharon Thornberry became the OFB's community food systems manager. In this essay, she recognizes that food banks everywhere face some tough questions about their work in feeding the hungry and their role in rural and urban food systems.

I began life on an eighty-acre family farm near Maxwell, Iowa. We lived in a large two-story farmhouse with a monstrous furnace in the basement that was fueled by corncobs. We had electricity, but the only "running" water in the house came from a hand pump by the kitchen sink. Our connection to the outside world was a crank telephone on a party line. We had milk cows and sold milk and cream to the dairy, but made our own butter and cottage cheese. We raised, traded, fished, or hunted for nearly everything we ate. Only staples were purchased in town. Fresh banana bread and citrus fruit were rare treats. From the time I could walk and carry a basket, with the guidance of my eighty-year-old great-uncle Arthur, I was responsible for feeding the chickens and gathering the eggs. Our house and farmyard sat on one of the highest points in the area up a long lane.

One of my earliest memories is of sitting on the front steps of that big house with my eyes closed listening to the community come to our farm near dawn. It was harvest time, and it was our turn. From my vantage point on the hill, I could hear and see tractors, trucks, and combines come onto the farm in multiple places. Soon after that, the women of the community would arrive in our front yard with vehicles loaded down with the bounty of our farms. Harvest was a community event, labor and equipment were shared by everyone, and it moved from farm to farm until everyone's crops were safely in the corncribs or delivered to the farmers' co-op in town. It was not until I was an adult that I truly appreciated how much planning and trust it took to make that work for all of the farm families involved. They were a community in the truest sense of the word. That value of community and the security it brought was indelibly etched on my heart and soul by the time I was five. My life's connection to community food systems had been determined.

We lost that farm in 1959 when I was six, and we began a series of moves from farm to farm as my father worked as a hired hand and then farm manager. We lived in towns settled by Norwegians, Danes, and Germans. I grew up on large family farms in Iowa and finally on a large corporate hog farm in eastern North Carolina, experiencing many variations of rural community food systems along the way. I learned a lot about communities and their relationships to food on that journey. I experienced communities that celebrated their traditions and honored their "old country" roots through the food they prepared and shared. I knew elders who were first-generation Americans and had ways of producing and consuming food that many of us long for. I experienced people who provided comfort and solace to the ill and bereaved in their communities through food. I experienced congregations that created community and fellowship through food.

As a young wife and parent, I lived on military bases in the United States, Okinawa, and Guantanamo Bay. When my husband left the Marine Corps, we moved to Houston, Texas. It was there that my children and I experienced real hunger for the first time and I glimpsed my first food pantry. When my marriage dissolved, I returned to eastern North Carolina and worked six years for Kroger's, where I gained yet another perspective of the food system. Then, twenty-six years ago, my family and I moved to Philomath, Oregon, and a year later I became a VISTA volunteer for the local community action agency working with low-income food-gleaning programs.

During those years, I worked at the local, regional, state, national, and international levels. I coordinated gleaning programs, organized food drives, designed repack programs, and developed food donors and public benefits outreach programs along with a myriad of other activities that are required in the emergency and supplemental food system. I even managed my community's local emergency food pantry for five years as a volunteer in my spare time.

In the early 1990s, I began to work with the Campaign to End Childhood Hunger, led in our state by the Oregon Food Bank (OFB). In 1990 the OFB and a coalition of human services and faith-based organizations advocated for the Oregon legislature to form the Oregon Hunger Relief Task Force. With the leadership of executive director Rachel Bristol, the OFB changed its mission: "To eliminate hunger and its root causes, because no one should be hungry." In 1993 the OFB became one of the first food banks in the nation to undertake advocacy for low-income people and root cause issues of hunger. Over the last two decades, the OFB, in partnership with the Oregon Hunger Relief Task Force, has conducted outreach on federal nutrition programs and advocated on issues that have included raising and indexing Oregon's minimum wage; regulating payday loans; simplifying application processes for food stamps (now SNAP); and many other state and federal issues.

In the late 1990s, Oregon was one of the hungriest and most food-insecure states in the nation. Oregon's place in the US Department of Agriculture's Food Security Index improved dramatically during the last decade, but the recession of 2008 returned the numbers closer to the original standing. The years of improvement were attributed to extensive SNAP and other federal nutrition program outreach efforts led by the Oregon Hunger Relief Task Force, the OFB, and many other public- and private-sector partners as well as faith-based organizations. Building positive relationships with the state's Department of Human Services, supported by the governor's office, made that outreach even more effective. In May 2012, 92 percent of those eligible, or about 810,000 Oregonians, participated in the SNAP program—an all-time high. SNAP benefits contribute over $1 billion in federal funds to Oregon's economy each year.

The Oregon Food Bank currently serves 240,000 people monthly through more than 900 partner agencies across the state—also an all-time high! It's an amazing effort that just seems to be growing and leaves us wondering how we will continue to meet the need. Too many of our neighbors face food insecurity, and the emergency food system seems to have been chosen as a way to address the problem. Still, the food banking system nationwide faces many criticisms. A few of them include:

- The food is unhealthy.
- Emergency and supplemental food programs are undercutting the food economies in inner-city and rural communities.
- Charitable food distribution and meal programs disrespect recipients and undercut self-sufficiency and community dynamics.
- Food banking does not speak up on behalf of the people it feeds.
- The existence of emergency food systems makes it possible for society and government to avoid dealing with the issues of hunger and poverty.

We need to look to the history of food banking to begin to understand and address these issues. It is important to remember that food banking began as an effort to keep food out of the landfill as much as it did to feed those in need. Many of those who became involved were convinced that it was a temporary endeavor until a permanent solution could be found. I have known food pantry volunteers who went to their graves asking what happened.

Ironically, the food industry has become so good at controlling its waste and excess inventory that food banks have now developed elaborate food rescue programs to recover and distribute the most perishable products. But a system that is based on the salvage from our nation's food system is going to directly reflect that food system. We are reminded daily that our food system is laden with unhealthy choices and that the healthy choices are often the most perishable and most expensive. Food banks across the country are engaged in efforts to supply more fruits and vegetables to those in need, including intentional production and community gardens as well as partnership with large-scale producers and distributors. Community partners are encouraged to distribute food through "client choice" or "shopping style" pantries to offer recipients more choice and dignity in a grocery store–like experience.

Many are establishing or partnering with community gardens that allow people in need to raise their own gardens and become more food-secure. Food banks now run or partner with nutrition education programs in concert with the national nonprofit organization Share Our Strength, USDA extension programs, and SNAP, among others.

Food banks do face some serious questions, however. They need to examine their role in rural and urban food systems. For example, free farmers' markets can be in direct competition with "Healthy Corner Store" initiatives to restore produce to inner-city neighborhoods. Rural grocers report that they can no longer sell bread because so much free bread comes to the community through local food pantries and other food distribution programs. In these situations, small businesses suffer and community members become more food-insecure. I don't think that food banks intend to be permanent food suppliers to these communities. The Oregon Food Bank, along with a few other food banks, engages in efforts to rebuild local food systems through assessment and community organizing. These initiatives improve access to healthy food for all community members and have the added benefit of creating economic opportunities, primarily for small business.

Food banks state that their mission is to "eliminate or end hunger." It is time to ask what that really means. It is clear that the distribution of emergency food will never end hunger. Feeding America and its network of food banks distributed 3 billion pounds of food a year to 37 million people, and yet the need continues to rise. It is clear that we need the emergency food system to help people for the short term, but it will never eliminate hunger. The first time I stood in line to get food to feed my children, that box was absolutely necessary, but no matter how many times I got emergency food, it did not provide a long-term solution or make me more food-secure. The things that would lift me out of poverty were much more complex, as are the solutions to end hunger and poverty today.

Most important, we need the political, social, and economic will to end hunger and poverty in this country. We need to put voice to that will. The tens of thousands of staff, board members, and volunteers of food banks across this country are frontline witnesses to the conditions of hunger and poverty and the devastating effect they have on people and communities. They could be that voice, but only a few food banks have been brave enough to go past program outreach and advocate for their own programs and funding. While "the emergency food system" is necessary for feeding people today, it will never provide long-term solutions. Imagine the power for change if food banks and their partner organizations engaged themselves and all of their donors and supporters in truly working to "eliminate hunger."

The conditions that have produced inexplicable hunger in a land of plenty will not be changed overnight, but they will never change at all unless we begin to address the real issues standing in the way of eliminating hunger, not just alleviating it. First, we need to realize and admit that the massive system we have built will not really eliminate hunger. It will require collective agreement, courage, and action to put voice to that fact. The change will not produce instant results, nor will it be as gratifying as handing out a food box or donating to a food bank or pantry, but it is absolutely necessary. We need to build a collective vision of a world in which the food banking system does not need to exist. Can we build the kind of community developed by the farm families of my youth, which were based on will, respect, and trust, to end hunger in America?

ᢙ

Sharon Thornberry is the community food systems manager of the Oregon Food Bank. She also worked for sixteen years on the Oregon Hunger Task Force.

CHAPTER 13

Hunger in New York City

What Local Government Can Do

JOSH GETLIN AND **SCOTT M. STRINGER**

FROM *A PLACE AT THE TABLE*

We need to bring government to do the right thing much more quickly, but the only way to do that . . . is by making government care.

—Raj Patel, author of **Stuffed and Starved: The Hidden Battle for the World Food System**

Hunger is a growing problem in New York, America's largest city. Here, Scott Stringer, the Manhattan borough president, and his director of communications, Josh Getlin, consider ways in which local government can get involved in more positive programs for poor and hungry New Yorkers.

All Sonya Simmons wanted to do was sell fresh fruits and vegetables at the small, community-based farmers' market she hosted every week in Harlem. The neighborhood had a shortage of grocers selling healthy produce, and Simmons was working with a group of upstate farmers to sell their products on a busy corner. She never dreamed it would take more than five years—and a frustrating battle with the city's Department of Transportation—to finally cut through red tape and get permits that would let her vendors park in front of the market without paying $100 tickets.

Despite her protests, police had been citing the farmers for illegal parking at the corner of West 145th Street and Edgecombe Avenue, where there were few available spaces. Soon Simmons began sleeping overnight in her car at the site, hoping to save spots for the mornings her market was in business. Simmons didn't get the permits she needed until our office made calls and media reports began surfacing. It was a small, albeit frustrating victory in a continuing battle to bring fresh food to the areas that need it the most.

For all its riches, hunger is a growing problem in the nation's largest city. One in five New Yorkers now live in poverty, and the estimated number of low-income people here is 1.65 million, which is greater than the population of Philadelphia. One in four children, nearly 500,000, live in food-insecure homes where families struggle to afford basic meals and do not know from day to day whether they will have enough money to do so. Last year, as the economic downturn took its toll, the demand at city food pantries and soup kitchens grew 12 percent. Some fifty emergency food programs shut down because of federal government cutbacks and a decline in private donations. Although 1.8 million New Yorkers get food stamps, an additional 500,000 eligible recipients are not enrolled. Our participation in school breakfast programs is low compared to Houston, Newark, Chicago, and other big cities.

The statistics are daunting, but a host of food policy experts say that an equally serious problem is that New York City has failed to articulate, adopt, and enforce a comprehensive program to fight hunger. Simmons's case is instructive and hardly unique: in a report my office issued on the red tape plaguing community-based farmers' markets, we found that entrepreneurs like her are hamstrung by a bewildering maze of regulations and costly departmental fees—some running as high as $1,600 annually—for the simple right to sell a head of lettuce in Harlem and other underserved communities. Sadly, this experience is repeated across local government in New York City, where some forty municipal agencies have jurisdiction over programs relating to food consumption, production, or distribution. They fail to communicate with each other, adopting conflicting priorities on policies that either attack hunger directly or deliver healthy food in hard-hit neighborhoods.

"There really needs to be a plan in New York City for connecting the dots," says Dr. Nevin Cohen, chair of environmental studies at the New School in Manhattan and an expert on the role of cities and local government in anti-hunger campaigns. "We need to start thinking holistically about the system. If all of the agencies in New York City were on the same page when it comes to food policy, we'd see a big difference in the level of hunger in this city, in improved nutrition, and in all the benefits that accrue from that. But there is no overall plan, no binding vision that pulls it together."

Such planning must start at the top—and Mayor Michael Bloomberg deserves credit for taking action on some key issues involving food policy. He has been a leader in pushing for the availability of more nutritious foods in New York City; his administration has ramped up outreach to get more New Yorkers enrolled in the food stamps program; he has increased the number of schools in breakfast programs; and he has sponsored projects to bring more healthy produce into "food deserts," or neighborhoods that lack easy access to supermarkets. Under his direction, New York City has produced "PlaNYC," a document laying out sustainability priorities through 2033. Finally, he is one of the few US mayors who has appointed a full-time food policy coordinator in his office.

But none of this adds up to a clear and enforceable blueprint for city-wide food policy, especially as it affects hunger. Nevins wrote in the *Gotham Gazette* last year that "PlaNYC," a 198-page document with two pages devoted to food, "lacks the force of law. . . . There is no assurance that any initiatives it mentions will be reflected in other agency plans, or that agencies will focus on the food system. Now that PlaNYC officially acknowledges food to be essential to a 'greener, greater New York,' food advocates should press for a comprehensive food plan and make sustainable food practices a permanent part of city government."

In the absence of such a plan, elected officials, advocates, community leaders, nonprofit organizations, academic experts, and others have proposed their own road maps to help the city attack hunger. Our office, for example, convened an unprecedented food and climate summit at New

York University in 2009, a daylong conference focusing on hunger, the impact of our food system on the economy, and the health of our communities. We issued a report several months later, "FoodNYC," that laid out a comprehensive set of food policies for New York City, ranging from urban agriculture and regional food production to procurement of regionally grown food. A key recommendation was that the city create a Department of Food and Markets that would tackle the job of coordinating and enforcing food policies.

Elsewhere, City Council speaker Christine Quinn produced her own report one year later, "FoodWorks: A Vision to Improve NYC's Food System." Dr. Cohen of the New School is working to craft a Five-Borough Farm Project, a plan for coordinating urban agriculture and other programs on a citywide basis. Just Food, an advocacy group, has focused on empowering local communities to attack the problems of hunger in the city. Fueled by a $2 million grant from the US Department of Agriculture, a collection of New York City anti-hunger organizations known as the Hunger-Free Communities Consortium is preparing to launch a Food Policy Council for New York, modeled after successful organizations in other cities across the country. Joann Shanley, executive director, says that her group hopes to lay out a blueprint and action plan that doesn't exist now. "Our hope is this council would be something the next [mayoral] administration could look at and use as a means of addressing hunger and food-related issues," she says. "This council could be the vehicle to get people talking to each other about hunger."

On a daily basis, the fight against hunger in New York City focuses more on immediate individual human need than broad policy debates. And the city is fortunate to have so many organizations delivering emergency meals and counseling people on how to combat day-to-day health problems related to food, such as obesity, high blood pressure, and diabetes. But it is hard to ignore larger issues at a time when the lines are lengthening at soup kitchens, when children in classrooms remain hungry, when food deserts plague residents, and when the need to create a citywide infrastructure for the packaging and delivery of food remains a huge challenge for local government. Here are some telling snapshots from New York City's daily battle against hunger:

THE YORKVILLE PANTRY—
FOOD STAMPS AND FOOD SECURITY

On a cool spring afternoon, less than a mile from some of Manhattan's pricier real estate, lines are already forming at the city's largest emergency feeding kitchen. Longtime customers and newly enrolled participants file into a small basement at the Yorkville Community Pantry, where they place orders for a biweekly assortment of fruits, vegetables, and meat. Upstairs, in a hectic kitchen, volunteers are reading newly placed orders on a computer screen and racing to fill them. Across the hall, caseworkers patiently interview new customers, whose ranks continue to grow. The Yorkville facility, a small, multi-story building just around the corner from Fifth Avenue and the northern border of Central Park, does not impose geographic restrictions on customers. Last year it served more than 1.8 million meals, and it has been grappling with the problem of hunger for thirty-three years.

Like many anti-hunger organizations, the Yorkville Pantry's mandate is more than simply putting food on a plate. The organization has mounted an ambitious nutrition education campaign for adults and partners with local government to teach young children about the importance of eating healthy foods. Last summer the Yorkville Pantry brought seventy kids to an East Harlem performance of "Super Sprowtz"—an interactive puppet show cosponsored by our office that featured colorful action heroes like Colby Carrot, Brian Broccoli, Suzy Sweetpeas, and Erica Eggplant doing battle with the evil Pompous Pollution. The pantry also provides counseling, emergency meals, and showers to those in need.

"We're the largest facility like this in New York, and that's a good thing and a bad thing all at once," says Daniel Reyes, director of Yorkville's programs and operations. "Good because we're working very hard to meet a need, but bad because we have to be here at all. Our numbers are not decreasing." As the economic downturn continues, the pantry has seen a large influx of formerly working people down on their luck. The stereotype that people coming to a soup kitchen are lazy or unmotivated is absurd, Reyes notes, because "we're seeing people who want more than anything to get back in the workforce. They face tough decisions: Should they pay the rent or save money for food? Many don't know if they're eligible for food stamps, and that's a huge issue."

If there is one thing anti-hunger advocates agree on in New York and other cities it's that federally funded food stamps—known as SNAP (Supplemental Nutrition Assistance Program) benefits—are a lifeline to hungry people. They offer more security than the emergency aid given out by community-based food programs, and New York City has pushed to increase SNAP enrollments at Human Resources Administration offices. Applications are also processed online at the Yorkville Pantry, where caseworkers screen applicants in a setting that seems more congenial than a government office. But no matter where they wind up applying for emergency aid, many New Yorkers encounter a disturbing disconnect between what the city says and, until recently, what it has actually done when it comes to food stamps.

Until May 2010, when Governor Andrew Cuomo proposed regulations to end the practice, New York City was the only US jurisdiction, along with Arizona, that required SNAP applicants to be fingerprinted as part of the process. The city's argument is that this cuts down on potential fraud. But there is little compelling evidence for this, and we strongly opposed the requirement, as have many anti-hunger advocates. Joel Berg, executive director of the New York Coalition Against Hunger, blasted the rule as "a mean-spirited, punitive crackdown on people who want to find jobs again and are only trying to survive." He blamed the requirement for New York's lagging participation in the program, saying that an estimated 500,000 people do not receive benefits to which they are entitled. Others believe that such a policy needlessly scares off undocumented immigrants who have been in the United States for five years and thus qualify for food stamps. "Why do this?" Berg asks. "It humiliates people who have to leave work and lose wages to apply for benefits. And in many cases they've already paid taxes to support getting those benefits."

The people applying for food stamps today in New York City reach across the economic spectrum. Many of the newest customers at the Yorkville Pantry recently lost their jobs and can't believe they're facing such dire economic straits, according to caseworker Tyler Weidig. "Unemployment insurance pays a maximum of $300 a week for many, and if applicants don't get food stamps, how can they possibly pay more than $1,000 for rent?" Nowadays Weidig sees a growing number of well-dressed families coming to the pantry for emergency aid: "What they all seem to be saying is, 'I may not look like I need food. But I do.'"

Just ask Jacqueline Dockery, a fifty-year-old food stamp recipient who lost her job as a food service worker at New York University. After eleven years of service, she could no longer perform her duties because of crippling back pain. She takes care of her son and gets $168 monthly in SNAP benefits. That, along with the food she gets at the Yorkville Pantry, keeps her family fed. Barely. "Try living in Manhattan on that kind of budget, and see how far you get," she says. "There are times when we're still hungry. I never thought I'd be facing this situation. And I know that I'm not the only one."

BREAKFAST IN THE CLASSROOM— FEEDING HUNGRY CHILDREN

As the school day begins at PS 102 in East Harlem, first-graders are climbing four narrow flights of stairs to a fifth-floor classroom. They're not just toting books and backpacks: each child carries a plastic bag with that morning's breakfast, which includes milk, dry cereal, a whole-grain muffin, a stick of cheese, and fruit juice. The students tear open the bags and begin eating the minute they reach their room, and schoolwork starts at the same time. Homework is checked, reports are passed in, and the teacher huddles with individual kids. By the time breakfast ends, at approximately 8:20 AM, the school day is well under way.

It's all part of the city's federally funded Breakfast in the Classroom (BIC) program, which is designed to boost the number of kids eating healthy meals each morning. The BIC program differs from other meals-in-school initiatives, which typically serve breakfast in a lunchroom with minimal supervision. What makes PS 102 distinctive is that it serves breakfast to all students in every classroom. In New York City, which has more than 1,600 public schools, 352 of them now serve breakfast in some of their classrooms. But only 52 schools offer it universally.

Overall, the city's participation rate in BIC ranks twenty-seventh out of the nation's twenty-nine largest school districts, according to a report by the Food Research Action Council. And this has spurred an ongoing debate in the nation's largest public school system: What should be the city's policy when it comes to universal classroom meals? Decisions about whether to participate in BIC are currently made by principals on a school-by-school basis, and for some this underscores the program's sadly unrealized promise. "There are reasons why principals might not implement it," says Triada Stampas, director of government relations for the Food Bank of New York City. "The cafeteria may not be big enough. You might not have sufficient refrigeration capacity to store food for long periods. There could be staffing and resource problems. But it's also a question of will, and whether you make this a priority."

Across the nation, Chicago, Houston, Newark, the District of Columbia, and other jurisdictions have achieved universal participation in Breakfast in the Classroom—and few doubt that the program plays a crucial role in boosting children's health and education. Numerous studies show that students who skip breakfast, no matter their age, suffer an academic disadvantage. Teachers report that such children seem less focused in class; they make more errors and do not remember things as well as kids who eat a healthy breakfast. The problems are exacerbated when students come from economically disadvantaged homes; quite often they don't get proper nutrients before school and depend on classroom breakfasts to function properly. There are other benefits: Classrooms where all of the students eat breakfast together have higher rates of academic participation, and the fact that all sit down together removes the problem of stigmatization, which can be a problem in less-structured meal programs. Perhaps most important, starting the day with breakfast builds healthy eating habits for a lifetime.

Sandra Gittens, principal of PS 102, has championed the BIC program for the last four years and says that the results are well worth whatever logistical adjustments she's had to make. It's hard to veto such a program, she notes, when teachers see daily reminders of the hunger problems plaguing their students. If a child routinely asks for more than one breakfast serving, Gittens says, that can be a red flag for educators. The message can be sent in other ways as well. Several years ago the *New York Daily News* wrote a story about elementary school students' Christmas letters to Santa, and the newspaper was startled to find hungry kids in the mix. "I need food," wrote one child at a Brooklyn elementary school. "I need . . . not to starve every morning, noon and evening. I just can't take it anymore. Me and my family are hungry."

Local school officials pushed in 2007 to increase the overall number of New York City schools participating in BIC to three hundred, and the number has grown incrementally since then. But the city's basic policy remains that individual principals decide what's best for their schools. That voluntary model has drawn criticism from some anti-hunger advocates: "We are the country's largest school district, and we need to do more to ensure that greater numbers of students participate in the school breakfast programs," says City Harvest's Kate Mckenzie. "The participation rate that we have in New York is not at all representative of our potential. A more head-on, focused approach is needed to boost the numbers."

Others say that pushing for universal participation right away may not always be the best tactic. "When we promote breakfast in the classroom programs, we encourage a school to start small and see how they can expand the effort over time," said Roxanne Henry, community outreach manager with the Food Bank for New York City. "The program is easier to implement if you have all of the resources, the plastic bags, and the staff available to commit to the program. We try to build support for this wherever we can."

A key forum is the School Meals Coalition, a group that the Food Bank for New York City convenes that includes elected officials, educators, union members, anti-hunger organizations, child welfare advocates, and community groups. The Food Bank also coordinates Cook School in 160 New York City schools; this program introduces children to the rudiments of nutrition and food. Minutes after their breakfast is done, the class of first-grade students at PS 102 begins a Cook School lesson about food groups. The discussion is about calcium, how it helps build strong bones and where it can be found—in leafy vegetables and dairy products. "How do we feel when we eat healthy food every day?" the teacher asks. "We feel *great!*" they answer.

MOBILE MARKETS—
FRESH PRODUCE FOR FOOD DESERTS

With a profusion of neighborhood stores less than one block away, the sidewalk in front of the Dyckman Houses in northern Manhattan might seem like an odd place to hold an emergency food distribution. But this community is one of New York's food deserts, and it's easy to see why: the local bodegas and corner groceries on nearby streets sell produce that looks tired and wilted, there is limited access to fresh fruits and vegetables, and residents live miles away from the Whole Foods, Fairway, or Trader Joe's stores in other parts of the borough. Living here is hard enough if you're a low-income family trying to make ends meet. But if you want to prepare healthy food for your kids, it's even more difficult.

Today more than three million New Yorkers live in areas that lack adequate supermarkets, and the number is growing as more property owners shutter grocery stores and sell to developers, according to industry analysts and city officials.

Transforming these underserved areas has become a priority for City Hall, and not just for food-related reasons. Forced to rely on cheap, subpar diets, thousands of residents in food deserts experience New York's highest rates of obesity and diabetes.

Local government has focused on the problem, but nonprofit groups also play a significant role—and that's why a large City Harvest van is parked in front of the Dyckman Houses, part of the New York City Housing Authority, on an unseasonably warm March morning. As a long line of people wait along a fence, volunteers unpack bags and boxes of fresh potatoes, onions, lettuce, and other vegetables and stack them on tables. The food, which has been trucked in from a Brooklyn warehouse, will be distributed free to recipients based on the number of people in their families.

It's called a "mobile market," and the only ID you need to get such a bounty is to show that you live in Dyckman Houses or belong to the community association. It's a blessing any way you slice it. "I'm on my way, dear Lord, I'm on my way," an elderly woman in a wheelchair sings as she inches closer to the front of the line. When she reaches the tables, a volunteer helps her collect several large bags of food. Standing behind her, a mother with three young children picks up four bags of vegetables and quietly thanks workers at the tables. Today there are more than 350 people waiting to get food, which is considered a good turnout.

The bimonthly, open-air market is part of City Harvest's Healthy Neighborhoods program—and it shows how much the nation's largest food rescue effort has grown in thirty years. City Harvest collects unwanted or discarded food every day from grocery stores, farmers' markets, businesses, and industries and brings it that same night to more than six hundred community food groups. Once a shoestring operation, it now has eighteen trucks—a fleet our office was proud to help fund—and delivers 30 million pounds of food each year.

"As we've grown, we needed to deliver more than just pounds of food to people," says director Kate Mckenzie. "We wanted to deliver food with good nutrient value, so it can contribute to your health. So a great deal of what we're delivering is fresh fruit and vegetables, along with low-fat dairy products, meats, whole grains, and other things we should all be eating. There's no reason why the people we serve shouldn't benefit from nutrition as well."

Just as important, City Harvest is launching a pilot program in the neighborhood called the Corner Store Initiative. Modeled after successful ventures elsewhere in the city and around the nation, the goal is to work with merchants and upgrade the quality of the produce sold in local bodegas. "When we deliver fresh fruit and vegetables and help them display it a certain way, the neighborhood stores here can take on a whole new look," says Sally Cooper, director of the Healthy Neighborhood program. "Customers can see the difference immediately. It's a win-win." The new initiative echoes the priorities of two existing city programs: under the Green Carts Program and the Healthy Bodegas Initiative, local government has endorsed the idea that building mega-markets isn't the only way to transform a food desert and revitalize a neighborhood's food economy. You can also meet the needs of underserved customers by working with local merchants to improve the quality of the produce they sell and enabling vendors to sell healthy food from street carts.

But once again, the city is sending mixed signals: On the one hand, the Green Carts Program and the Healthy Bodegas Initiative seek to strengthen local food merchants in neighborhoods that need them. On the other hand, the administration's strong support for the entrance of a retailing behemoth like Wal-Mart into New York City works at cross-purposes with these initiatives. Although Wal-Mart, the world's largest retailer, has become a leading grocery outlet—selling $132 billion in groceries in fiscal year 2010—there is little doubt that it would compete directly with existing New York City fresh food retailers and eventually drive many of them out of business.

Although Wal-Mart has not revealed where and when it plans to open its first New York City store, there have been persistent media reports that a large site at the corner of Lenox Avenue and West 125th Street in Harlem—just a few miles from the Dyckman Houses—is under strong consideration. Last year our office decided to study the potential impact of such a store on the neighborhood's retail food landscape. We surveyed merchants within a one-mile radius and identified 24 supermarkets, 17 greengrocers, and 157 bodegas selling fresh produce. This data was then analyzed through the lens of a 2009 study by Loyola University in Chicago that tracked, over three years, business closures within a four-mile radius of a new Wal-Mart store on the city's west side. The Chicago study found that 25 percent of all competing businesses in a one-mile radius went out of business in the first year; by the second year, 40 percent had closed.

Using the Chicago model, we projected in a 2011 report, "Food for Thought," that in the first year after a new Wal-Mart opened in Harlem, anywhere from thirty to forty-one fresh food retailers could go out of business, representing a loss of 110,300 to 126,300 square feet of fresh food retail space. By the second year, an additional eighteen to twenty-five stores could shutter, for a total loss of approximately 176,530 square feet of fresh food retail. Even if Wal-Mart opened its largest urban store of 120,000 square feet in Harlem, it would mean a net loss of 54,500 to 82,000 square feet of fresh retail food outlets.

It's hard to imagine the loss of so many retail food outlets in a New York City neighborhood that needs them. But that seems to be the inescapable consequence of welcoming Wal-Mart into Harlem or any other community that wants to protect its fragile food economy. "The culture of New York is not necessarily about big stores—it's about enhancing corner stores and small businesses that anchor so many of our neighborhoods and offer a huge market opportunity for the sale of healthy food," says City Harvest's Mckenzie. "We really need to get our priorities right."

MAKE WAY FOR THE VEGGIE VAN— AND FOOD INFRASTRUCTURE

When the delivery truck finally pulls up, a roomful of volunteers at the Isabella Geriatric Center in Washington Heights gets ready. A driver begins carting in boxes of fresh fruits and vegetables, and the usually quiet coffee shop becomes a blur of people packing, unpacking, sorting, and bagging food. Welcome to Your Upper Manhattan Market (YUMM), which brings a cornucopia of food every Wednesday to a neighborhood that has surpassed the South Bronx in its rate of food-related diseases like diabetes and obesity. The fruits and vegetables, bundled in clear plastic bags, have been ordered well in advance, and it's easy to see why YUMM has become so popular. It's the best food bargain in Manhattan.

A huge "family size" bag costs $20, and on this morning each one includes hefty portions of oranges, apples, mangoes, strawberries, plums, mustard greens, parsley, yucca, cucumber, turnips, and green peppers. Volunteers, who include senior citizens and local high school students, stagger under the weight of the bags, which are quickly sorted into separate delivery piles, bound for five different sites in the neighborhood. It's a bear hug of produce, and a reminder that recipients would be hard-pressed to find equivalent quality—or value—in local grocery stores or bodegas.

The program is operated by GrowNYC, which runs the nation's largest outdoor network of urban farmers' markets, and director Michael Hurwitz hopes to expand it in the coming years. But he points out that YUMM is not just about putting healthy meals on people's plates. Like many other anti-hunger advocates, he talks about the importance of infrastructure—and the need to build a citywide food network that supports local farmers. In the summer of 2012, Hurwitz had high hopes for the "Veggie Van," a novel expansion of the YUMM food box program. With this new refrigerated vehicle, the organization will transport locally grown produce to communities that don't participate in the program, like the Lower East Side and East Harlem. The Veggie Van—which our office helped initiate and fund—will bring a new dimension to the delivery of fresh fruits and vegetables to New York neighborhoods. With any luck, it may soon become as familiar a sight as a Mr. Softee truck in the dog days of summer.

"We'll be increasing the number of neighborhoods that can get these fruits and vegetables," says Hurwitz. "But the larger point is that we need to build an infrastructure that supports the purchase and delivery of food from regional and upstate farmers, which is a huge priority for us." The Veggie Van, he says, is a good example of what can be done on a micro level: it allows for easier distribution and storage of food and will make deliveries more efficient. But there is much more that needs to be done. The city must begin to develop an upstate-downstate connection so that millions of New Yorkers can benefit from healthy produce, while farmers generate economic activity—and jobs—by selling their products in underserved New York City neighborhoods.

A top priority for many food activists, for example, is the development of a large farmers' market at Hunts Point in the Bronx. This sprawling, 113-acre facility, New York's main food distribution hub and the world's largest produce market, supplies food to 22 million people in a fifty-mile radius. It sells 3.3 billion pounds of produce worth $2 billion annually, but almost none of that—barely 2 percent—comes from New York State. A 2005 study showed that the unmet demand among city food retailers, restaurants, and distributors for local produce was $649 million, a number that has surely grown since then. For meat and poultry, the unmet demand was $48 million; for eggs and dairy, it was $44 million.

The case for building a wholesale farmers' market at Hunts Point is strong: It would provide a main distribution point for locally grown food in New York City, a terminus that doesn't exist now. It would also forge new links between the city and the state's 36,000 farms, which grow agricultural products worth $5 billion annually. The city is now negotiating a lease extension with the vendors who operate Hunts Point, and a multi-million-dollar modernization may be in the cards. But the administration has been silent on the creation of a wholesale farmers' market at the site. "PlaNYC," the city's planning blueprint, talks of the need to modernize the facility, but says nothing else about it. Meanwhile, New York City's Economic Development Corporation is handling the Hunts Point issue as a real estate question instead of as a key link in the city's food economy.

Local government must play a more affirmative role. It owns the infrastructure at Hunts Point and can green-light the construction of a farmers' market. If it did, New York would take a giant step toward sourcing more of its food from regional farms. We would give an economic shot in the arm to farmers and bring more fresh produce to city markets. Just as important, the city would be cutting the cost of distributing healthy, locally grown food to many of our most underserved neighborhoods. It's time for us to act.

HUNGER IN NEW YORK CITY: WHAT'S THE PLAN?

There is no shortage of innovative ideas to fight hunger in the Big Apple. Berg, with the Coalition Against Hunger, proposes that the city select an experimental model block in a neighborhood where hunger and its related diseases have reached epidemic proportions. He'd call it a "Harlem Food Zone," and the idea would be to target that block with every successful anti-hunger strategy—food stamp enrollments, Breakfast in the Classroom, nutrition education, access to farmers' markets, Green Carts vendors, exercise classes, and medical care—to see if hunger plummets.

Dr. Cohen, looking into a crystal ball to imagine what might be accomplished in the next ten years, envisions a city that sources more of its food from upstate farms. Currently the Department of Education serves more than 800,000 school meals every day and is second only to the Pentagon in the amount of food it purchases annually. Surely, he says, New York City can leverage that buying power to mandate the purchase of locally and regionally grown foods, with all the attendant economic and health benefits.

Elsewhere, promising projects that start in one borough could have an equally positive impact in other parts of the city. The Go Green Programs in northern Manhattan pioneered by our office have boosted the growth of farmers' markets and encouraged links with upstate farmers. Instead of simply teaching kids about the importance of nutrition, we created the Youthbucks Program, in which students get coupons worth $2 that they can use on visits to farmers' markets to buy fresh fruit instead of junk food. We have offered proposals to build needed reforms into the New York City charter, including, as mentioned earlier, the creation of a Department of Food and Markets.

There are many more ideas, to be sure, but they all have one unifying thread: local government must play a more aggressive role in laying out food policy in New York City and enforcing it. For someone like Sonya Simmons, the city should roll out the red carpet and cut through the red tape, encouraging her to sell fresh produce. When it comes to food stamps, there should be no further impediments to enrolling people so desperately in need. Our school system can and must do a better job of feeding hungry children. We should protect local food retailers in food deserts and build the infrastructure needed to support local farmers in New York.

President Obama recently set a goal of eliminating child hunger in America by 2015. Surely we in local government can follow his lead—and eliminate hunger in New York City once and for all.

⸎

Scott Stringer, a Democratic elected official, grew up in the Washington Heights neighborhood of Upper Manhattan and graduated from the John Jay College of Criminal Justice. He served thirteen years in the New York State Assembly and has been Manhattan borough president since 2006. A leader on progressive food policy, he has addressed the impact of food on the health of New Yorkers in several reports on food policy, including "Food in the Public Interest" (February 2009, available at: http://mbpo.org/uploads/policy_reports/FoodInThePublicInterest.pdf); and "Red Tape, Green Vegetables" (April 2011, available at: http://www.liberty control.net/uploads/mbpo/RTGVReport.pdf).

Before joining the Manhattan Borough President's Office as communications director, **Josh Getlin** was the New York bureau chief for the *Los Angeles Times*. During a nearly thirty-year career at the paper, he was a national correspondent covering New York politics, media, publishing, and culture; he was also a Washington, DC, correspondent covering Capitol Hill as well as congressional and presidential campaigns.

CHAPTER 14

Getting Off the Anti-Hunger Treadmill

ANDY FISHER

FROM *A PLACE AT THE TABLE*

The '80s created the myth that (a) hungry people deserved it, and (b) well, we could fill in the gaps with charities.

—Joel Berg, executive director of the
New York City Coalition Against Hunger

Andy Fisher created and publicized the concept of community food security and played a key role in building the community food movement. From 1994 to 2011, he led the Community Food Security Coalition (CFSC), a national alliance of groups working on access to local food. Here he traces community food responses to hunger over the last three decades and examines the corporate influence on charities that dispense emergency food.

Last December, Orion, my third-grader, came home excited about his school's Christmas food drive. "There's a contest for which class can raise the most money and donate the most pounds of food for Oregon Food Bank. I want our class to win," he said as he started scouring the cupboard for the heaviest food items he could find. My wife stopped him from stripping our cupboard bare. A week later, as I was headed out the door on a shopping trip, he pleaded with me to buy some more heavy food, as his classroom's donation barrel wasn't very full. At the store, I looked for nutritious food that was heavy and inexpensive. Tempted by the cheapness and weight of half-gallon bottles of soda, I took the higher road of purchasing some cans of organic beans and whole wheat flour on sale.

As I was shopping, I realized that the food drive at Orion's school was a microcosm of one thing that really irritates me about food banks: they measure their success in the millions of pounds of food that they distribute. Here's a sample from the website of the Regional Food Bank of Oklahoma (a food bank that I admire for its food systems activity): "In Fiscal Year 2011, the Regional Food Bank of Oklahoma distributed a record-breaking 46.2 million pounds of food and product through a network of more than 825 partner agencies and schools throughout 53 central and western Oklahoma counties."[1]

I get it. On a very basic level, there are millions of people struggling to make ends meet, and the more food gets distributed, the better fed they are. But we're treating hunger like a sporting contest, a numbers game. It's not a game we can win by just pumping more food through the charitable food sector. Hunger is the result of both a failure of the political will to resolve an entrenched problem and a failure of the marketplace to meet the needs of the poor.

Every food banker worth his or her salt will tell you that they are trapped in a broken system, a Sisyphean challenge that cannot be resolved by more charitable food donations. Why can't we donate our way out of hunger?

First, the number of poor and hungry is too big for the charitable food sector to handle. Forty-nine million people are at risk of hunger, based on the fact that they qualify for food stamps. The charitable food sector would have to increase in size more than sixfold to even feed all of these persons for a week every month.[2] Second, even if we could manage this feat, the impacts on society and individuals are less than desirable. Charity, subject to the continued interest and ability of donors, is inherently unsustainable. For example, food banks have seen donations drop as manufacturers sell dented cans on the salvage market rather than donate them. As Sharon Thornberry points out in her essay (see Chapter 12), in some rural communities in Oregon struggling grocery stores lose crucial business when residents receive their free boxes of food.

Finally, food bank critics have long argued that distributing free food fosters dependence when in fact society should be encouraging self-reliance by creating jobs.

⁓

Every food bank annual report or website that heralds the millions of pounds the organization distributes each year leads us a step deeper into a labyrinth from which escape becomes an increasingly distant dream. The more we celebrate our charitable food achievements, the further we define these achievements as the solution to hunger rather than as an unfortunate activity we are morally obligated to undertake because of our societal failure to prevent hunger in the first place.

Yes, the millions of pounds that food banks gather and distribute are a testament to the generosity of our communities and should be celebrated as such. At the same time, however, these truckloads of free food are a reflection of our inability to create an economy and a safety net that meet Americans' basic food needs. Every increase in the amount that food banks distribute is a measure not of their success but of their—and our—collective dysfunction.

Going back twenty years or so, the unsustainability of the emergency food system was front and center in the minds of a small cadre of anti-hunger dissidents working on food and nutrition projects in low-income neighborhoods across the country. As a graduate student in urban planning at UCLA, I was part of a team that completed a comprehensive study of the food situation in inner-city Los Angeles in 1993. My colleagues and I saw that the food banks' "medical model" of solving hunger through providing doses of food, as if hunger were a disease carried by an individual, was a humane but inadequate way to address a more systemic problem. Instead, we believed that hunger could be prevented from happening in the first place by taking a public health approach that included public education, policy advocacy, and other interventions that addressed the root causes of hunger and poverty.

Hunger wasn't the only concern of this ragtag band of academics, policy advocates, and practitioners. We saw plenty of problems in the way food was produced and retailed: too few sources of healthy and affordable food in low-income neighborhoods; small farmers going out of business because they couldn't get a fair price for their crops; subdivisions replacing food as the primary "crop" on some of the nation's best farmland; rampant pollution from overuse of agrichemicals; and increasing concentration of the ownership of the nation's food supply into the hands of a few massive multinational companies. As a result, consumers were getting further and further alienated from the source of their food. Diet-related diseases among persons of color were on the rise, and they were higher than rates for whites. At the same time, we also saw the potential of alternative food production and distribution projects as tools for widespread social change. For example, we knew that urban farming could increase access to healthy food and provide economic opportunity.

Using the framework of a food system—the set of activities that lead to the production of food, its distribution, its consumption, and the handling of waste—we soon realized that the same food system that harmed low-income consumers also marginalized family farmers. We developed a conceptual framework that we called "community food security," which held that the transformation of the food system through reorienting food production and distribution around the needs and assets of communities and family farmers was a pathway to creating a healthier, more ecological, and more democratic society.

This idea morphed into a national alliance of groups from a wide range of sectors involved in food and farming, uniting them under an immediate goal of gaining passage of a community food security–oriented grants program in the 1996 Farm Bill and a longer-term agenda of building a community-based food movement. We won the inclusion of the Community Food Projects Competitive Grant Program (CFPCGP) in the Farm Bill, with mandatory funding. Although the CFP distributed only $2.5 million of federal funds per year to nonprofits, it was one of the few bright spots in an otherwise regressive piece of legislation.

Since 1996, the USDA has provided $66 million to nonprofit organizations for roughly four hundred grassroots projects aimed at meeting the food needs of low-income people while fostering self-reliance in communities to meet their own food needs.[3]

Following are a few examples of the diverse types of projects funded under this program:

- Along the Arizona-Mexico border, the Tohono O'odham tribe received funding to reintroduce traditional crops through farming and gardening projects. These traditional foods can help reduce the surging rates of diabetes among tribal members.
- In rural Missouri, Patchwork Family Farms received a grant to support a sustainable hog-farming operation that distributes pork through buying clubs. The project also brought together rural white farmers with African American church congregations.
- In western Massachusetts, Nuestras Raices supported Puerto Rican gardeners and farmers in local food production and created a regional food policy council.
- The National Farm to School Network received a training and technical assistance grant to support the development of farm-to-school projects across the nation.
- In Los Angeles, SEE-LA received a grant to establish a teaching and retail kitchen that emphasizes fresh produce consumption, job training, and food and nutrition education targeted to low-income residents.

Although community food projects often seek to improve the nutritional status of low-income households, they are not anti-hunger projects. They aim to improve the food security of their participants, but within a broader context of transforming an inequitable and unsustainable food system. They typically engage individuals at a more intensive level than food pantries, but the number of people they reach is much smaller.

CFPs cannot solve the massive and entrenched problem of hunger in the United States. They can, however, provide a glimpse of a very different approach to the same problem.

Community food projects are small investments in innovation in the context of the failure of the mainstream food system to meet the needs of marginalized communities and individuals. In other words, the Community Food Projects program would not have been born if the marketplace had been working as intended. Despite the diversity of programs funded, the CFPs are linked by the fact that they create methods of food production and distribution grounded in community needs and values. The only comprehensive analysis of these grants, conducted for a five-year period starting in 2005, indicates an astonishing impact for only $25 million in federal money:[4]

- The production of 19 million pounds of food, valued at $19.7 million
- The farming or gardening of over 56,000 acres of land, including 9,100 community garden plots
- Receipt of food by 2.5 million persons through a community food project
- Implementation of 183 policies in communities, affecting 33 million Americans
- Creation of 2,300 jobs
- Creation of 1,000 new businesses and support given to 2,600 existing businesses
- Preservation of 3,000 acres of land
- Formation of 40 food policy councils

Not only have these community food projects been highly effective in achieving their legislatively mandated goal of transforming the food system, but they have been transforming their communities and participants in unforeseen ways. The following is a brief description of some of these accidental benefits of community food projects.

At the neighborhood level, some CFPs have fostered a sense of community pride. The process of transforming a vacant lot in an underserved neighborhood into a thriving urban farm or community garden can imbue residents with an increased sense of ownership and foster their desire to care for their community. The City Farms Project in New York City provides a concrete example of the way in which residents of marginalized neighborhoods have reclaimed control over their space through collaborating in creating and caring for community gardens.

CFPs have helped to reinvigorate lost traditions, foster intergenerational communication, and rebuild connections between communities and their environments. Support to the Tohono O'odham nation in southern Arizona has helped them to re-create their traditional food system by increasing the cultivation of tribal lands for such crops as drought- and insulin-resistant tepary beans. The project has also engaged the elders to revive the long-lost custom of harvesting the fruit of the tree-size saguaro cactus, a ritual that includes the singing of songs that haven't been heard on the reservation for decades.

CFPs use food as a tool to bring together persons from different geographic areas, ethnicities, and socioeconomic standings. In doing so, these projects build increased social capital and a more nuanced understanding of the diverse cultures that make up our country. For example, the Food Project in Boston connects inner-city youth with suburban youth through food production, processing, and retailing. Youth gain not only valuable business and food production skills but also a greater understanding of each other's cultures. The project also helps to foster increased social capital—or personal connections—between communities that normally would be socially and geographically isolated from each other.

At the individual level, the intention of many CFPs has been to shape project participants' knowledge or behavior within the confines of the marketplace. For example, they have sought to improve small farmers' marketing expertise or to encourage individuals to become better consumers through increased knowledge of nutrition. Yet, interestingly, these projects are also fostering food citizenship by encouraging individuals to fully participate in their communities.

For example, the Watts Growing Project in Los Angeles, funded in 1996, largely failed to meet its goals of increasing incomes for Central American and Mexican immigrant community gardeners, but it yielded an unexpected crop: food democracy. Project staff had pushed hard to strengthen an existing but dysfunctional garden club as a tool for decision-making. Staff encouraged a democratic process with full participation by all gardeners, helping them develop written rules and hold regular elections for officers. By the end of the two-year project, the gardeners were much more engaged in the operation of the site. They were holding their leaders accountable to following the rules, such as no consumption of alcohol on the premises, and for the wise use of garden dues. Regular meetings were being held in an orderly fashion. The gender bias that had initially diminished the role of the women gardeners was substantially overcome by the end of the project. The garden did not turn into a model of democratic process, but it was clear that the project had helped the gardeners, many of whom were probably undocumented, become citizens, in the Athenian meaning of the word.

Sixteen years after the first Community Food Project grants were made, the importance of this seminal program as it relates to the mainstream corporate food system can be summed up in three primary ways.

First, as mentioned earlier, CFPs have filled in the cracks where the market has failed. They have provided services such as access to healthy food in underserved communities and helped small farmers stay on the land by providing them with new channels to market their products.

Second, CFPs play a research and development (R&D) function for the food movement to experiment with complex food systems programs for low-income communities. Increasingly, these grants are going to projects that seek to increase the scale of their impact by bringing in more powerful partners or shaping local policy. These policies tend to be less about defining the rules of the marketplace to constrain big agri-food interests and more about creating pathways for noncorporate, community-based players (such as farmers' markets) to thrive.

Third, CFPs challenge the basic premise of the mainstream food system: that food is a commodity. This premise holds that ten pounds of russet potatoes is ten pounds of russet potatoes, without regard to how those potatoes were grown, who grew them, and where they were produced. CFPs, like much of the local food movement, reject that notion, instead holding that the values embedded in food production, distribution, and retailing differentiate their products from those of the corporate-run marketplace. In other words, the process by which food is produced is of equal importance to the characteristics of the foodstuff itself. The utmost expression of this phenomenon is the Tohono O'odham and other Native American community food projects in which food is sacred, integral to the web that links environment, culture, and community.

So far, we have examined the work of nonprofit groups responding to the lack of political will and marketplace failures to produce healthy people, communities, and environments. Let's switch our focus to consider the role of those who have caused this situation and who benefit from it—large agri-food production, processing, and retailing multinational corporations. Supermarkets have increased their profits by focusing on middle-class customers and redlining low-income communities and communities of color.

Fast-food companies (among others) have made a fortune marketing super-sized, low-nutrient, high-profit foods. Companies such as Cargill, ConAgra, and Archer Daniels Midland have built vertical and horizontal monopolies of numerous key sectors of the food system across the globe. They have lobbied hard to keep their inputs, such as corn and soy, as cheap as possible so that they can maximize their profits on such products as beef and pork. By not paying employees a living wage, Wal-Mart saves billions of dollars annually, pushing the costs off onto taxpayers, who foot the bill for Wal-Mart employees' food stamps and other federal benefits.

As if this weren't bad enough, these companies are co-opting and managing civil society's responses to their harmful activities to minimize the impact of those responses to their bottom line. Food companies such as Dean Foods and Smucker's long ago co-opted the organic food movement's challenge to agribusiness by gaining a narrow definition of organic in USDA label standards. These standards now focus solely on production practices rather than on other integral aspects of the long-held definition of organic food, such as it coming from small community-oriented farms. The food industry is replicating this strategy with the new challenge of "local food."

In the anti-hunger movement, corporations have penetrated the food banking sector through and through. Food banks are dependent on large manufacturers and retailers for a significant percentage—if not a majority—of the food they distribute. (The actual totals vary by food bank.) Such multinationals as Wal-Mart, Tyson's, ConAgra, and Kraft have donated hundreds of millions of dollars in cash to food banks. There is scarcely a food bank website that is not plastered with the logos of its multinational corporate donors and partners.

More significantly, representatives from corporations make up roughly half of all board members of food banks affiliated with Feeding America, inevitably forging closer ties to corporations than to community activists. Similarly, the organizational culture of food banks is becoming more corporate as employees of the for-profit sector are hired into senior positions.

The close ties between the corporate world and the charitable food sector have diminished the participation of food bank clients and community activists on these boards and are an indicator of food banks' limited accountability to the clients they serve. Pittsburgh-based anti-hunger advocate Ken Regal points out that, "historically, food banks used to have a strong social justice orientation. Now they are mainstream community institutions, and the same people who serve on the boards of local museums also sit on their boards."[5]

Corporate participation on food bank boards is a double-edged sword. It reinforces the respectability of food banks, while providing access to corporations' excess food and philanthropic largesse. These resources are essential to help food banks meet the increasing demand from those affected by the latest recession. The more mainstream a food bank becomes, the more money it can raise to feed hungry people.

On the other hand, the policy changes needed to reduce or eliminate hunger are anathema to the wealthy and the corporations on food bank boards. Such policy changes might result in increased operational costs or federal taxes for businesses. Thus, the high degree of corporate participation on food bank boards deters advocacy for any redistributive policies that would provide a real solution for poverty reduction but go against the interests of the business sector.

⁓

As a nation, we have increasingly privatized our response to hunger over the past thirty years. Through this transfer of responsibility from the public sector to nonprofit-business partnerships, we have created a system that is effective in feeding hungry individuals but not in ending hunger. It is a system doomed to succeed in the short term—by lulling the public into the false belief that their charitable donations are fixing the problem—and doomed to fail in the long term as well.

Food bankers are like hamsters on a treadmill. They have been running faster and faster just to keep up with demand over the past thirty years. To get more food to feed more hungry people, they have had to compromise their values by partnering with corporations, some of which, such as Wal-Mart, are causing hunger through their labor practices.

These compromises have kept hunger at bay, but they do not advance us any further toward our goal. We need to stop the treadmill long enough to find another path to reach our vision of a hunger-free America.

The moment is ripe now. The attention on income inequalities in the 2012 elections provides the right moment to rethink our approaches to this persistent problem. To stop the treadmill we must rethink the way we address hunger as a nation; create new policies, programs, organizations, and partnerships for the long term; and revise our goals—perhaps even dropping the term "hunger" as the overarching metaphor. This new framework should focus on the root causes of hunger, such as ending poverty, and on health, since hunger and obesity are flip sides of the same malnutrition coin. Like the community food projects, the new framework must also embrace innovation and transformation at the community level. I look forward to the day when food banks measure their success not in pounds of food distributed to the poor but in the number of people they *don't* serve—those who are healthy and have enough food for their families.

P.S.: Orion's class did win the contest, not for poundage but for most money raised. Their prize was a party with the eighth-graders.

Andy Fisher led the Community Food Security Coalition, which he co-founded, from 1994 to 2011, and he led the Farm Bill campaign to gain passage of the Community Food Projects Program. He has written extensively on such topics as food from farm to school, farmers' markets in low-income communities, and local food policy. He lives in Portland, Oregon, with his wife and two children.

PART III

BEYOND FEEDING
THE HUNGRY

FROM *A PLACE AT THE TABLE*

We don't have a food policy in this country to address hunger, we never have had one. We have a welfare system that is very limited in its ability to get people on their feet, which is what you really want. . . . You want to empower people to be able to make enough money to buy their own food and take care of their own needs. We don't have anything that does that.

—*Marion Nestle*

In our country we put a lot of emphasis on self-reliance, on everybody fending for themselves, liberty, and those are all great strengths, but as a nation it has not been our strength to do what we can to reduce poverty.

—*David Beckmann*

CHAPTER 15

Childhood Hunger

A Battle That Can Be Won

BILL SHORE

With a $2,000 cash advance on a credit card, Bill Shore and his sister Debbie started Share Our Strength in 1984. Today it is one of America's leading organizations working to end childhood hunger and has funded hundreds of anti-hunger organizations across the country, awarding more than $100 million in grants by 2010. But Shore found that something was missing. "Everything we did delighted everyone—except ourselves," he says. "We got to a point where we didn't want to just feed people. We wanted to end hunger. And that required an entirely different approach. We heeded the advice of the social science writer Jonathan Kozol, who said that one should 'pick battles big enough to matter, but small enough to win.' The battle to end childhood hunger in the United States was just such a battle."

My six-year-old son Nate is fortunate to spend much of the summer in Maine at a small cottage we have on the water at a place called Goose Rocks Beach. Last summer a man I'd never met before walked over to where I was standing, pointed to Nate, and asked, "Is that your little boy?" For a moment, I was seized by the apprehension all parents share in wondering what their child has done now. But he said, "I had an interesting talk with your son. I was building a sand castle down by the water's edge with my son, and your son came over to us, hands on hips, and said, 'Just so you know, I've seen a lot of these and they're always gone by morning.'"

Many of us might express a similar sentiment about some of the causes and campaigns that we've seen come and go, be it the war on poverty, the war on drugs, climate change, even hunger. But of the many things *A Place at the Table* says about hunger in America, perhaps the most subtle yet important is that this issue is different because this battle can be won. Although the film stops short of laying out a policy prescription for solving hunger in America, it offers compelling evidence that hunger in the United States is solvable. Before a single word is spoken on camera, the sweeping views of fertile farmland and fields of grain that begin the film make everything that comes after seem incongruous and unnecessary in the America of 2012. Ours is not a country that lacks food, the ability to produce it, or even food and nutrition programs for those not able to afford food on their own.

For that reason, the dream of ending hunger in America is not built on sand. In fact, it's got a more solid foundation than anything I've seen over the past quarter-century of engagement with the issue. Here's why: Hunger is a problem, but it is a problem with a solution. And the solution combines the same blend of idealism and pragmatism echoed in young Nate's words. Let's look at the scope of the problem, its root cause, and the strategy being successfully deployed to attack it.

The extent of the hunger problem is as great as it's ever been in modern times: 46.2 million Americans live below the poverty line, and 20 million of them live in deep poverty, which, for a family of four, is defined as living on less than $11,500 a year.

The child poverty rate in the United States grew by 18 percent between 2000 and 2009: 15.7 million of our children now live in poverty.[1] More than twice that number live in homes where no parent has a full-time job. Poverty rose in thirty-eight of our fifty states over the last decade. Some urban areas face catastrophe. For example, 67 percent of Detroit's children live in a neighborhood of concentrated poverty.

According to spring 2012 estimates, 46.4 million Americans are on food stamps, and half of them are kids. For the first time in our nation's history, a majority of fourth-graders in the United States are enrolled in the school lunch program, having crossed the threshold to 52 percent from the 49 percent of fourth-graders who were enrolled in 2009. The total number of students receiving subsidized lunches now exceeds 21 million. Millions of kids from once solidly middle-class families are getting free lunches for the first time because of changed economic circumstances and lost jobs.

Secretary of Agriculture Tom Vilsack, whose department administers most of the public food and nutrition programs, says that one of every two kids in this country will be on food assistance at some point during their childhood. Today's generation of children faces hard times worse than anything since the Great Depression.

But hunger, particularly childhood hunger, does have a solution. That solution is based on these two facts:

First, children are not hungry because we lack food or food programs, but because they lack access to those programs. Twenty-one million kids get a free school lunch, and even though they are eligible for extra help, only nine million get breakfast and only three million get meals in the summer when the schools are closed. Sometimes they lack access because they aren't aware of the program, but most times the state or city where they live hasn't set the program up, hasn't made it accessible, or has failed to remove the stigma of being in the free-lunch line to which kids are particularly sensitive. At lunchtime children are already at school, but for breakfast they must get there earlier, which might mean changing bus schedules, and in the summer when schools are closed, the jurisdiction must identify alternative sites.

Second, even in this era of government deficits and tight reins on spending, the funds for school lunch, school breakfast, and summer meals have been authorized and are available. When they are drawn down to reimburse schools and communities for feeding children, it is a win-win for all because the money buys milk from local dairy farmers, bread from local bakeries, and other supplies that stimulate the local economy. But the money doesn't flow until the kids actually participate in these programs.

So what's the catch? Why wouldn't every child who needs it be getting this important resource? Why aren't the seemingly manageable obstacles overcome by determined ingenuity? The reason is that these kids are not only vulnerable but voiceless. They don't make campaign contributions, they don't belong to advocacy organizations, and they don't have lobbyists. Most governors are not even aware of the degree to which children in their own state are under-enrolled, nor of how many tens of millions of dollars they leave on the table in Washington as a result. Hungry children don't make it onto the radar screen of even well-intentioned policymakers.

When our banks are in trouble, Congress and the White House act. It's the same when auto companies or insurance firms need help. During the debt ceiling crisis, there was enormous concern over whether the markets would suffer. But when it comes to children, who are the most vulnerable and most voiceless, poverty and hunger statistics are greeted by sounds of silence. Where are the White House summits with the Speaker of the House? Where is the legislation that could help ensure a safety net for desperately poor children?

In a *New York Times* report about the team guiding President Barack Obama's reelection campaign, his top political adviser, David Plouffe, asserted that Obama offered the American people the choice "of a president who says, 'Every decision I make is focused on the middle class.'"

What about the rest of the country? What about those who have fallen out of the middle class and are now part of the 46-plus million Americans struggling to survive below the poverty line? What must it feel like for them to hear that they are not even in the scope of the president's work, let alone a priority? We have reached a new low when political leaders and their spokespeople actually brag about representing, not all of the nation, but only a portion of the population, albeit a politically powerful one. Political calculation has morphed into political callousness.

There is no greater testament to just how invisible and voiceless these children are than the fact that several billion dollars a year have been allocated for their needs and they are not getting it. These are federal entitlement programs, but not the programs that have given entitlements a bad reputation. They are not drivers of the national debt. They represent the bipartisan wisdom of previous generations, the wisdom that says kids are the most vulnerable to, and the least responsible for, the situations in which they find themselves, and something as basic as whether or not they eat should not be subject to the prevailing political winds.

Children's food and nutrition programs were not cut in the 2011 budget deal that accompanied the debt ceiling increase and were specifically exempted from the automatic "sequestration" cuts that would be triggered if the congressional joint "super committee" failed to reach an agreement. As other essential services, especially in health and education, are cut, the safety net represented by the child nutrition entitlement programs stands out as all the more vital an oasis in the desert.

Much of the nation has begun to rally around the No Kid Hungry campaign launched by Share Our Strength and dozens of partnering anti-hunger organizations around the country to work with governors and mayors, nonprofits and businesses, in public-private partnership to identify and eliminate the barriers to kids' participation in programs like summer meals and school breakfast. These partnerships work with community organizations to set up additional sites, where necessary, and put ads on radio stations to make parents aware of where their kids can get food. The results have been promising.

- *Maryland:* In 2010 there was a 45 percent increase in participation in summer meal programs over the previous year.
- *Arkansas:* From 2010 to 2011, the number of summer meals sites where families could gain access to free meals nearly doubled.
- *Colorado:* In 2010 and 2011 there was a 66 percent increase in the number of kids participating in school breakfast programs.
- *Washington:* There has been a 64 percent increase in participation in the state's SNAP program.

From the time when our military leaders recommended such nutritional assistance after World War II, there has been broad bipartisan support for the school lunch and school breakfast programs. Even lack of access is a problem with a practical and affordable solution. Innovations like breakfast in the classroom and grab-and-go breakfast programs have enabled tens of thousands of children to benefit.

These programs work, which is why they have been around for more than thirty years and are continually reauthorized. At a time when so many doubt that government works at all, this is a shining example of public-private partnerships at their best.

This may sound good, and it is. But good is not good enough. Martin Luther King Jr. once said, "In this unfolding conundrum of life and history there is such a thing as being too late. Procrastination is still the thief of time. The tide in the affairs of men does not remain at flood, it ebbs." Despite our success, there are still too many children for whom we are too late. The spectacular results we are getting in Arkansas have not found their way to Texas. The progress we have seen in Maryland has not reached Mississippi.

There is no substitute for changing the nation's current narrow political agenda. Through No Kid Hungry, we are working with governors across the country to ensure that they at least do everything possible to enroll more children in vital food and nutrition programs like school breakfast and summer meals. That is necessary, but not sufficient—others in the nonprofit community and the business community as well must become advocates and join in urging policymakers to pursue an agenda aimed at reversing the growth in child poverty. Otherwise, no matter how much good these private efforts are accomplishing, it may not be good enough.

At the end of 2011, Share Our Strength received a $50 contribution from eight teachers in Fairfax County's Family and Early Childhood Education Program (Head Start) with a note that said: "Please accept this donation to the No Kid Hungry campaign on behalf of the eight of us, all Early Childhood Resource Teachers in the FECEP/Headstart program in Fairfax County Public Schools, Fairfax, VA. We work with children and families of poverty each day and know their struggles. This year we decided to forgo our own gift exchange and donate to your cause instead. We appreciate all that you are attempting to do for these kids and their families!"

These teachers were telling us that they support our program because having their students enrolled in public food and nutrition programs is one of the most important ways to advance their own work. When children are fed, they are healthier, our schools and teachers have students who are better able to pay attention and are ready to learn, and better students and better schools lead to an economy that is more competitive globally. Ending childhood hunger, in other words, has the potential to become an education issue, a health issue, and an economic issue, thus gaining a larger constituency than we might have imagined.

All successful movements—from civil rights to the environment—succeed when they are able to cross over and appeal to a broader constituency than their original passionate but small base. Children represent one of America's few areas of common ground, where Democrats and Republicans, liberal advocates and conservative corporations, can all be found. In today's bitterly divided political landscape, such common ground becomes sacred ground.

It turns out that is one of the few things Democrats and Republicans have been able to agree on. And so do teachers and doctors and Fortune 500 CEOs and economists and chefs. So this problem of hunger has a solution. Private efforts can't take the place of vital public policy, but engaged and active citizens who put people ahead of politics can show Washington the way.

ᔕ

A Place at the Table doesn't tell the viewer what to do. At the end of the film, you want to do something because there is simply no excuse for the suffering and struggling you've just seen on the screen. Bearing witness in this manner lays the foundation and creates the urgency for social change.

But the greatest driver of urgency comes not from politics or a documentary film, as critically important as they are. Rather, it comes from the research labs of cutting-edge scientists whose groundbreaking new discoveries in child development coincide with historic levels of child poverty.

A December 2011 *New Republic* article about babies and brains titled "The Two-Year Window" summarizes the work of researchers from Harvard, Tulane, and the University of Maryland who have demonstrated that lack of proper nourishment and stimulation for infants not only stunts development but actually physically changes the architecture of the developing brain.

In the developing child, neurons send signals that create circuits. Those circuits proliferate and strengthen when used and stimulated. When not stimulated, they fade away through a natural process called "pruning," just as a town bypassed by a new interstate loses businesses and resources, leading to isolation and limited opportunities for its residents. New technology enables us to map the effect of stimulation on the developing brain—think Google Earth for young brains—to see what we haven't seen before in detail, and the picture is spectacular and sobering.

This research allows us to go beyond oft-stated generalities such as "hungry children can't learn" or claims that they have more trouble paying attention. Instead, we now know that hungry children are being disabled and damaged in ways that are specific and measurable, but also avoidable.

New knowledge creates new responsibility. For better or for worse, we can no longer deny knowing that every child we fail to reach is a child whose brain, education, and economic potential have been compromised, just as if we'd deprived them of oxygen. It may be the second-grader in Colorado whose school we've not yet convinced to adopt a breakfast in the classroom program, or the siblings in New Mexico with no access to summer meals.

The failure to invest in at-risk kids early enough creates and perpetuates a cycle of poverty. And yet, for the first time, 2012 will be the second year in a row that Congress has cut appropriations for children. The *New Republic* article concluded: "When it comes to early childhood, public policy is lagging far behind science—with disastrous consequences."

This means there is a greater imperative than ever to help our nation close the gap between what we know and what we do.

⌎⌏

The fight to end hunger in America has come too far to be swept away like sand castles on the beach by incoming tides of special interest and cynicism. It's come too far to let our legacy be an America in which record numbers of kids go to bed hungry, wake up hungry, show up at school hungry, and become part of an economy and society weakened by such neglect.

A Place at the Table suggests that we have an opportunity to show my son Nate and American children everywhere that this time will be different—this time what we build together will be there in the morning, and will be there for the next generation.

This time we not only have a vision but a voice, and raising our voices together on behalf of those whose voices are not heard can change the national conversation as we insist that partisan politics stop not only at the water's edge but at the doorstep of any home where young children need a chance and are depending on us to give it to them. Our hopeful voices can finally achieve an America in which no child is hungry.

Bill Shore is the founder and executive director of Share Our Strength, the nation's leading organization to end childhood hunger in America. He currently serves on the board of directors of the Timberland Company and of Venture Philanthropy Partners. Shore has been an adjunct professor at New York University's Stern School of Business and the program adviser for the Reynolds Foundation Fellowship program at the John F. Kennedy School of Government's Center for Public Leadership. He is the author of three books.

CHAPTER 16

Beyond the Charity Myth

JOEL BERG

Joel Berg, a passionate, longtime activist in the campaign to end hunger in America, is executive director of the New York City Coalition Against Hunger. Since 2001, Berg has led the Coalition, which represents the more than 1,100 nonprofit soup kitchens and food pantries in New York City and the nearly 1.5 million low-income New Yorkers who live in households that cannot afford enough food. He served for eight years in the Clinton administration in senior executive service positions in the US Department of Agriculture, creating a number of high-profile initiatives that fought hunger and implemented national service projects across the country. One of the boldest thinkers in the fight against hunger, here he argues that, as it did in the fight to wipe out yellow fever and malaria, the only entity capable of organizing political and social action that would eliminate hunger in America is the federal government.

Many Americans believe that we can end US hunger one person at a time, one donated can of food at a time. They are well meaning. But they are wrong.

US history proves that major societal problems can only be solved by massive, coordinated, society-wide action, led by the only entity capable of organizing such action: the government.

Yes, the government. I'm perfectly aware that, in today's political climate, it's downright shocking to claim that government must take the leading role in solving a major social problem such as domestic hunger, but history proves that claim is demonstrably true.

America's dominant political narrative now tells us that our own government is somehow an evil, alien, occupying force that does nothing except steal our money. We're told that government is the antithesis of community. And we're told that government programs rarely, if ever, work.

That narrative is problematic for many reasons, not the least of which is that it's utterly untrue.

Although the Tea Party movement seeks to claim that centralized government programs are a violation of the US Constitution, the truth is that the original Constitution was created to replace the weak Articles of Confederation precisely so that the federal government would be more capable of engaging in coordinated action on behalf of the states and the people.

In a democracy such as the United States, government is the most legitimate embodiment of community. Of course, all the components of civil society—including businesses, nonprofit groups, civic and religious congregations, families, and individuals—have important roles to play in addressing social problems such as hunger. Yet the leaders of nonprofit organizations aren't elected by the public. Neither are business leaders. These kinds of leaders are generally picked by small, self-selected boards of directors. In contrast, the reason we call "elected officials" by that name is that they were elected by a plurality of voters. Whether you like your elected leaders or not, the fact remains that they are the only leaders empowered by the community to act on behalf of the interests of the entire community.

How can government be the enemy if we all are the government?

Moreover, the knee-jerk hatred of all things governmental ignores the historical reality that the government's efforts have often been extraordinarily successful at accomplishing its goals.

WHAT YELLOW FEVER, CHOLERA, AND MALARIA TELL US ABOUT US HUNGER

If you don't believe me when I say that government has solved major problems in the past, let me ask you a question: have you ever had cholera? If not, the reason is that cholera—not to mention other major diseases such as malaria and yellow fever—was wiped out almost entirely in America, owing mostly to government-led efforts.

Throughout the first few hundred years of US history, yellow fever, cholera, and malaria were persistent killers, with the deaths mostly clustered in low-income neighborhoods and communities. Yellow fever was as miserable and scary as it was deadly. It turned people's skin yellow, forced them to vomit black bile, and made them ooze blood out of every orifice and pore.[1] (If you are reading this over breakfast, I apologize.) In 1795, yellow fever killed 732 people in New York City, or about one out of every 68 people. As a point of comparison, when the AIDS death rate in New York was at its highest in the mid-1990s, it killed about one out of every 1,000 residents.

Yellow fever killed more than 41,000 people in New Orleans alone between 1817 and 1905. In 1878 a report described how the disease had ravaged the town of Granada, Mississippi: "Deserted stores, empty houses, abandoned fields and public roads, unmarked by a wagon-track, extended one hundred miles."[2]

Cholera was an even more deadly mass killer, claiming the lives of tens of thousands of Americans, including former president James Polk.

Malaria infected US presidents from Washington to Lincoln. During the American Civil War, malaria accounted for 1,316,000 illnesses and 10,000 deaths. An estimated 50 percent of the white soldiers and 80 percent of the African American soldiers contracted malaria.[3]

The public, believing that these diseases were simply a natural part of existence and there was nothing mere mortals could do to stop them, left it up to private charities to do the best they could to marginally ease the horrible (but inevitable) suffering. Many even believed that the diseases were sent by God to punish poor people for drinking too much or not washing enough. In 1832 wealthy New Yorker John Pintard wrote: "At present [the cholera] is almost exclusively confined to the lower classes of intemperate & filthy people huddled together like swine in the polluted habitations. A visitation like the present may work beneficially to promote temperance by proving a blessing instead of a curse."[4]

Few people thought that human actions could end these diseases.

Indeed, those three diseases are still rampant in many parts of the developing world. Over the last few decades, the number of yellow fever epidemics has actually risen, and more countries are reporting cases. Yellow fever still causes 200,000 illnesses and 30,000 deaths across the globe.[5] Cholera is still a huge problem worldwide, and in 2007 more than 2,000 Iraqis contracted the disease.[6] Up to 7,000 people may have died in a recent cholera outbreak in Haiti.[7] Even more staggering, in 2010, 216 million people contracted malaria, which caused an estimated 655,000 deaths.[8]

Yet these diseases no longer exist in the United States, except in the very rare instances when someone brings them to the country from overseas. Why? Given that yellow fever, cholera, and malaria are generally warm-climate diseases, and given that the United States has gotten warmer in the last few hundred years, one would think these diseases would only have increased here. Yet they went away.

What happened to them?

The US government wiped them out. *Yes, the government solved major problems facing the country.*

When cholera was found to be caused by dirty water, government authorities devoted vast sums of money to a massive effort to create public works projects to bring fresh water into—and take wastewater out from—US cities and towns nationwide. They also created and enforced a wide variety of sanitary and public health laws.

As for yellow fever, scientists, led by US Army general Walter Reed, discovered that the disease was caused by mosquitoes and then sent public health officials to destroy mosquito breeding grounds, clean local water supplies, and fumigate.

During World War II, the US government began serious efforts to end malaria because increasing numbers of soldiers stationed in the South needed to be protected. In 1947 the National Malarial Eradication Program, a cooperative effort by state and local governmental health agencies and the US Public Health Service, conducted more than 4.6 million anti-mosquito spray applications, and within a few years the United States was declared "free of malaria." That effort launched the modern US Centers for Disease Control and Prevention (CDC).[9]

New York City provided the best example of how government-led efforts eradicated cholera. In 1832 cholera killed 100 city residents every day in the month of July, and the year's death toll equaled 3,500 people (about one in 57 of the city's residents). If the same proportion of New York City residents died today, it would be the equivalent of 112,000 deaths per year—enough people to fill Madison Square Garden six times over.

In response, starting in 1835, state and city officials started planning a colossal reservoir and aqueduct system—rivaling the engineering marvels of the ancient Romans—to bring fresh water from upstate New York to the city. The system began operation in 1844 (and still operates today). Within twenty-five years, cholera in New York City was almost entirely a thing of the past.

Considering that most Americans today believe that government can't do something as simple as deliver trailer homes to disaster areas (and under President George W. Bush, it couldn't), most Americans would be surprised to understand just how effective past governments were in annihilating deadly diseases.

What does this have to do with hunger? A lot. The beliefs held by the American public about those diseases—that they were inevitable and unstoppable and that the best humans could do was apply a little charity to slightly reduce the misery—were almost identical to the beliefs that Americans hold today about hunger, which they think can be ameliorated by charitable acts but which they also believe is so ingrained as a permanent part of the natural environment that it can never be eliminated.

HOW THE UNITED STATES ALMOST ENDED HUNGER

Americans were wrong in the nineteenth and early twentieth centuries about disease, and they are wrong today about hunger. Major diseases were eliminated then, and government took the lead in doing so. Hunger also can be eliminated, if Americans band together to demand that their government once again solve big problems.

Hunger is a human-made problem, and it can be a human-ended problem. There have been times in US history when hunger was far greater than it is today, as well as times when it was significantly less—the difference being the state of the nation's governmental and economic policies. Likewise, today there are countries around the globe with massive amounts of starvation (like North Korea and many nations in sub-Saharan Africa) and others with virtually no hunger (like the countries of

Scandinavia). Although one explanation of the differences between these nations lies in natural conditions, such as drought, most of the difference is created by the actions of human beings.

As late as the 1960s, the United States still had pockets of Third World–style malnutrition. In 1967 a team of doctors headed by Dr. Robert Coles and funded by the Field Foundation traveled to the Mississippi Delta to study hunger there. Their findings of extreme hunger and malnutrition startled the nation:

> We saw children whose nutritional and medical condition we can only describe as shocking—even to a group of physicians whose work involves daily confrontation with disease and suffering. In child after child we saw: evidence of vitamin and mineral deficiencies; serious, untreated skin infections and ulcerations; eye and ear diseases, also unattended bone diseases secondary to poor food intake; the prevalence of bacterial and parasitic disease, as well as severe anemia, with resulting loss of energy and ability to live a normally active life; diseases of the heart and lungs—requiring surgery—which have gone undiagnosed and untreated . . . and finally, in boys and girls in every county we visited, obvious evidence of severe malnutrition, with injury to body's tissues—its muscles, bones and skin as well as an associated psychological state of fatigue, listlessness, and exhaustion. . . . We saw homes with children who are lucky to eat one meal a day. . . . We saw children who don't get to drink milk, don't get to eat fruit, green vegetables, or meat. . . . Their parents may be declared ineligible for the food stamp program, even though they have literally nothing. . . . We do not want to quibble over words, but "malnutrition" is not quite what we found. . . . They are suffering from hunger and disease and directly or indirectly they are dying from them—which is exactly what "starvation" means.

In response to these shocking findings, two things occurred. First, the national media (led by the CBS documentary *Hunger in America*) focused seriously and repeatedly on this issue. Unlike the media coverage today, which often gives the false impression that charity can solve the problem, the coverage then made it unapologetically clear that the United

States had so much hunger because the US government was failing to do its job properly and that the only sensible way to solve the problem was intensified government leadership.

Second, Dr. Martin Luther King Jr. launched the Poor People's Campaign, and one of the central demands of that movement was for the federal government to do more to combat domestic hunger. Although conventional history today tells us that the campaign petered out after King's death and was essentially a failure, that's not entirely true. In the years following the movement's encampment on the Mall in Washington, DC, the president and Congress jointly expanded the Food Stamp Program and the federal summer meals program for children from relatively small pilot projects into massive programs, and they also created the National School Breakfast Program and the Women, Infants, and Children (WIC) program, which provided nutrition supplements to low-income pregnant women and their small children.

These expansions succeeded spectacularly in achieving their main goal: ending starvation conditions in America. In 1979 the Field Foundation sent a team of investigators back to many of the same parts of the United States in which they had previously found high rates of hunger in the late 1960s. Finding dramatic reductions in hunger and malnutrition, they concluded: "This change does not appear to be due to an overall improvement in living standards or to a decrease in joblessness in these areas. . . . The Food Stamp Program, the nutritional components of Head Start, school lunch and breakfast programs, and . . . WIC have made the difference."[10]

These programs proved beyond a shadow of the doubt that government programs, properly targeted and effectively managed, can be extraordinarily effective. Perhaps that's the real reason why conservatives so desperately seek to discredit them.

It is also important to note that government actions not only reduced hunger but reduced the poverty that causes hunger. Between 1960 and 1973, the US poverty rate was cut fully in half—and 16 million people climbed out of poverty and into the middle class. Surely a significant cause of that reduction was broad-based economic growth and increasing wages for workers. Most Americans now assume that such economic growth was solely a result of the independent productivity of the private sector. But government efforts, most notably the original GI Bill, played a critical role in that growth. The GI Bill enabled millions of returning soldiers to obtain government help to pay for college and become the first in their families to obtain higher education, including my father.

There is no question government efforts—most notably government-enforced protections for union organizing and collective bargaining—played a significant role in bolstering high wages for workers.

It is no coincidence that the most massive reductions in US poverty coincided with the height of the Great Society and War on Poverty programs initiated by the Johnson administration in the 1960s. Today the attacks on these programs in the media and in our political system have been so pervasive that it is now accepted conventional wisdom that all those programs failed. The truth is that most of them were working spectacularly. We were actually winning the War on Poverty.

By the late 1970s, a combination of factors—the growth of the American economy and living wage jobs, the massive increase in federal nutrition safety network programs, and the dramatic decrease in poverty—had almost entirely ended hunger in America.

The only reason we have so much hunger and food insecurity in America today is that our economic and social policies have gone backward.

THE BUCKET BRIGADES

Before the mid-1800s, the most common way of fighting fires in the nation's cities and towns was the bucket brigade, made up of volunteers. When a fire was spotted, the cry of "throw out your buckets" would be sounded, and a bucket brigade would be formed, two lines of people stretching from the town well to the fire to deliver as much as sixty gallons of water per minute.[11] Such brigades epitomized the very best of the fledgling nation—the kind of voluntary community association that foreign observers such as Alexis de Tocqueville said made the United States so different from old Europe. But there was one small, intsy-tinsy glitch in this system: The bucket brigades almost never worked. Major cities would simply burn to a crisp within hours.

Today urban fires no longer destroy entire cities or towns. What changed? Government—yes, government (do you detect a theme, dear reader?)—took effective actions to prevent fires and limit their damage.

Buckets were replaced by modern fire trucks (which now can deliver up to one thousand gallons of water per minute); untrained volunteers were replaced by professional, full-time government firefighters; and fire safety codes were enacted by local lawmakers to make buildings safer.

Yet when it comes to fighting hunger, America has moved away from coordinated, guaranteed government antipoverty programs of proven effectiveness and instead has increasingly returned to reliance on social service bucket brigades—volunteer-run food pantries and soup kitchens.

When Ronald Reagan entered office in 1981, there were only a few hundred emergency feeding programs in America, most of which were traditional soup kitchens serving mostly the people who had been the most hungry historically—single men, many of whom suffered from substance abuse or mental illness problems. Yet, as a direct result of the economic policies and social service cuts set in motion by Reagan, the number of emergency feeding programs in America skyrocketed and continued to do so even after he left office. There are now about 38,000 such programs in America—across urban, suburban, and rural areas—and roughly two-thirds of them are food pantries where parents and their children, the elderly, and working people obtain free groceries. In 2009 food pantries and soup kitchens served 37 million Americans, including 14 million children.[12]

Rather than using modern sorting machines, these charities typically sort their food donations by hand, one can at a time. Rather than being staffed by trained social service professionals paid to work regular business hours, they are usually run by untrained volunteers available to provide food only a few times a month when they have no other obligations. And rather than serving as a last resort that would be secondary to more serious government hunger-prevention efforts such as boosting the minimum wage or hiking food assistance, these charitable feeding agencies have increasingly become the nation's first line of defense against hunger.

And unfortunately, these grassroots feeding programs are similar to the original bucket brigades in one other important way—they are mostly failing to solve the problem. Although the unpaid volunteers and underpaid staff who run these agencies engage in inspiring efforts every day, and though their efforts do supplement government programs enough to prevent Americans from starving (certainly a vital role), they have not—and cannot—end hunger in America.

As I often say in speeches, "Trying to end hunger with food drives is like trying to fill the Grand Canyon with a teaspoon." One time an audience member challenged that assertion by claiming that you could indeed fill the Grand Canyon with a teaspoon if you had enough time. My retort: "No, you can't, because the Grand Canyon would erode faster than you could fill it." Indeed, since 2001, as the number of people using charitable feeding agencies has skyrocketed, so has the number of Americans facing hunger and food insecurity.

The truth is that these agencies simply don't have anything close to the resources needed to meet demand. The organization I manage, the New York City Coalition Against Hunger, found that in 2011 close to 60 percent of the approximately 1,100 soup kitchens and food pantries in the city were forced to ration food because they lacked resources; they had to reduce portion size, limit hours of operation, or turn away hungry families. These agencies are so underfunded that nearly fifty of them were forced to close in New York City in just the last few years.[13]

The fact is that pantries and kitchens, despite the tireless work of volunteers, have their failings. Sociologist Janet Poppendieck, in her seminal book about the emergency food system titled *Sweet Charity*, lists what she calls the "Seven Deadly 'ins'" of the network:

*In*sufficiency (not enough food)

*In*appropriateness (people don't get to pick what is best for their families)

Nutritional *in*adequacy (too much high-sugar, high-sodium, high-fat junk food)

*In*stability (feeding agencies can't always predict when they will be open and when they will run out of food)

*In*accessibility (agencies can be particularly hard to get to in rural areas, or for seniors, people with disabilities, or people with no car)

*In*efficiency (the agencies require a massive, three-tier system just to give out free food)

*In*dignity (at even the best-run agencies, obtaining emergency food is usually a degrading experience)[14]

All these problems concern me, but perhaps the worst is the inadequacy, since the average amount of food given out by a pantry is generally dwarfed by the amount of food a family could be getting from today's food stamp program. For example, in 2007 a family who got food from the South Texas Food Bank based in Laredo generally received $50 worth of groceries per month. Compare that with the average monthly household food stamps benefits of $239 in Texas that year.[15]

Still, most Americans hold tight to the myth that neighbor-to-neighbor generosity and compassion is the best support system for those in need, and certainly better than government aid. In response to an article on food stamp benefits in an upstate New York newspaper, an anonymous blogger posted the following: "There is a big difference between the guy with food stamps and the organizations that I donate my time, money, and energy to. The guy with the food stamps took my money at the point of a gun, he obtained it by force. I had no choice in the matter. The charities and the people they support received my money and efforts of my own free will and desire to help. . . . They receive zero government dollars."

That comment encapsulates how many Americans feel, but the blogger ignores two vital points: First, those receiving food stamps (now called SNAP, for Supplemental Nutrition Assistance Program) did not take his money at the point of a gun; they legally received aid allocated to them by government officials who were democratically elected to represent his community. Second, I can virtually guarantee that the charity of which he speaks receives at least some of its food (and possibly even some of its money) from government. People often say that they prefer "community" aid and "neighbors helping neighbors" to government, but that ignores the reality that, in a democracy, government *is* community, and efficient programs such as SNAP (funded by the tax dollars of people who are neighbors) actually are the single fairest, most efficient way in which neighbors help neighbors.

Even though food banks, soup kitchens, and food pantries are ubiquitous in today's media, they are actually a relatively small part of the nation's response to hunger. All the food they distribute provides less than one-fifteenth of the dollar amount of food distributed by federal nutrition assistance programs, despite the fact that those safety net programs are incredibly underutilized. Today, even if all the nation's food charities somehow accomplished the Herculean task of doubling their food distribution, this feat would barely dent the nation's hunger problem. In contrast, an easily achievable increase in the government safety net programs could wipe out the problem entirely.

When the American people were asked in 2011, "How much of the time do you think you can trust the government in Washington to do what is right?" only 10 percent answered, "Just about always or most of the time"—down from 36 percent in 2007.[16] That belief leads many people to falsely assume that charities provide more food than government does, and that they provide it more efficiently and economically. Perhaps if they knew the truth—that government feeds more people and does so more cost-effectively than charities—they surely would feel differently about government's ability to do the right thing.

First, it's vital to note that much of the food distributed by charities was paid for by government in the first place. Second, because charities create a system of food distribution that is in addition—and parallel—to the existing commercial food distribution system, they have to spend additional money on overhead. When a national food manufacturer donates food to a national organization, which then ships it to a local food bank, which, in turn, trucks it to local food pantries, such logistics often involve two or three sets of trucks and fuel costs, two or three sets of warehouses, and two or three sets of administrative and fund-raising staffs. The late Dick Gabel, one of the pioneers of the food banking system, once told me that the emergency food system is the "most inefficient system in the world. I should know. I helped create it."

While it is often a great burden to enroll in SNAP, once someone receives the benefits, it is usually relatively easy to use them, especially since paper coupons have long since been replaced by easy-to-use EBT (electronic benefits transfer) cards. The government merely transfers the money electronically onto EBT cards, and then, at virtually no additional cost to the government other than the benefits themselves, recipients are able to use the money solely for food. That's why the vast majority of money in SNAP goes to food, not to administrative overhead. I calculated that, before the current recession, only about 15 percent of the spending in the entire program went to administrative overhead. Since then, because the spending on benefits has soared while the spending on caseworkers to administer the program has remained relatively flat, the administrative overhead is now less than 10 percent.

In contrast, some food banks have overhead rates of up to 20 percent. When you add in the overhead of a national organization that distributes to food banks as well as the overhead for local community-based pantries and kitchens that directly feed people, the total overhead for the entire system—from original donation to final distribution—is far greater than 20 percent.

Case closed: the government's food safety net is more cost-efficient than charities. Unfortunately, many feeding charities unconsciously—and sometimes deliberately—perpetuate the false impression that they are more effective and efficient than government. Many have even convinced themselves that this is true. In their marketing materials, they often make extreme claims—seldom supported by the facts—as to how many meals they can provide in exchange for each dollar donated. Such claims matter because, if people believe that ending hunger is as easy as giving just five bucks to an ultra-efficient charity that leaves government in the dust, why would they ever support government policies that spend their tax dollars to tackle the problem?

It's clear that charity—no matter how vast or small—cannot substitute for systematic, progressive social change that would reduce poverty and inequality nationwide. Until that time, we should make sure that the charities have the resources they need to fill the gap.

❧

Some well-meaning people suggest that we could end domestic hunger if more low-income people grew their own food in their own gardens. That's preposterous. Even if all low-income people had enough time (which they don't) to grow all their own food, and even if they had access to land on which to do so (which they don't), such efforts would produce only a small amount of the vegetables and fruits they need and would be very unlikely to produce the grains, dairy products, meats, and other proteins necessary for a healthy, balanced diet. It would be nearly impossible for most low-income people to produce themselves the many parts of a healthy diet other than produce. Besides, most people, myself included, enjoy eating fifty-two weeks out of a year, not just the handful of weeks that constitute the growing season in most parts of the United States. Thus, while community gardens can be a very positive addition to a neighborhood—by reclaiming empty lots for community use and providing a laboratory for nutrition and environmental education—they cannot be an adequate mass response to ending food insecurity for the 50 million Americans who suffer from it.

The only way to truly end US hunger is by advocating for fundamental change that includes living wages jobs and a robust safety net.

BEYOND THE BUCKET BRIGADES

Today hunger, poverty, and homelessness are soaring nationwide. Most elected officials are either ignoring these maladies or taking actions that actually make them worse. The reason they get away with that is that there is no broad-based, grassroots anti-hunger movement to counteract them.

The recent moment that encapsulated the weakness of anti-hunger fighters was our collective inability to stave off defeat on the recent federal Child Nutrition Reauthorization (CNR) bill. Anti-hunger advocates had all hoped that the bill would contain massive new investments in child nutrition programs and move the nation toward President Obama's previously stated pledge to end child hunger by 2015. Yet the final bill contained few serious expansions of anti-hunger programs. The vast majority of the money was used to increase the quality of school lunches for middle-class and low-income students (certainly a worthy goal), but relatively little of the bill's money went to ensuring that more hungry children would even get to eat school breakfasts, summer meals, or after-school snacks in the first place.

To add insult to injury, because of a last-minute deal to protect corporate welfare, the final CNR bill was almost entirely paid for with billions of dollars' worth of cuts in SNAP, a program in which half the recipients of benefits are children, all of whom are low-income. Ironically (but predictably), Congress has since attempted to gut even the higher-quality school meals.

Thus, the CNR bill took away money for feeding low-income children in order to pay for improvements in existing meals for middle-class and low-income children—improvements that may not even fully come to pass. In a cruel irony, the bill that we had hoped would help end child hunger in America will probably increase child hunger in America.

The president and Congress have recently enacted other cuts in anti-hunger funding (including cuts in WIC and the Federal Emergency Management Agency's Emergency Food and Shelter Program, the main source of federal cash for feeding charities). The bucket brigades of pantries and kitchens have never been more outgunned.

Yet it could get even worse. As I write this in September 2012, the Democratic-run Senate has passed another $4.5 billion in SNAP cuts and the Republican-controlled House Agriculture Committee passed $16 billion in additional cuts.

❧

My hope is that this all could be a blessing in disguise, giving the nation the final jolt we need to once again ignite a grassroots movement to end hunger.

In the late 1960s and early 1970s, when advocates were able to harness significant grassroots activism (including the prominent participation of low-income people) and obtain significant (on-message) media coverage, not only were they able to turn President Nixon from a hunger-denier to an anti-hunger champion, but they were able to prompt the creation of the modern nutrition safety net, which almost ended domestic hunger. Popular movements emerge from the daily struggles of thousands of citizens.

Progress is never easy, but as we've seen with the government activities that wiped out cholera, yellow fever, and malaria in the United States, if society has the will, it has the way. If enough people push for change, then the governmental and other institutions can solve big problems. We are at a moment in US history when we must expect and demand real change. It is simply not acceptable to have hungry people amid such skyrocketing wealth. We must start feeding the solution.

What seemed inevitable in one age is unthinkable in another. When we look back in our country's history, we can't allow ourselves to imagine how bad things really were. Take child labor. Can we imagine that the country was so heartless as to often allow "breaker boys" as young as six years old to work in anthracite coal mines, separating slate rock from the coal, for fourteen to sixteen hours day, six days a week, frequently losing fingers or dying from black lung—all for just a few dollars per month? No, we can't imagine it.

Or slavery. Can we truly remember that America used to be so barbaric that it was acceptable to buy and sell human beings? Can we even conceive of the fact that we split up families for profit? We can't imagine that either.

We must work together so that, in the not-too-distant future, we simply won't be able to imagine a time when US children had to go through dumpsters to get breakfast, or when tens of millions of our neighbors were forced to use food pantries and soup kitchens.

How did we end child labor and slavery? Through mass movements that forced our political system to change. True, it also took a war to end slavery, but it only did so because the abolitionist movement had made the notion of slavery abhorrent to the majority of Americans.

Most contemporary Americans have been brainwashed into believing that our government and political system are so broken that citizen action simply doesn't matter. But history proves that's not true. Collective action works.

Together, we can ensure that all Americans have enough to eat. But it's up to each of you to join the movement needed to do so.

The Underground Railroad gave millions hope, enabled slaves to follow the North Star to freedom, and emboldened the national movement to end slavery entirely. Today, we must restore our moral compass by ending hunger in America.

Dr. Martin Luther King led a highly successful movement to ensure that people of all skin colors and backgrounds had an equal place in America's political system. But in 1969, King said, "What does it profit a man to be able to eat at an integrated lunch counter if he doesn't earn enough money to buy a hamburger?" It's time for us to launch another movement, this time to ensure that all Americans have physical and economic access to all the nutritious food their families need. It's time for all Americans to have an equal place at the table.

Joel Berg is a nationally recognized leader and media spokesperson in the fields of domestic hunger, food insecurity, obesity, poverty, food-related economic development, national service, and volunteerism. He is also the author of *All You Can Eat: How Hungry Is America?* (Seven Stories Press, 2008).

His New York City Coalition Against Hunger works not only to meet these residents' immediate food needs but also to enact innovative solutions to help society move "beyond the soup kitchen" to self-sufficiency. The Coalition recently launched pilot national service projects in seventeen states from coast to coast, making the work of the organization national in scope. The Coalition's latest handbook is *Ending Hunger through Citizen Service* and is available at http://www.hungervolunteer.org.

Prior to his work with the Coalition, Berg served for eight years in the Clinton administration in senior executive service positions at the US Department of Agriculture. For two years, he acted as USDA coordinator of community food security, a new position in which he created and implemented the first-ever federal initiative to better enable faith-based and other nonprofit groups to fight hunger, bolster food security, and help low-income Americans move out of poverty.

A native of Rockland County, New York, and a graduate of Columbia University, Berg now resides in Brooklyn.

Federal Programs Can Do More

FOOD RESEARCH AND ACTION CENTER

The United States is a prosperous country and an influential leader on the global stage. It is a country where no person should suffer from hunger or malnourishment. President Barack Obama has committed to ending childhood hunger by 2015. Our country can achieve this goal by ensuring that all Americans get a fair share of economic growth, by ensuring that parents and others who work full-time get paid enough to support a household, and by bolstering the country's federal food assistance programs. On the economic front, the country needs to raise the federal minimum wage, expand the Earned Income Tax Credit (EITC), and provide affordable health insurance. On the nutrition front, the country needs to strengthen and broaden the reach of effective programs like SNAP, the school nutrition programs, WIC, summer and after-school meals, and child care meals.

Let's start with the National School Breakfast Program, which served 3.5 million low-income children in 1990, 6.3 million in 2000, and almost 10 million in the 2010–2011 school year. That growth is impressive, and yet, for every one hundred children who eat school lunch, there are still only forty-eight who eat breakfast. There are many ways to increase that number: the most dramatic and effective is to move school breakfast from the typical cafeteria-before-school setting to the classroom when the bell rings. The cafeteria breakfasts, offered before class time, don't always reach those kids who are deterred by the stigma attached to a cafeteria program seen as being "for the poor kids" or who are racing around on the playground, too caught up in the excitement of play to remember to eat. Nor do these breakfasts reach those children who get to school just as the bell rings. If more breakfasts were offered in the classroom, as is the case at Alsup Elementary in Colorado, then more children would start the academic day on a full stomach, ready to learn.

The federal after-school and summer meals programs also have yet to realize their full potential. The programs are flexible, in that they work in partnership with schools, community groups, boys' and girls' clubs, community recreation centers, and other local organizations. However, more work needs to be done to inform and help these local groups build the capacity needed to act in partnership with the federal government and feed hungry children.

SNAP is the largest and most expansive of all the federal food aid programs. This program, too, must be made even more effective in combating hunger. One way to do this is to increase the monthly food allotment that SNAP provides to families. As much as SNAP helps families put more food on the table, the monthly allotment is not enough to carry households through to the end of the month.

SNAP's monthly allotment isn't sufficient because it's predicated on an outdated food plan called the "Thrifty Food Plan," which was developed during the Depression in the 1930s "as a restricted diet for emergency use." It is updated for inflation, but its predicate is flawed. The plan has never represented the purchasing power needed to keep a household on a healthy diet for a month.

Children's HealthWatch and two other organizations recently gathered grocery store pricing data in Philadelphia and found that SNAP's maximum benefit doesn't pay for a full month's worth of healthy meals. In fact, the Thrifty Food Plan shopping list in sixteen of the surveyed Philadelphia stores costs a household of four almost $200 more than the maximum benefit. A similar grocery store pricing project conducted by the Food Research and Action Center's DC Hunger Solutions Initiative in Washington, DC, also found that SNAP's maximum benefit wasn't nearly enough. The project's manager, Jasmine Mickens, says that a few staple, healthy items are cost-prohibitive for those who shop on the Thrifty Food Plan budget: "Healthy meat, like lean beef, is really expensive, and so is frozen fish. Another really important basic food that's very expensive is whole wheat bread. At many of the stores where we visited, the price of one loaf was over four dollars. Think about how quickly a family of four goes through one loaf of bread."

The grocery pricing study in Washington, DC, found other troubling barriers similar to those found in urban and rural "food deserts" around the country: there were few full-service grocery stores in low-income neighborhoods, and some stores did not stock some basic items that are critical to a low-budget, healthy diet, including whole-grain pasta, whole-grain flour, and different varieties of beans. Jasmine Mickens says: "I visited four corner stores in one low-income part of town, and I could only find fresh apples in one of them. As for vegetables, these stores had potatoes and onions, and that's it. You couldn't even find frozen vegetables."

SNAP also needs to reach more people. Three out of ten people who are eligible for the program are not enrolled. Some people don't enroll in the program because they may not know they are eligible. The hassle of wading through bureaucratic red tape discourages many others from applying. More public education campaigns, outreach, and application assistance are needed.

Low-income people held to tight, unforgiving work schedules may not be able to afford several visits to the application office during work hours, only to encounter long lines and overwhelmed staff who inform them that they need to return the next day with more paperwork. States and localities administer SNAP, and many states and cities are trying to make the application process more bearable by reducing wait lines, expanding office hours, framing the application interview in respectful tones, and asking only what's needed to determine eligibility. They are also cutting back on overly burdensome verification and documentation requirements, replacing interviews at the application office with telephone or at-home interviews and granting longer certification periods.

Vermont is one of the states at the forefront of the movement to make the Food Stamp Program more attractive to eligible Americans by giving it a public relations makeover. Vermont gave the program a new, catchy-sounding name—"3Squares VT," for three square meals a day. The director of Vermont's program, Renee Richardson, says that her staff markets the program as a nutrition program, not a welfare program. When Richardson talks to people about the program and why it's good for families and residents, she emphasizes the health benefits: "I tell people to think of the program the same way they think about Medicare. Medicare is a health program, and so is 3Squares, because nutrition and health are directly connected. People don't worry about stigma when they use Medicare to book doctors' appointments. Well, people needn't worry about using their EBT card in the grocery store to buy nutritious food."

Richardson and her staff have worked closely with community advocacy groups to get the word out about 3Squares VT, and enrollment has skyrocketed in recent years.

The enrollment increase can also be attributed to the painfully slow economic recovery and to the fact that the state took advantage of an opportunity, granted by the federal government, to broaden eligibility. Starting in 2009, Vermont changed its eligibility to allow more near-poor families to apply for the benefits. Richardson says that her state decided to include more near-poor families because her staff saw so many families with incomes at that level who were struggling to pay for groceries: "Working families have so many out-of-pocket expenses like rent, day care, the car and gas, and bills. With all these payments, they have a hard time keeping it all together. We wanted to help them." When Vermont made the change, roughly 33,000 households participated in SNAP. Twelve months later, the number of participants had risen to 42,000, and by December 2011 the number had increased to roughly 48,500. Vermont's program now helps one in every six people in the state.

Despite the tremendous advantages that WIC affords low-income mothers and their children, the program is not reaching all those who are eligible. About 4.8 million children are enrolled, but about 7.5 million are eligible. If WIC was funded at a higher level, the benefits could reach more of these children. A recent administrative change to the program puts WIC in a position to easily reach more children. States can now keep children enrolled in the program for one year instead of six months. If states adopt this change and partner with advocacy groups to market it to families, more children could receive the nutritional benefits.

CHAPTER 17

The One-Word Strategy for Ending Hunger

MERGERS

ROBERT EGGER

When Robert Egger was growing up in Washington, DC, he wanted to open the greatest nightclub for the best bands where he could use music to change the world. He was on his way to fulfilling this dream when, one rainy night, he and his future wife, Claudia, helped a church group feed the homeless. They witnessed a group of well-meaning people buying food from an expensive grocery store and handing it out of a truck to people who lived on the streets of the nation's capital. Egger knew that restaurants threw away tons of food every day. He got a grant from a private foundation to buy a refrigerator truck, and on January 20, 1988, the day George H. W. Bush was inaugurated as president of the United States, he opened the DC Central Kitchen, giving out hot meals. Then he empowered his clients by training them to be chefs. Today his kitchen has an annual budget of $7.4 million and employs more than fifty people, creating jobs and making meals at the same time. But, as he argues here, charity cannot end hunger. Still a visionary, he proposes a radical alternative—a grand merger of all nonprofits to create a new world of sustainable philanthropy that would "completely redesign the machine" and, at the same time, end hunger.

In so many, many ways, I'm exceptionally lucky.

First and foremost, I was born a white man in America. That in and of itself gave me unlimited potential and promise. There were zero limits put on my imagination. Nobody ever suggested that I couldn't do anything I put my mind to. When any teacher asked, "What do you want to be when you grow up?" I could raise my hand and pick any profession or accomplishment, and no matter how far-fetched it was, nobody would ever suggest that my goal was beyond my reach.

I also grew up witnessing the liberating work of Dr. King and Cesar Chavez . . . as well as listening to the liberating sounds of The Beatles, Jimi Hendrix, and The MC5. Between these two powerful, amplified movements, I grew up fully baptized in the idea and promise of the American dream of freedom and opportunity for all.

But I couldn't help but notice how hard that dream would be to actually achieve. As I entered young adulthood, the leaders I admired were assassinated. The bands I adored broke up. And the hippies I longed to join cut their hair. Sure, most people genuflect to the notion of freedom and justice, but few are willing to explore their own role. As Richard Pryor once famously quipped: "When white folks talk about justice, that's what they mean . . . just us."

So I started studying tactics, and I discovered Gandhi's notion that *both* the oppressed and the oppressor are equally afflicted. He put forth the bold idea that you must liberate both if your liberation movement is to succeed.

For the longest time, I wanted to use entertainment to follow that idea. I wanted to open a nightclub that would use the power of music, comedy, theater, and dance to disguise tough ideas and gently but purposefully use their power to help people overcome the fear of change and embrace new ideas.

I pursued this idea with a young man's passion for over a decade, working in punk clubs and jazz dives, trying hard to learn every aspect of the biz.

But all that came to an unexpected end when I went out one night to "serve the homeless" on the streets of DC. I've told that story too many times to repeat it here, but in a nutshell: that night, on the rainy streets of

DC, I witnessed how we fought hunger in DC. Well-intended volunteers, with hearts full of love, took food purchased from an expensive local store and served it to people on the streets, then went home, justifiably happy that they had helped another human make it through another day.

But I didn't see anybody truly elevated by the experience. What I saw was a system designed to provide redemption for the giver, not liberation for the receiver.

So I came back with a business plan based on FedEx . . . and the power of mergers.

I proposed bringing foods donated by the very nightclubs I was raised in, as well as from caterers, hotels, and other food service businesses, and using it to fuel a culinary job training program that would teach skills to unemployed men and women—the homeless, addicts, or those coming home from prison—while also helping serve those further down the ladder than them. In short, I wanted to use what we threw away to set the stage and expose Washington, as well as the rest of America, to the radical idea that nothing should be wasted—not food, not people, not money or time. Nothing. More important, I wanted to illustrate the idea that everyone has a role in the solution.

But I didn't want to do it myself—I just wanted to help those who were already doing it to take my ideas so they could feed better food to more people, for less money, while shortening the line by the very way it was served by training folks for jobs. To say that I was shocked when my suggestions were rebuffed would be an understatement. I was thunderstruck by the resistance I met. Again, I don't want to retell this story so much as to set the stage for the topic at hand.

As you probably know or can tell by the tone of my tome, I ended up leaving nightclubs, and on inauguration day in 1989, January 20, I opened the DC Central Kitchen.

Ever since then, my coworkers and I have remained passionately dedicated to innovation, flexibility, and being open-source about our work and our experiments in empowerment and nutrition. We didn't have time to waste being proprietary or parochial about our approach or our commitment to liberating people: we wanted to share what we learned, and to learn from others as efficiently and powerfully as we could.

But we knew there were bigger fish to fry than just running or replicating our model.

False modesty aside, we were monsters of love, purpose, sweat, and butter. We were out-front innovators of job training, food recovery, utilization of volunteers, exploration of social enterprise, and ways to embrace advocacy as well as early adapters who used the Internet to communicate with colleagues to share breakthrough ideas every day rather than wait for the annual conference. Nobody could touch us. But we knew that no matter how big our programs grew, or how many cities adopted our model, what we were doing could never end hunger.

No charity can. Which is the point I'd like to make in this essay.

Charity in America was built on extra—extra food, extra buildings, extra clothes, and most important, extra money. Following World War II, our food system fed the world, and our industrial base helped rebuild it. Whatever people wanted or needed, we grew, made, or sold. And that era produced a cornucopia of "extra." More than enough, in fact, to convince many that if we just built more charities, or pumped more money into the growing charitable system, we could end hunger and poverty and create a more open and just society.

We can't. The charitable system can't. No charity can. And besides, the era of "extra" is over in America. If we couldn't do it by now, with all the "extra" we've had at our disposal, then we have to launch a bold new effort for a tight new era.

That's why I left the day-to-day management of the Kitchen to others and began writing and speaking about a new opportunity that we—the hunger fighters, service providers, activists, artists, administrators, and all the other nonprofit employees—have to explore. It starts with mergers.

Normally, when I mention that word, I see colleagues wince. They assume that I mean "two become one," which isn't an illegitimate idea. Simply put, no city can afford an unlimited number of organizations, each doing its own thing, but that's just the beginning of what I propose.

Nonprofits in America employ 10 percent of the workforce. We are 10 percent of the economy. We engage almost 80 million volunteers annually, and we are the third-biggest employer in America.

Imagine if, for example, we merged our banking business. With $3 trillion in assets and over $300 billion in annual revenue, we'd be as big as Bank of America. We could loan each other money rather than have to bow and scrape for grants or gifts. We could have access to capital and build housing, start businesses, employ people at good wages—even issue credit cards at reasonable rates to help clients own their own fates.

Imagine if we merged our marketing power. If we know that low wages are the reason the majority of people require food assistance, imagine what would happen if we issued a "Nonprofit Seal of Approval" for businesses and said to 80 million volunteers, "Thanks, truly, for helping, but if you want less hunger and more opportunity, fewer fund-raising letters and lower taxes, then look for our seal. The businesses that have it pay a living wage. They have health insurance or provide day care. They have green policies and reinvest profit back into the community."

For years we've turned to the boycott to punish companies. Why don't we try to reward and incentivize businesses that we admire and then use market forces to compel others to compete for our combined commerce? That's sustainable philanthropy. That's the "buycott."

But let's take it to one more level. What if we merged our voting power to bust through the notion that nonprofits must avoid direct political engagement?

To be direct—there is no profit in America without nonprofits. We set the stage for communities to thrive. Without health care, education, arts and culture, communities of faith, and a clean environment, no business can thrive. We need to own that and to openly offer to help support and elect people who propose ideas that celebrate these contributions and offer economic alternatives to the outdated notion that "dot-com businesses drive the economy while dot-org charities do good deeds."

When you read history, you sometimes shake your head at the impression that "servants," though they so vastly outnumbered their "masters," allowed bondage to continue. But it is only when "servants" quit fighting each other and stand together to fight a common "enemy" that they can begin to liberate themselves or others.

Nonprofits in America—whether they fight hunger, celebrate art, build homes, or lift spirits—have the keys to their economic chains. They have the ability to completely redesign the machine. They always have. They just need to stand back, stand together, and march forward.

Then, and only then, will we move beyond charity and begin to explore true justice and the economic opportunities that come with it.

∽

Robert Egger travels throughout America, speaking about the DC Central Kitchen (www.dccentralkitchen.org), social enterprise, nonprofit unity, political engagement, and other changes needed to reach the goal of a hunger-free nation.

PART IV

WHAT YOU CAN DO
ABOUT IT

CHAPTER 18

The Accidental Activist

KELLY MEYER

Kelly Meyer is a passionate environmentalist, cofounder of the Women's Cancer Research Fund, and an active leader in veterans' affairs as well as in several national and local environmental organizations. She is a trustee of the Natural Resources Defense Council and sits on the board of southern California's Heal the Bay. In January 2011, Kelly Meyer was appointed by Secretary of Labor Hilda Solis to the Advisory Committee on Veterans' Employment, Training, and Employer Outreach. She was instrumental in the passage of the Environmental Education Initiative (EEI), a groundbreaking piece of legislation that requires environmental education in grades K–12 in all public schools in the state of California. Most recently, she cofounded Teaching Gardens, a group that seeks to eliminate childhood obesity by integrating nutrition and fitness into schools. Now a nationwide program with 140 gardens, it has been adopted by the American Heart Association as part of its obesity prevention campaign. Kelly is married to Ron Meyer, president and COO of Universal Studios. They have four children and live in Malibu, where she enjoys hiking, surfing, and stand-up paddling. Here she writes about how she became involved with hunger and obesity in America.

For several years now, as part of my environmental activism, I have been interested in how food is produced and how it gets to our plates. More recently, I learned the alarming statistics of hunger and obesity and the direct links to the crops we grow and the kind of processed foods produced from those crops. Then I understood that the true costs of the way we produce and market our food also include the hidden medical costs of diabetes, heart disease, and other obesity-related diseases. As individuals, we pay the human tax that allows giant corporations and the agriculture industry to maintain their profits under the false pretense that they are providing a product that we must consume to survive. This perfect storm of malnutrition, skyrocketing health care costs, rising numbers of lifestyle-related diseases, and a huge increase in the number of hungry children was enough to spur me into action.

I looked at the macro and activated the micro. For all of us, there is always a place to help make a difference. For me, it was the Teaching Gardens.

I came up with the idea in the middle of the night. Instead of just tossing and turning, I got up and wrote a simple idea on one sheet of paper, an explanation of what I wanted to see happen for children. I wanted children to have the opportunity to learn what being healthy really means. Put in the food context, I wanted them to learn about growing vegetables. I wanted to connect them to a whole-food source by planting gardens in schools, with local support from communities coupled with physical fitness and nutrition introduced and inspired by local sports figures and chefs.

My message was to link good food, exercise, and a basic understanding of nutrition.

I grew up in Colorado near military bases, and I had heard about people planting the legendary "victory gardens" during World War II. As a result of my recent work with veterans returning from Iraq and Afghanistan, I wanted to include them in helping us to build, maintain, and sustain these gardens. I wanted them to bring their sense of purpose and service into the school communities to help with this movement. I wanted to plant these gardens at elementary schools on military bases to help support military families in the struggle to eat well.

This didn't seem too difficult. I knew that many garden programs in schools and local communities already existed and that many of them were very successful. But for me, it was not only about the garden but also about spreading the word and amplifying the message of health in response to the rising rate of obesity among children. My goal was to start a conversation, create an awareness in schools, about health and fitness and to inspire kids to think about their food choices. I wanted kids to invest in their own health, literally from the ground up. Michelle Obama's amazing vegetable garden at the White House further inspired me to give kids everywhere the chance to experience the magic of growing your own food.

The principal of my children's elementary school in Malibu had always indulged my environmental projects and was more than willing to jump on board. Her knowledge of how to work with schoolteachers and her understanding of how and where to find the teachers and staff who would support the project were invaluable.

We grew a variety of vegetables—carrots, kale, radishes, and tomatoes. Soon after the garden became a success, a number of private groups offered financial support, and we were able to start Teaching Gardens in less-privileged neighborhoods of East and South Central Los Angeles. Aimed at first- through fifth-graders, the program teaches children how to plant seeds, nurture growing plants, harvest the produce, and ultimately understand the value of good eating habits.

The success of Teaching Gardens locally attracted the attention of the American Heart Association (AHA), which adopted us into its education and nutrition program about obesity and heart disease and has generously supported us ever since.

With funding in place, we chose school locations nationwide. The designated school had to complete a comprehensive survey committing to the program, and it had to also establish a Teaching Gardens committee. Before the first planting, the committee would receive special training and an AHA Teaching Gardens tool kit.

With the AHA's support, we started to plant gardens across the country. For example, in the summer of 2012, with one of the grants from the AHA, students at the Rosa Parks Elementary School planted the first Teaching Garden in Indianapolis. Thanks to the AHA, Rosa Parks Elementary is now just one of 140 schools across the country that share the common ground of learning about nutrition from Teaching Gardens.

The Teaching Gardens program is not a solution to the problem of hunger, but it is a step in the direction of defeating food ignorance. The gardens teach kids not only about planting but also about math and science outside the classroom. They help children learn about the cycle of life and about delayed gratification. Through gardening, children also learn discipline and the importance of a good work ethic. After all, the garden is a metaphor for life: if it is not attended to, it will not thrive. The entire experience provides an extraordinary learning opportunity while also supplying fresh healthy vegetables that can be harvested and eaten.

Teaching Gardens are also green billboards, if you like, that help to counter the irresponsible advertising of junk food to children, food that has been engineered to attract consumption, regardless of its nutritional value.

On many occasions, we have found that children went home and asked for healthier food. They asked their parents if they, too, could plant a garden. Children know when given the opportunity to eat better that they feel better. The smallest exposure to what it feels like to be healthy can inspire a child to take action to make healthier choices.

Of course, we are not all fortunate enough to have gardens or to be able to spend time cultivating them. But we should at least know about them and have the opportunity to appreciate the marvel of food grown naturally and harvested well.

Just as my children, like their forebears, learned to love to plant, I hope that the Teaching Gardens program can give other children, some of whom may never have had the chance to watch food grow, a stake in the process of growing what soon might become a salad they would actually be interested in eating. My goal is very simply to connect children to the environment in a real way through the food on their tables. For more information, please visit Teaching Gardens on the AHA website: www.heart.org/HEARTORG/GettingHealthy/HealtheirKids/TeachingGardens.

CHAPTER 19

Seven Steps to
Ending Child Hunger by 2015[1]

FOOD RESEARCH AND ACTION CENTER

Every one of us has a role to play in reducing and eventually ending hunger in America. Many of us contribute to emergency food providers, and that's a start. Food bankers will be the first to tell you, however, that the "heavy lifting" is being done by federal programs and that improving those programs is the key strategy to end hunger. That is also the message of *A Place at the Table*.

We need to protect and improve those federal food aid programs, like SNAP and school meals, that are doing the heavy lifting. There are many allies to be had in this fight: a recent poll finds that a solid majority of Americans believe that the Food Stamp Program is important for the country and that the federal government should be spending as much money on solving hunger as it is currently, or even more.

To do your part, keep informed about national and state legislation and rules that affect SNAP, school meals, summer and after-school meals programs, WIC, and child care meals. A good place to start is the web page for FRAC's Legislative Action Center, http://frac.org/leg -act-center.

Write and call your members of Congress, and meet with them (both senators and representatives) when they come home on recesses. Join local anti-hunger, anti-poverty, and children's advocacy groups and community associations to organize meetings. Ask the members to step up their support for SNAP, WIC, and other programs. A review of strategies that are helpful when advocating for these programs can be found at FRAC's advocacy tools web page, http://frac.org/leg-act-center/advocacy -tools.

Be a squeaky wheel. Contact your senator or representative not just when a big vote comes up that will affect federal food programs but throughout the year. Invite members of Congress to accompany you on a visit to nutrition program sites, such as locations where SNAP outreach and application assistance is conducted or school breakfast or summer food is being served.

Remind lawmakers and others that a solution is within reach. Federal nutrition programs have the infrastructure, the public support, and the partners to get the job done. They need to reach more people, with more adequate benefits, but they have the potential to rid America of hunger. We now need to endow these programs with the funding and political might necessary to finish the job.

౽

Today America's anti-hunger groups agree that one central goal must be ending childhood hunger by 2015. Here are seven essential strategies to achieve that goal, excerpted from an analysis by the Food Research and Action Center.

1. Restore economic growth and create jobs with better wages for lower-income workers.
2. Raise the incomes of the lowest-income families.
3. Strengthen the SNAP/Food Stamp Program.
4. Strengthen the child nutrition programs.
5. Engage the entire federal government in ending childhood hunger.
6. Work with states, localities, and nonprofits to expand and improve participation in federal nutrition programs.
7. Make sure all families have convenient access to reasonably priced, healthy food.

1. RESTORE ECONOMIC GROWTH AND CREATE JOBS WITH BETTER WAGES FOR LOWER-INCOME WORKERS

Although our nation certainly is affluent enough that it could have acted to end hunger even in the recent times of deep recession, it is more practical and politically viable to implement key strategies to do so as the nation's economy regains strength and continues to grow again.

Moreover, while solving the childhood hunger problem is the paramount goal, how it is solved is extraordinarily important and will help determine the permanence of the solution. The solution must be built on jobs and family supports, not on overstretched charities. As we bolster the economy, the nation must strive to ensure that all Americans get a fair share of economic growth, which generally has not occurred over most of the last thirty years. Whenever possible, parents want jobs and good wages and benefits as the means to support their families. To do that will require fiscal and monetary policies that restore and sustain growth; robust private- and public-sector job creation and job training, with new attention to making the economy work for all, including disadvantaged populations; full-time jobs at good wages that create family-supporting incomes; benefits and leave provisions that are consistent with family well-being; and strong child care supports.

Moving forward, moreover, it will not be enough, ethically or practically, just to feed children and leave parents in crisis. When parents themselves are struggling with hunger, it has negative effects on the development, behavior, health, and learning of their children. Food insecurity during pregnancy, for example, is associated with poor birth outcomes, and parental food insecurity—and the resulting stress, depression, poor health, and other outcomes for the parent—continues to adversely affect children throughout childhood.

2. RAISE THE INCOMES OF THE LOWEST-INCOME FAMILIES

President Obama's "Tackling Domestic Hunger" analysis made the important point that "the most effective way to eliminate childhood hunger and reduce hunger among adults is through a broad expansion of economic opportunity." To do that, he outlined a range of initiatives "to reduce and alleviate poverty, including providing permanent tax relief for working families, expanding the Earned Income Tax Credit, raising the minimum wage, and providing affordable, accessible health insurance."

FRAC agrees with this approach. Some significant steps along this path have occurred since 2008. Nutrition programs alone can't carry the whole burden of government supports to end childhood hunger when employment falls short. There must be decent family incomes on which to build. If a full-time minimum-wage job pays only two-thirds of the poverty level, even substantially improved food stamp and school meals programs, while they can reduce suffering, won't end hunger.

3. STRENGTHEN THE SNAP/FOOD STAMP PROGRAM

This is the nation's most important direct defense against hunger. The program is fundamentally strong, but needs some key reforms and improvements to carry its share of the weight in reaching the 2015 goal:

- Update and improve benefit levels. Benefit levels are too low to stave off hunger for a month, much less allow a family to purchase a healthy diet. The monthly allotment is predicated on the "Thrifty Food Plan," which was developed during the Depression in the 1930s "as a restricted diet for emergency use." The allotment typically carries even the most careful of families only three-quarters or four-fifths of the way through the month. Although the temporary boost passed in 2009 (which should be permanent) helped to improve the food security of households, it still doesn't make benefits adequate. The amount of the federal government's own "Low-Cost Food Budget"—the lowest of three government budgets for normal use—is approximately 25 percent higher than the Thrifty Food Plan and should be the basis for SNAP allotments. The Low-Cost Food Budget is generally in line with what low- and moderate-income families report that they need to spend on food, as opposed to the lower amount a food stamp allotment would provide.

- Adjust benefit amounts in a timely manner. Although the benefit allotment is adjusted for inflation each year, the increases come only after a time lag, so the allotment reflects not current prices but the prices of the (already inadequate) Thrifty Food Plan from between four and sixteen months earlier.
- Expand eligibility and improve benefit computation rules. Policymakers should also: extend the program to children and parents now excluded from benefits by arbitrary eligibility rules; fully allow SNAP benefits to increase when high housing costs consume more of a family's income (a provision that was cut back for families with children by 1996 legislation); reduce unnecessary red tape that deters participation; improve earnings disregards and other benefit computation rules; and otherwise improve access and responsiveness to the needs of families with children.

4. STRENGTHEN THE CHILD NUTRITION PROGRAMS

The president's "Tackling Domestic Hunger" paper emphasizes also that the child nutrition programs (school lunch and breakfast, after-school and summer food, WIC, child care food) are essential tools for ending childhood hunger. The paper correctly notes that these programs and SNAP do more than address hunger: "They reduce poverty, prevent obesity, strengthen schools and child care programs, and boost children's health, development and school achievement." They are among our nation's most important and cost-effective public interventions, but they must be bolstered in important ways as part of a campaign to eliminate childhood hunger. Here are some of the necessary steps:

- Increase participation in the federal free and reduced-price school meals programs, especially breakfast, which is severely underutilized. Part of the answer is for schools, localities, and states to work aggressively to enroll into the meals program the many eligible but not participating children. (One way to do this is more effective automatic enrollment of SNAP-recipient children, bolstered by the 2010 child recipient law.) Wherever possible, paperwork for parents should be reduced or eliminated. Red tape is also a problem for schools: paperwork for participating schools (and nonprofits like after-school and summer programs) should be reduced so that they need not file multiple applications to serve children nutritious food year-round. The federal government should also move to: provide more support to initiatives that offer lunch and breakfast free to all children in schools with substantial numbers of low-income children (this will reduce red tape and stigma and boost participation); support initiatives to serve breakfast in the classroom (an increasingly successful nutritional and educational strategy); and provide federal commodities (as well as cash reimbursements) for school breakfasts, as is now done with school lunches.

- Expand access to nutrition in after-school and summer programs. Only fifteen children receive lunch in the summer from the federal nutrition programs for every one hundred low-income children who get lunch during the school year. One barrier is the difficulty for many after-school and summer programs in meeting an "area eligibility test" for nutrition program reimbursement that is too strict (particularly after congressional cutbacks). The government should make the eligibility requirement for such funding the same as in education and after-school programs like the Department of Education's Title 1 and 21st Century Community Learning Center programs. Start-up grants and transportation grants (especially for rural areas) also are essential.

- Robustly implement the new (as of late 2010) program of federal support for after-school meals served in after-school programs in schools, public agencies like parks and recreation programs, and community-based nonprofits and faith-based institutions.

- Expand nutrition programs for children in child care. The federal Child and Adult Care Food Program (CACFP) should be adjusted to make far more low-income preschoolers in child care centers and family child care eligible for a day's worth of federally funded meals and snacks. This will require changes in the eligibility test (currently less than half of all child care facilities participate in CACFP) and a rollback of a shortsighted rule enacted by Congress limiting the number of meals for preschoolers to two a day no matter how many hours a day they are in care.

- Improve WIC. We should provide children in the WIC program with the full fruit and vegetable allotment recommended by the Institute of Medicine, rather than the slightly smaller one adopted in 2008 with a reduction driven by budget considerations.
- Improve meal quality. The government must improve the quality of meals provided in child care settings, summer and after-school, and schools; provide reimbursement rates and structures adequate to support healthy eating; improve the healthfulness of commodities donated to schools; and enforce the nutrition and safety standards already in effect, improve those standards, and apply them to all foods offered or sold in schools.

Some improvements in the child nutrition programs were made in the 2010 child nutrition "reauthorization" law, but more work is needed after reauthorization to make the programs robust enough to fully play their part in meeting the president's 2015 goal.

5. ENGAGE THE ENTIRE FEDERAL GOVERNMENT IN ENDING CHILDHOOD HUNGER

All agencies that touch the lives of low-income children, families, and communities must be engaged in the campaign to end childhood hunger, not just the Department of Agriculture. The Treasury Department can do more outreach to increase the utilization of important refundable tax credits for low-income working families. The Department of Education and the Justice Department, which fund after-school programs, can incorporate anti-hunger efforts into their program rules. They can, for example, encourage or require their grantees to participate in federal nutrition programs and thereby provide healthy food to hungry children in their care. The Department of Health and Human Services can take similar steps with the tens of thousands of child care providers who receive its funds. This type of coordination could be facilitated by streamlined application and documentation processes. The Department of Defense should expand its program that gets healthy commodities into schools. The Corporation for National and Community Service should make ending childhood hunger a priority as it places volunteers and carries out its important domestic programs. In addition, many offices in the White House and the Executive Office of the President have significant expertise that could help identify and implement solutions to childhood hunger. They include the Office of Social Innovation, the Domestic Policy Council, the Office of Urban Affairs Policy, the Council on Women and Girls, and the Office of Faith-Based and Neighborhood Partnerships.

6. WORK WITH STATES, LOCALITIES, AND NONPROFITS TO EXPAND AND IMPROVE PARTICIPATION IN FEDERAL NUTRITION PROGRAMS

The federal income support and nutrition programs need to be strengthened, but the intermediaries for those programs also need to take better advantage of them. Today the rate of participation in SNAP among eligible people ranges from about 50 percent in some states to more than 90 percent in others. The situation is similar with school feeding programs: in some states, only thirty-three low-income children get school breakfast for every one hundred who get school lunch; in others, that rate is much higher.

Even in the best states, rates often aren't high enough, and low enrollment rates in most states contribute enormously to the hunger problem. They are due to a variety of factors. The differences in both official attitudes and results among the states point to one important reason to have even stronger federal programs with robust federal funding and clear national program rules: whether or not a child is hungry—and healthy and able to learn—shouldn't depend on an accident of birth or family mobility, where she is from or where she goes to child care or school.

Strengthening the national framework, therefore, is essential, but so is encouraging full use of federal programs and available federal funds:

- Expand outreach and education. The federal government, as well as state and local governments, foundations, and other private-sector stakeholders, should increase outreach efforts for nutrition programs, as they have done for child health insurance and the Earned Income Tax Credit. This effort should include expanding support for nonprofit advocacy groups, food banks, and other direct service providers that struggle to improve federal nutrition program participation.

- Restore support for the Community Food and Nutrition Program, a federal initiative that for many years supported successful and cost-effective local outreach and advocacy but was defunded beginning in fiscal year 2006.
- Improve and expand performance bonuses. Federal initiatives that reward states for excellent performance in such areas as reaching higher rates of SNAP-eligible families should be made more robust and extended to all nutrition programs.
- Create incentives for participation in nutrition programs. The federal government should find new ways to encourage or require schools, child care providers, and out-of-school-time providers funded by government agencies to participate in the federal nutrition programs.

7. MAKE SURE ALL FAMILIES HAVE CONVENIENT ACCESS TO REASONABLY PRICED, HEALTHY FOOD

Many neighborhoods and towns across America lack decent-sized stores that sell a good variety of food, including fresh produce, at reasonable prices. Living in one of these "food deserts" makes it far harder, if not impossible, for a struggling low-income family to stave off hunger and stay healthy. They often must forgo healthy food or spend scarce resources traveling to food stores, pay more than average amounts for food, and get food of lesser nutritional quality.

Community gardens and school gardens, farmers' markets and "green-carts," and improvements to the offerings of corner stores can help combat this. But we must take steps to make decent grocery stores accessible to all Americans. President Obama's Healthy Food Financing Initiative (HFFI) is making important strides in this direction by providing grants and loans for food markets in low-income, underserved areas—a national fresh food financing initiative. In addition, all grocery stores should participate in the food stamp and WIC programs in order to give low-income families better access to high-quality food. Other strategies to help low-income households afford adequate and healthy food are outlined in FRAC's "Review of Strategies to Bolster SNAP's Role in Improving Nutrition as Well as Food Security."

Attaining the 2015 goal is certainly possible, but it will require using every day of next year to adopt and implement smart strategies. FRAC is eager to engage public officials, experts, other advocates, and all who care about addressing hunger and poverty in this country in this important enterprise.

We welcome comments and thoughts on the seven strategies described here. And we welcome the commitment of all who want to engage in this extraordinarily important effort.

Food Research and Action Center
1875 Connecticut Avenue NW, Suite 540, Washington, DC, 20009
202-986-2200
www.endingchildhunger2015.org
Send comments on this chapter to: 2015@frac.org.

CHAPTER 20

Directory of NGOs

This list, compiled by Sarah Newman, Participant Media's researcher on *A Place at the Table,* includes national organizations with examples of some of the best local and regional groups:

30 Project

http://www.30project.org

Background: The 30 Project was founded by Ellen Gustafson, who previously was with the FEED Foundation. Her new organization is intended to address the obesity-hunger connection. The 30 Project brings together key organizations and activists working around the world on addressing hunger, obesity, and agriculture issues to talk about their visions for the food system and the next thirty years.

Area of focus: Obesity, hunger, food system

Programming: Hosting dinners to share knowledge and ideas

Level of engagement: Local, brainstorming

Twitter (@the30project http://Twitter.com/#!/the30project): 744 followers; Facebook (http://www.Facebook.com/30Project): 659 followers

Alliance to End Hunger

alliancetoendhunger.org

Background: The Alliance to End Hunger, the interfaith NGO arm of Bread for the World, develops innovative partnerships among its members, political commitment among its leaders, and global connections among groups working to end hunger worldwide.

Area of focus: Eradicating hunger

Programming: Bringing organizations together; increasing political focus on hunger

Level of engagement: National, international

Facebook: 66 likes, 80 member organizations

American Academy of Pediatrics

www.aap.org

Background: The American Academy of Pediatrics, the major professional association of pediatricians, takes the position that childhood hunger is a determining factor in long-term health and social outcomes.

Programming: Advocacy, resources for professionals

Facebook: 6,586 likes; Twitter: 5,031 followers

Members: 60,000 pediatricians

American Association of Retired Persons (AARP)

http://drivetoendhunger.org

Background: AARP is a nonprofit lobbying group working on behalf of older Americans.

Area of focus: Seniors, hunger

Programming: Striving to end hunger

Level of engagement: National

Facebook: 12,420 likes; Twitter: 4,391 followers

Members: Over 40 million

American Federation of State, County, and Municipal Employees (AFSCME)

http://www.afscme.org

Background: The AFSCME is one of the largest labor unions in the United States and a key SNAP supporter.

Area of focus: Education, health care, housing, hunger

Programming: Advocacy, lobbying

Members: 1.6 million

American Federation of Teachers (AFT)

http://www.aft.org

Background: The AFT is a labor union representing teachers at all levels of education, government employees, and health care workers; like the AFSCME, it is a key SNAP supporter.

Area of focus: Education, health and safety, health care

Programming: Advocacy, lobbying

Members: 1.5 million

Ample Harvest

http://www.ampleharvest.org

Background: AmpleHarvest.org diminishes hunger in America by educating and enabling gardeners to donate their excess harvest to the needy in their community.

Area of focus: Farmers, food pantries

Programming: Connecting farmers' extra produce to hungry people through food pantries

Level of engagement: Direct services

Anti-Hunger and Opportunity Corps

http://antihungercorps.posterous.com

Background: The Anti-Hunger and Opportunity Corps is an AmeriCorps VISTA project.

Area of focus: Hunger

Programming: Volunteer recruitment and management, fund development, markets and gardens initiative, benefits access plans

Level of engagement: National

BeeLocal.org (One Economy)

http://beelocal.thebeehive.org/about

Background: Hunger is a popular search request on this site for finding public services.

Area of focus: Public services access

Programming: Project of One Economy

Level of engagement: Local, national

Boys' & Girls' Clubs of America (BGCA)

http://www.bgca.org/Pages/index.aspx

Background: BGCA is committed to enabling all young people, especially those most in need, to reach their full potential as productive, caring, and responsible citizens.

Area of focus: Health, fitness, character/leadership

Programming: Mentoring, educational programs, sports groups

Level of engagement: National

Bread for the World

http://www.bread.org

Background: Bread for the World, a key SNAP supporter, is a collective Christian voice urging the nation's decision-makers to end hunger at home and abroad. (Its interfaith NGO coalition arm is the Alliance to End Hunger.)

Area of focus: Hunger, policy change

Programming: Mobilizing people of faith to do advocacy, anti-hunger policies

Level of engagement: National

Twitter (@bread4theworld): 6,375 followers; Facebook (http://www .Facebook.com/breadfortheworld): 10,105 followers

The California Endowment

http://www.calendow.org

Background: The California Endowment funds hunger relief and regional food system programs in California.

Area of focus: Health care, the obesity epidemic

Programming: Advocacy, funding, regional outreach

Level of engagement: State

Campaign: SAVE for All

http://www.chn.org/save4all/index.html

Background: A coalition supported by key hunger NGOs and run by Coalition on Human Needs, Strengthening America's Values and Economy (SAVE) for All is a coalition of national, state, and local advocacy groups, service providers, faith-based organizations, policy experts, and labor and civil rights groups working to protect important services from harmful federal budget cuts and to save the federal capacity to spur economic recovery and progress for the benefit of all.

Area of focus: Poverty, housing and homelessness, health, food and nutrition

Programming: Developing materials, engaging grassroots advocates, employing media strategies, contacting members of Congress

Center on Budget and Policy Priorities

http://www.cbpp.org

Background: A key SNAP supporter, the Center on Budget and Policy Priorities works at the federal and state levels on fiscal policy and public programs that affect low- and moderate-income families and individuals.

Area of focus: Poverty, fiscal issues, welfare

Programming: Strengthening low-income program policy, assisting federal agencies, identifying often overlooked effects, disseminating information

Level of engagement: National

Chefs Collaborative

http://chefscollaborative.org

Background: The Chefs Collaborative is a network that connects chefs to sustainable food growers.

Programming: Educational programs for chefs, farmer-chef connections, seafood solutions

Level of engagement: National

Twitter (http://Twitter.com/#!/chefscollab): 7,727 followers

Children's HealthWatch

http://www.childrenshealthwatch.org

Background: Children's HealthWatch provides research and analysis from the front lines of pediatric care, linking nutrition and other issues to children's health. Its research plays a crucial role in forming government policy regarding food and nutrition assistance programs.

Area of focus: Health
Programming: Research, policy, advocacy—connecting latest research in
pediatric health with government policies
Level of engagement: National

City Harvest
http://www.cityharvest.org
Background: Based in New York City, City Harvest works with restaurants to donate their excess food to food banks. The organization collects 28 million pounds of excess food from all segments of the food industry, including restaurants, grocers, corporate cafeterias, manufacturers, and farms. This food is then delivered free of charge to nearly six hundred community food programs throughout New York City. City Harvest also addresses hunger's underlying causes by supporting affordable access to nutritious food in low-income communities, educating individuals, families, and communities.
Area of focus: Nutrition education, hunger, communities
Programming: Bringing excess food from restaurants and other segments of the food industry in New York City to community programs serving the hungry
Level of engagement: Local, direct services
Twitter (@CityHarvest): 8,800 followers; Facebook (http://www.Face book.com/CityHarvestNYC): 30,762 likes

Coalition on Human Needs
http://www.chn.org
Background: Another key SNAP supporter, the Coalition on Human Needs is an alliance of 102 national organizations working together to promote public policies that address the needs of low-income and other vulnerable people.
Area of focus: Child nutrition, SNAP
Programming: Research, advocacy
Level of engagement: National policy recommendations
Twitter (@CoalitiononHN): 1,034 followers
Facebook (http://www.Facebook.com/pages/Coalition-on-Human-Needs /144519585571873): 1,188 likes

Community Food Security Coalition (CFSC)

http://www.foodsecurity.org

Background: The Community Food Security Coalition is a North American coalition of diverse people and organizations working from the local to international levels to build community food security and sustainable food systems; through this work, CFSC serves as a bridge between the nutrition and hunger communities. The group works on national legislation, with an emphasis on the need to reorient the food system to support policies based in social justice.

Area of focus: Food security, food access

Programming: Advocacy for national legislation, annual conference, healthy corner store network

Level of engagement: National coalition with many local branches

DC Central Kitchen

http://www.dccentralkitchen.org

Background: DC Central Kitchen uses a community kitchen as a central location to recover unused food, prepare and deliver meals to partner social service agencies, train men and women for jobs in the food service industry, and engage volunteers.

Area of focus: Food banks, job training

Programming: Providing food to DC residents, food bank, job training

Level of engagement: Local, direct services

Twitter (@dcck): 6,629 followers; Facebook (http://www.Facebook.com /dccentralkitchen): 3,617 likes

Donors Choose

http://www.donorschoose.org/donors/search.html?subject2=28

Background: DonorsChoose.org is an online charity that makes it easy for anyone to help students in need. It works with the FEED Foundation to provide donor cards for people to use to support the building of school salad bars.

Area of focus: Range of projects, including nutrition, fitness, special needs, math, and music and the arts

Programming: Connecting donors with classroom projects in need of funding
Level of engagement: Local
Twitter (@DonorsChoose): 121,684 followers
Facebook (http://www.Facebook.com/DonorsChoose): 111,000 likes

Do Something's "Feed the Need" Campaign
http://www.dosomething.org/tackle-hunger
Background: DoSomething.org, one of the largest organizations in the United States that helps young people pursue causes they care about, is a driving force in creating a culture of volunteerism.
Area of focus: Local food drives
Programming: Web-based contest encouraging people to raise the most amount of food in their local communities
Level of engagement: Local focus

End Hunger Network
http://www.endhunger.com
Background: Founded by actor Jeff Bridges and other entertainment industry leaders in 1984, the End Hunger Network has a long record of innovative initiatives aimed at encouraging, stimulating, and supporting action to end childhood hunger.
Area of focus: Hunger, childhood hunger
Programming: Los Angeles World Hunger Event, End Hunger Televent, Live Aid, US Presidential End Hunger Awards, Primetime to End Hunger, Fast Forward to End Hunger, Hunger in America Film
Level of Engagement: National

Environmental Working Group (EWG)
http://www.ewg.org
Background: The mission of the Environmental Working Group (EWG) is to use the power of public information to protect public health and the environment. A leader in farm bill advocacy to reduce commodity crop subsidies, this environmental organization publishes all Farm Bill subsidies online.
Area of focus: Toxic material in food

Programming: Sharing information with the public and advocacy
Level of engagement: National
Twitter (@ewgtoxics): 18,691 followers; Facebook (http://www.Facebook .com/ewg.org): 137,952 likes

Esperanza

www.esperanza.us

Background: Esperanza provides Hispanics with services that accurately reflect their needs, build ownership, and provide opportunities to gain assets for long-term change.
Programming: Community engagement on a range of social issues
Level of engagement: National and local

Fair Food Network

http://www.fairfoodnetwork.org

Background: Fair Food Network is dedicated to building a more just and sustainable food system. It works to improve healthy food access, inform public policy, strengthen funding strategies, and expand networks and sharing knowledge.
Programming: Incentives for purchasing healthier food with SNAP, public policy, connecting organizations
Area of focus: Sustainable healthy food access
Level of engagement: Domestic
Facebook (http://www.Facebook.com/FairFoodNetwork): 3,304 likes

Farmers' Market Coalition

http://farmersmarketcoalition.org

Background: The Farmers' Market Coalition seeks to strengthen the capacity of farmers' markets to serve farmers, consumers, and communities by providing the rapidly growing movement with information and representation at the state and federal levels.
Area of focus: Local food, farmers' markets
Programming: Resources, advocacy, webinar
Level of engagement: Local

FEED Foundation

http://feedusa.thefeedfoundation.org

Background: The FEED Foundation supports programs and organizations that are working to fight hunger and eliminate malnutrition throughout the world. In America, FEED USA includes school garden and cooking programs. The FEED Nature Fund gives support to areas that have been affected by natural disaster by providing much-needed school meals to kids in these regions as well as planting trees through community programs.

Area of focus: Sustainable solutions to food-, agriculture-, and nutrition-related causes; international school programs

Programming: The cornerstone of FEED USA is the funding of teacher-led, school-based interventions that allow local activists to see the challenges to improving nutrition in their own schools.

Area of focus: Improving school food across America

Level of engagement: Throughout America, school-based

Twitter (@FEEDprojects): 8,936 followers; Facebook (http://www.Face book.com/feedprojects): 37,872 likes

Feeding America

http://feedingamerica.org

Background: The largest NGO hunger relief provider in the United States, Feeding America is the nation's leading domestic hunger relief charity. It works closely with companies such as ConAgra and Wal-Mart and is a key SNAP supporter.

Area of focus: Food banks, hunger

Programming: Providing food through a number of programs and working with preexisting food banks

Level of engagement: National, direct services

Twitter (@FeedingAmerica): 54,682 followers; Facebook (http://www .Facebook.com/FeedingAmerica): 235,128 likes

Food and Water Watch

http://www.foodandwaterwatch.org

Background: Food and Water Watch works on issues related to commodity crop subsidies, sustainable food systems, organics, food safety, and consumer education.

Area of focus: Food and water

Programming: Legislative advocacy at the local, state, and national levels; consumer education

Level of engagement: Local, campus, national

Twitter (@foodandwater): 17,512 followers; Facebook (https://www .Facebook.com/FoodandWaterWatch): 3,409 likes

FoodCorps

http://www.food-corps.org

Background: The vision for FoodCorps is to recruit young adults for a yearlong term of public service in school food systems. Once stationed, FoodCorps members build farm-to-school supply chains, expand food system and nutrition education programs, and build and tend school food gardens. The ultimate goal of the organization is to increase the health and prosperity of vulnerable children while investing in the next generation of farmers and public health leaders.

Area of focus: Farm to school, nutrition education

Programming: Recruiting AmeriCorps volunteers to work in schools building farm-to-school supply chains

Level of engagement: Local, in-school

Food Research and Action Center (FRAC)

http://frac.org

Background: A national hunger advocacy and lobby group, the Food Research and Action Center (FRAC) is the leading national nonprofit organization working to improve public policies and public-private partnerships to eradicate hunger and undernutrition in the United States. FRAC works with Feeding America, Bread for the World, and hundreds of other national, state, and local nonprofit organizations, public agencies, corporations, and labor organizations to address

hunger, food insecurity, and their root cause—poverty. FRAC is a key
SNAP supporter.

Area of focus: Hunger, poverty, food insecurity

Programming: Ending childhood hunger by 2015, ending obesity and
hunger

Level of engagement: Research, advocacy, national

Twitter (@fractweets): 1,296 followers; Facebook (http://www.Facebook
.com/foodresearchandactioncenter): 1,076 likes

Food Trust

http://www.thefoodtrust.org

Background: Working with neighborhoods, schools, grocers, farmers, and
policymakers, this Philadelphia organization offers sustainable, innovative ways to address food deserts and obesity.

Area of focus: School nutrition, community access to healthy food

Programming: School-based programs ranging from policy to bringing
farms to schools, community-based programs such as bringing farmers'
markets and healthy groceries to communities without them

Level of engagement: Local, direct services, advocacy

Twitter: (@thefoodtrust): 11,868 followers; Facebook (http://www
.Facebook.com/thefoodtrust): 4,816 likes

Healthy Corner Stores Network (HCSN)

www.healthycornerstores.org

Background: The Healthy Corner Stores Network (HCSN) supports efforts to increase the availability and sales of healthy, fresh, affordable
foods through small-scale stores in underserved communities.

Areas of focus: Healthy food, food deserts

Level of engagement: Local

Programming: Bimonthly webinars, in-person meetings, listserv, access
to consultants

Healthy Eating, Active Communities (HEAC)

http://www.healthyeatingactivecommunities.org

Background: Healthy Eating, Active Communities (HEAC) shows
how communities can reshape the food and physical activity envi-

ronment to improve children's health. Schools, community groups, and public health departments collaborate at HEAC sites in six low-income communities.

Area of focus: Healthy communities

Programming: Market Makeovers, a division of HEAC, provides an online tool kit (pictures, docs, videos) about how to transform a corner store market into a healthy eating space.

Level of engagement: Local, six sites across California

Institute for Agriculture and Trade Policy (IATP)

http://www.iatp.org

Background: Initially established to protect family farmers, IATP works on globalization, building sustainability, and safe and healthy ecosystems.

Area of focus: Trade, rural communities, food and health, local foods, food and justice

Programming: Advocacy and access (farm to school, local markets, etc.)

Level of engagement: Local and national

MAZON: A Jewish Response to Hunger

http://mazon.org

Background: MAZON: A Jewish Response to Hunger is a national nonprofit organization that allocates donations from the Jewish community to prevent and alleviate hunger among people of all faiths and backgrounds. In addition to providing immediate relief, the group also works with congregations to donate money instead of canned foods. MAZON, a key SNAP supporter, works on the hunger-obesity connection by trying to connect local food banks with local providers of healthier foods.

Area of focus: Hunger, food banks

Programming: Giving grants to hunger relief organizations

Level of engagement: National

Twitter (@StopHunger): 11,073 followers; Facebook (http://www .Facebook.com/mazonusa): 1,275 likes

Meals on Wheels Association of America

http://www.mowaa.org

Background: The Meals on Wheels Association of America aims to end senior hunger. A key SNAP supporter, it serves as a network of local organizations that provide meals for the elderly who are hungry.

Area of focus: Senior hunger

Programming: Providing meals to hungry elderly who cannot drive or leave their homes

Level of engagement: Local, direct services

National Anti-Hunger Organizations (NAHO) Coalition

www.wecanendhunger.org

Background: A coalition of anti-hunger groups that build public awareness and support for activities and policies addressing problems of hunger and poverty in America. NAHO is a key SNAP supporter.

Area of focus: Hunger, coordinating NGOs

Programming: Projects include "A Blueprint to End Hunger" and "A Roadmap to Ending Childhood Hunger."

National Sustainable Agriculture Coalition (NSAC)

http://sustainableagriculture.net

Background: The NSAC is an alliance of grassroots organizations that advocate for federal policy reform to advance the sustainability of agriculture, food systems, natural resources, and rural communities. The group works primarily on protecting small farmers and ranchers.

Area of focus: Family farmers, the food system

Programming: Direct and grassroots advocacy and public education

Level of engagement: National

Facebook (http://www.Facebook.com/pages/National-Sustainable -Agriculture-Coalition/154052595576): 4,834 likes

New York City Coalition Against Hunger (NYCCAH)

http://www.nyccah.org

Background: NYCCAH serves to meet the immediate food needs of low-income New Yorkers and enact innovative solutions to help them move "beyond the soup kitchen" to self-sufficiency. The group also works on addressing systemic changes to solve hunger in New York City.

Area of focus: Hunger, food access, and food pantries and soup kitchens

Programming: Policy lobbying, assisting citizens with signing up for SNAP, AmeriCorps partnership

Level of engagement: Direct and local services

Twitter (@NYCCAH): 1,228 followers; Facebook (http://www.Facebook .com/NYCCAH): 1,346 likes

Parent Earth

http://www.parentearth.com

Background: Parent Earth's mission is to answer parents' questions about food and work with partners to create a world that nurtures healthy, thriving children. It distributes videos in clinics, hospitals, and doctors' offices about food, nutrition, cooking, etc.

Area of focus: Family and child nutrition

Programming: Online videos to answer parents' questions about nutrition

Level of engagement: Online

Twitter (@parentearth): 2,400 followers; Facebook (http://www.Facebook .com/ParentEarth): 1,467 likes

People's Grocery

http://www.peoplesgrocery.org

Background: People's Grocery's mission is to improve the health and economy of West Oakland through programs, advocacy, and leadership development.

Area of focus: Improving the economy and health of West Oakland

Programming: Advocacy, leadership development, food distribution, urban agriculture programs

Level of engagement: Direct services

Twitter (@peoplesgrocery): 3,369 followers; Facebook (http://www .Facebook.com/PeoplesGrocery.org): 3,844 likes

Public Health Law and Policy (PHLP)

www.phlpnet.org

Background: PHLP is a team of attorneys, policy analysts, and urban planners dedicated to building healthy communities nationwide.

Area of focus: Law, health

Programming: Policy research, workshops, training, and advocacy

RAMP America

http://www.rampamerica.org

Background: RAMP (Rockin' Appalachian Mom Project) is a charity dedicated to improving the well-being of poor families in Appalachia.

Area of focus: Poverty, food security

Programming: Providing micro loans and mentoring families in Martin County, Kentucky, partnering with Whole Foods and Rockin' Water to raise funds

Level of engagement: Local

Twitter (@RAMPAmerica): 194 followers

The Rural Grocery Initiative

www.ruralgrocery.org

Background: The Rural Grocery Initiative help to establish rural grocery stores.

Area of focus: Food deserts

Programming: Creating more rural grocery stores and supporting existing ones

Level of engagement: Local

Save the Children

www.savethechildren.org

Background: Works with other organizations, governments, nonprofits, and local partners to improve the lives of children faced with poverty, hunger, illiteracy, disease, and natural disasters around the world and in the United States.

Programs in the United States: Supports education policies for children in low-income communities and collaborates with local partners to prevent and reduce childhood obesity through the Campaign for Healthy Kids.

Service Employees International Union (SEIU)

http://www.seiu.org

Background: The SEIU represents health care, public services, and property services workers. The union is a key SNAP supporter.

Level of engagement: National, local

Share Our Strength

http://www.strength.org

Background: Share Our Strength's highest priority is to make sure that every child in America gets the nutritious food that he or she needs to learn, grow, and thrive. The organization has a range of programs, from summer meals to No Kid Hungry to nutrition education. Share Our Strength is a key SNAP supporter.

Area of focus: Child hunger

Programming: Working closely with the culinary industry to create programs that raise funds for advocacy and grant making (e.g., the Great American Bake Sale, the Great American Dine Out)

Level of engagement: National

Slow Food USA

http://slowfoodusa.org

Background: Slow Food USA is a national group with local chapters that support sustainable food programming.

Area of focus: Sustainable food

Programming: Sustainable food education and action

Level of engagement: Local

South Los Angeles Healthy Eating, Active Communities Initiative (HEAC)

http://www.healthyeatingactivecommunities.org/grantee _showcase1_5.php

Background: South LA students in this HEAC chapter spearhead corner store conversions, capturing their success in online videos. They work with store owners to carry healthy food items and display them for sale and then follow up to ensure that the makeovers are sustained. The efforts of these South LA teens have received international attention.

Area of focus: Availability of healthy food choices in neighborhoods that have traditionally lacked fruits and vegetables

Programming: Youth-led "store makeovers" of locally owned corner stores that did not previously carry healthy food choices

Level of engagement: Local (South LA)

United Food and Commercial Workers (UFCW)

http://www.ufcw.org

Background: The UFCW represents grocery and food processing workers and is a key SNAP supporter.

Area of focus: Hunger, workers' rights

Programming: Making change at Wal-Mart, feeding the hungry, voter registration

Level of engagement: National, local

United Way

http://liveunited.org

Background: United Way improves lives by mobilizing the caring power of communities around the world to advance the common good.

Area of focus: Education, financial stability, promoting healthy lives

Programming: Changing health policy, connecting volunteers to organizations, working with local partners

Level of engagement: Local (in the United States) and international

Twitter (@live_united): 13,577 followers

US Department of Agriculture Faith and Neighborhood Partnerships

http://www.usda.gov/wps/portal/usda/usdahome?navid=FBCI

Background: USDA resources can be accessed through the USDA Center for Faith-Based and Neighborhood Partnerships, which works with community partners to end hunger, revitalize rural communities, preserve natural resources, and promote fitness. This program works on SNAP participation through faith and community events and organizations.

Area of focus: Hunger, rural communities, natural resources, fitness, nutrition, farmers

Programming: Online resources, housing development programs, connecting volunteers to organizations

Level of engagement: National, local

The Wallace Center

www.wallacecenter.org

Background: The Wallace Center supports entrepreneurs and communities as they build a new, twenty-first-century food system that is healthier for people, the environment, and the economy.

Area of focus: Food quality, access, animal treatment, enterprise

Programming: Connecting food and farm innovators, sharing information, providing financial resources, collaborating as a national food hub

Level of engagement: National

The White House Project: Plate to Politics

thewhitehouseproject.org/platetopolitics

Background: A coalition of the White House Project, Midwest Organic and Sustainable Education Service (MOSES), and the Women, Food, and Agriculture Network (WFAN), the White House Project: Plate to Politics works to advance women's leadership in sustainable agriculture and food systems development. The group also works on childhood nutrition and access, especially in "food deserts."

Area of focus: Advocacy

Programming: Cultivate Summit 2012

Level of engagement: Local and national

Wholesome Wave

http://wholesomewave.org

Background: Wholesome Wave seeks to nourish neighborhoods by supporting increased production and access to healthy, fresh, and affordable locally grown food for the well-being of all.

Area of focus: Local agriculture, communities, and farmers in "food deserts"

Programming: Farm-to-community programs in "food deserts"

Level of engagement: Local, national
Twitter (@wholesomewave): 4,480 followers; Facebook (http://www .Facebook.com/wholesomewave): 3,683 likes

WhyHunger
http://www.whyhunger.org

Background: A key SNAP supporter, WhyHunger is a leader in building the movement to end hunger and poverty by connecting people to nutritious, affordable food and by supporting grassroots solutions that inspire self-reliance and community empowerment.
Area of focus: Hunger, poverty, community food security
Programming: Supporting community-based organizations that deal with hunger, enlisting performing artists to raise funds and awareness.
Level of engagement: Grass roots
Twitter (@whyhunger): 5,510 followers; Facebook (http://www.Face book.com/WhyHungerFans): 3,889 likes

Witnesses to Hunger
http://www.witnessestohunger.org

Background: Founded by Dr. Mariana Chilton, Witnesses to Hunger is a group of mothers seeking to end childhood hunger through photography, advocacy, and dialogue, using forty cameras distributed by the Drexel University School of Public Health to forty mothers in Philadelphia to document hunger.
Area of focus: Hunger, children, nutrition, poverty
Programming: Online videos, photography exhibitions, providing resources for federal programs
Level of engagement: Grass roots

Digital Tools

Ample Harvest

http://www.ampleharvest.org/iPhone.php

Connects gardeners to local food pantries to donate products.

We Feed Back

http://wefeedback.org

Facebook, iPhone, and Windows phone apps for users who can enter their favorite food and calculate how many starving children that would feed. Then users are urged to donate that amount.

GAMES

FreeRice.com

http://freerice.com/about

Vocabulary game website that donates ten grains of rice to the World Food Program for every round played.

FreePoverty.com

Geography game in which every correct answer results in ten cups of water being donated to people in poverty.

FreeFlour.com

Answer a question correctly and one spoon of flour is donated to help world hunger.

BeeLocal.org

http://beelocal.thebeehive.org/about

A public services finder, BeeLocal.org is a project of One Economy. Hunger is a popular search request on the site.

Half in Ten Submit Stories

http://halfinten.org/stories/submit

Half in Ten is collecting stories that highlight the ways in which federal programs successfully build economic security and meet the needs of vulnerable populations.

Hunger Is Unacceptable

http://www.austinfoodbank.org/hunger-is-unacceptable/stuck-in -the-middle.html

Calculates the disparity between the federal poverty line and the cost of living, which leads to problems like hunger and other consequences of poverty.

Jewish Family Service of Los Angeles (JFSLA)

http://www.jfsla.org/page.aspx?pid=323

JFSLA conducts a virtual food drive.

New York Times Food Stamp Interactive Map

http://www.nytimes.com/interactive/2009/11/28/us/20091128-food stamps.html

This map can be searched by demographics and region.

SNAP: Retail Locator

http://snap-load-balancer-244858692.us-east-1.elb.amazonaws.com /index.html

Finds local SNAP retailers.

Stop the Hunger
http://www.stopthehunger.com
> Website with constantly updating domestic and international statistics on hunger problems.

We Feedback Calculator
http://wefeedback.org/calculator
> Enter your favorite food and estimated cost. How many hungry children will it feed? You'll be surprised! Then make it happen—click on "Feed Them Now!"

VIDEOS

Call2Action
http://www.call2action.com/gallery?spark=297&version=1
> Video of Matt Damon and Feeding America food banks

Hunger Prevention—Ana Ortiz
http://www.youtube.com/watch?v=gbVywLq-zAU
> PSA in Spanish

Hunger Prevention—Matt Damon
http://www.youtube.com/watch?v=PIBM8D0ZyMk

Hunger Prevention—Taye Diggs
http://www.youtube.com/watch?v=AOBSnm34gBs&NR=1

The Price of Immigration
http://www.youtube.com/watch?v=2s03JdyD4ds&feature=channel_video_title
> Short film on the experience of hunger for an immigrant

"ONE CLICK TO GIVE" SITES

Care 2
http://www.care2.com/click-to-donate/children/thank-you
Same as The Hunger Site. Click one button and sponsor one child with no personal expense. Can only click once per day.

Click to Give
http://clicktogive.com/Feed-The-Poor/Thank-You.aspx?Return Url=/Feed-The-Poor&time=23062011142641
Gives option to help a number of causes with one click at no cost.

The Hunger Site
http://www.thehungersite.com/clickToGive/home.faces?siteId=1
Clicking one button gives 1.1 cups of food to the hungry at no expense to the participant.

Your Food Environment Atlas Interactive
http://ers.usda.gov/foodatlas/atlas
"Food deserts," food access in individual counties

A Place at the Table: To Learn More—Books, Websites, and
Organizations Offering Further Insights into Hunger in America

Adamik, Kate. *Lunch Money: Serving Healthy School Food in a Sick Economy.* New York: Food
Systems Solutions LLC, 2012.

Alkon, Alison Hope, and Julian Agyeman, eds. *Cultivating Food Justice: Race, Class, and Sustainability.* Cambridge, MA: MIT Press, 2011.

Allen, Will. *The Good Food Revolution: Growing Healthy Food, People, and Communities.* New
York: Gotham Books, 2012.

Allen, Will, Diana Balmori, and Fritz Haeg. *Edible Estates: Attack on the Front Lawns.* New
York: Metropolis Books, 2010.

Astyk, Sharon, and Aaron Newton. *A Nation of Farmers: Defeating the Food Crisis on American Soil.* Gabrioli Island, BC: New Society Publishers, 2009.

Beckmann, David. *Exodus from Hunger: We Are Called to Change the Politics of Hunger.*
Louisville, KY: Westminster/John Knox Press, 2010.

Berg, Joel. *All You Can Eat: How Hungry Is America?* New York: Seven Stories Press, 2008.

Berry, Wendell. *Bringing It to the Table: On Farming and Food.* Berkeley, CA: Counterpoint,
2009.

Cooper, Ann, and Lisa Holmes. *Lunch Lessons: Changing the Way We Feed Our Children.* New
York: William Morrow, 2006.

Egger, Robert. *Begging for Change: The Dollars and Sense of Making Nonprofits Responsive,
Efficient, and Rewarding for All.* New York: Harper Business, 2004.

Gootlieb, Robert, and Anupama Joshi. *Food Justice.* Cambridge, MA: MIT Press, 2011.

Guthman, Julie. *Weighing In: Obesity, Food Justice, and the Limits of Capitalism.* Berkeley:
University of California Press, 2011.

Harrington, Michael. *The Other America: Poverty in the United States.* New York: Touchstone, 1962.

Hesterman, Oran B. *Fair Food: Growing a Healthy, Sustainable Food System for All.* New York:
PublicAffairs, 2011.

Kalafa, Amy. *Lunch Wars: How to Start a School Food Revolution and Win the Battle for Our
Children's Health.* New York: Jeremy P. Tarcher/Penguin, 2011.

Lappé, Anna, and Bryant Terry. *Grub: Ideas for an Urban Organic Kitchen.* New York: Jeremy P. Tarcher/Penguin, 2006.

Levine, Susan. *School Lunch Politics: The Surprising History of America's Favorite Welfare Program.* Princeton, NJ: Princeton University Press, 2008.

McMillan, Tracie. *The American Way of Eating: Undercover at Wal-Mart, Applebee's, Farm
Fields, and the Dinner Table.* New York: Scribner, 2012.

Miles, Sara. *Take This Bread: A Radical Conversion.* New York: Ballantine Books, 2008.

Morgan, Kevin, and Roberta Sonnino. *The School Food Revolution: Public Food and the Challenge of Sustainable Development.* Sterling, VA: Earthscan, 2008.

Nestle, Marion. *Food Politics: How the Food Industry Influences Nutrition.* Berkeley: University of California Press, 2003.

Nestle, Marion, and Malden Nesheim. *Why Calories Count: From Science to Politics.* Berkeley: University of California Press, 2012.

Patel, Raj. *Stuffed and Starved: The Hidden Battle for the World Food System.* Hoboken, NJ: Melville House, 2008.

Pollan, Michael. *Food Rules: An Eater's Manual.* New York: Penguin, 2009.

Poppendieck, Janet. *Sweet Charity: Emergency Food and the End of Entitlement.* New York: Viking, 1998.

———. *Free for All: Fixing School Food in America.* Berkeley: University of California Press, 2010.

Richardson, Jill. *Recipe for America: Why Our Food System Is Broken and What We Can Do to Fix It.* Brooklyn, NY: Ig Publishing, 2009.

Roberts, Paul. *The End of Food.* Boston: Mariner Books, 2009.

Schwartz-Nobel, Loretta. *Growing Up Empty: The Hunger Epidemic in America.* New York: HarperCollins, 2002.

Shore, Bill. *The Cathedral Within: Transforming Your Life by Giving Something Back.* New York: Random House, 2001.

Simon, Michelle. *Appetite for Profit: How the Food Industry Undermines Our Health and How to Fight Back.* New York: Nation Books/Random House, 2006.

Weber, Karl, ed. *Food, Inc.: How Industrial Food Is Making Us Sicker, Fatter, and Poorer—And What You Can Do About It.* New York: PublicAffairs, 2009.

Wilson, Michael. *Hunger: Food Insecurity in America* (In the News). New York: Rosen Publishing Group, 2010.

Winne, Mark. *Food Rebels, Guerrilla Gardeners, and Smart-Cookin' Mamas: Fighting Back in an Age of Industrial Agriculture.* Boston: Beacon Press, 2010.

US HOUSEHOLD FOOD SECURITY SURVEY MODULE:
THREE-STAGE DESIGN, WITH SCREENERS
Economic Research Service, USDA
July 2008

<u>Transition into Module</u> (administered to all households):
These next questions are about the food eaten in your household in the last twelve months, since (current month) of last year, and whether you were able to afford the food you need.

<u>Optional USDA Food Sufficiency Question/Screener: Question HH1</u> [HH = Household] (This question is optional. It is not used to calculate any of the food security scales. It may be used in conjunction with income as a preliminary screener to reduce respondent burden for high-income households.)

HH1. [IF ONE PERSON IN HOUSEHOLD, USE "I" IN PARENTHETI-CALS, OTHERWISE, USE "WE."]

Which of these statements best describes the food eaten in your household in the last 12 months: —enough of the kinds of food (I/we) want to eat; — enough, but not always the <u>kinds</u> of food (I/we) want; — sometimes <u>not enough</u> to eat; or, —<u>often</u> not enough to eat?

[1] Enough of the kinds of food we want to eat
[2] Enough but not always the kinds of food we want
[3] Sometimes not enough to eat
[4] Often not enough to eat
[ ] DK or Refused

<u>Household Stage 1: Questions HH2-HH4</u> (asked of all households; begin scale items).

[IF SINGLE ADULT IN HOUSEHOLD, USE "I," "MY," AND "YOU" IN PARENTHETICALS; OTHERWISE, USE "WE," "OUR," AND "YOUR HOUSEHOLD."]

HH2. Now I'm going to read you several statements that people have made about their food situation. For these statements, please tell me whether the statement was <u>often</u> true, <u>sometimes</u> true, or <u>never</u> true for (you/your household) in the last 12 months—that is, since last (name of current month).

The first statement is "(I/We) worried whether (my/our) food would run out before (I/we) got money to buy more." Was that <u>often</u> true, <u>sometimes</u> true, or <u>never</u> true for (you/your household) in the last 12 months?

[ ] Often true
[ ] Sometimes true
[ ] Never true
[ ] DK or Refused

HH3. "The food that (I/we) bought just didn't last, and (I/we) didn't have money to get more." Was that <u>often</u>, <u>sometimes</u>, or <u>never</u> true for (you/your household) in the last 12 months?

[ ] Often true
[ ] Sometimes true
[ ] Never true
[ ] DK or Refused

HH4. "(I/we) couldn't afford to eat balanced meals." Was that <u>often</u>, <u>sometimes</u>, or <u>never</u> true for (you/your household) in the last 12 months?

[ ] Often true
[ ] Sometimes true
[ ] Never true
[ ] DK or Refused

Screener for Stage 2 Adult-Referenced Questions: If affirmative response (i.e., "often true" or "sometimes true") to one or more of Questions HH2-HH4, OR, response [3] or [4] to question HH1 (if administered), then continue to *Adult Stage 2;* otherwise, if children under age 18 are present in the household, skip to *Child Stage 1,* otherwise skip to *End of Food Security Module.*

NOTE: In a sample similar to that of the general U.S. population, about 20 percent of households (45 percent of households with incomes less than 185 percent of poverty line) will pass this screen and continue to Adult Stage 2.

Adult Stage 2: Questions AD1-AD4 (asked of households passing the screener for Stage 2 adult-referenced questions).

AD1. In the last 12 months, since last (name of current month), did (you/you or other adults in your household) ever cut the size of your meals or skip meals because there wasn't enough money for food?

[ ] Yes
[ ] No (Skip AD1a)
[ ] DK (Skip AD1a)

AD1a. [IF YES ABOVE, ASK] How often did this happen—almost every month, some months but not every month, or in only 1 or 2 months?

[ ] Almost every month
[ ] Some months but not every month
[ ] Only 1 or 2 months
[ ] DK

AD2. In the last 12 months, did you ever eat less than you felt you should because there wasn't enough money for food?

[ ] Yes
[ ] No
[ ] DK

AD3. In the last 12 months, were you every hungry but didn't eat because there wasn't enough money for food?

[ ] Yes
[ ] No
[ ] DK

AD4. In the last 12 months, did you lose weight because there wasn't enough money for food?
[ ] Yes
[ ] No
[ ] DK

Screener for Stage 3 Adult-Referenced Questions: If affirmative response to one or more of questions AD1 through AD4, then continue to *Adult Stage 3;* otherwise, if children under age 18 are present in the household, skip to *Child Stage 1,* otherwise skip to *End of Food Security Module.*

NOTE: In a sample similar to that of the general U.S. population, about 8 percent of households (20 percent of households with incomes less than 185 percent of poverty line) will pass this screen and continue to Adult Stage 3.

Adult Stage 3: Questions AD5-AD5a (asked of households passing screener for Stage 3 adult-referenced questions).

AD5.   In the last 12 months, did (you/you or other adults in your household) ever not eat for a whole day because there wasn't enough money for food?

      [ ] Yes
      [ ] No (Skip 12a)
      [ ] DK (Skip 12a)

AD5a. [IF YES ABOVE, ASK] How often did this happen—almost every month, some months but not every month, or in only 1 or 2 months?

      [ ] Almost every month
      [ ] Some months but not every month
      [ ] Only 1 or 2 months
      [ ] DK

Child Stage 1: Questions CH1-CH3 (Transitions and questions CH1 and CH2 are administered to all households with children under age 18) Households with no child under age 18, skip to *End of Food Security Module.*

SELECT APPROPRIATE FILLS DEPENDING ON NUMBER OF ADULTS AND NUMBER OF CHILDREN IN THE HOUSEHOLD.

Transition into Child-Referenced Questions:
Now I'm going to read you several statements that people have made about the food situation of their children. For these statements, please tell me whether the statement was OFTEN true, SOMETIMES true, or NEVER true in the last 12 months for (your child/children living in the household who are under 18 years old).

CH1.   "(I/we) relied on only a few kinds of low-cost food to feed (my/our) child/the children) because (I was/we were) running out of money to buy food." Was that <u>often</u>, <u>sometimes</u>, or <u>never</u> true for (you/your household) in the last 12 months?

      [ ] Often true
      [ ] Sometimes true
      [ ] Never true
      [ ] DK or Refused

CH2.   "(I/We) couldn't feed (my/our) child/the children) a balanced meal, because (I/we) couldn't afford that." Was that <u>often</u>, <u>sometimes</u>, or <u>never</u> true for (you/your household) in the last 12 months?

[ ] Often true
[ ] Sometimes true
[ ] Never true
[ ] DK or Refused

CH3. "(My/Our child was/The children were) not eating enough because (I/we) just couldn't afford enough food." Was that <u>often</u>, <u>sometimes</u>, or <u>never</u> true for (you/your household) in the last 12 months?

[ ] Often true
[ ] Sometimes true
[ ] Never true
[ ] DK or Refused

<u>Screener for Stage 2 Child Referenced Questions:</u> If affirmative response (i.e., "often true" or "sometimes true") to one or more of questions CH1-CH3, then continue to *Child Stage 2;* otherwise skip to *End of Food Security Module.*

<u>NOTE:</u> In a sample similar to that of the general U.S. population, about 16 percent of households with children (35 percent of households with children with incomes less than 185 percent of poverty line) will pass this screen and continue to Child Stage 2.

<u>Child Stage 2: Questions CH4-CH7</u> (asked of households passing the screener for stage 2 child-referenced questions).

<u>NOTE:</u> In Current Population Survey Food Security Supplements, question CH6 precedes question CH5.

CH4. In the last 12 months, since (current month) of last year, did you ever cut the size of (your child's/any of the children's) meals because there wasn't enough money for food?

[ ] Yes
[ ] No
[ ] DK

CH5. In the last 12 months, did (CHILD'S NAME/any of the children) ever skip meals because there wasn't enough money for food?

[ ] Yes
[ ] No (Skip CH5a)
[ ] DK (Skip CH5a)

CH5a. [IF YES ABOVE ASK] How often did this happen—almost every month, some months but not every month, or in only 1 or 2 months?

[ ] Almost every month
[ ] Some months but not every month
[ ] Only 1 or 2 months
[ ] DK

CH6. In the last 12 months, (was your child/were the children) ever hungry but you just couldn't afford more food?

[ ] Yes
[ ] No
[ ] DK

CH7. In the last 12 months, did (your child/any of the children) ever not eat for a whole day because there wasn't enough money for food?

[ ] Yes
[ ] No
[ ] DK

END OF FOOD SECURITY MODULE
User Notes

(1) Coding Responses and Assessing Household Food Security Status:
Following is a brief overview of how to code responses and assess household food security status based on various standard scales. For detailed information on these procedures, refer to the *Guide to Measuring Household Food Security, Revised 2000*, and *Measuring Children's Food Security in U.S. Households, 1995–1999*. Both publications are available through the ERS Food Security in the United States Briefing Room.

Responses of "yes," "often," "sometimes," "almost every month," and "some months but not every month" are coded as affirmative. The sum of affirmative responses to a specified set of items is referred to as the household's raw score on the scale comprising those items.

• Questions HH2 through CH7 comprise the U.S. Household Food Security Scale (questions HH2 through AD5a for households with no child present). Specification of food security status depends on raw score and whether there are children in the household (i.e., whether responses to child-referenced questions are included in the raw score).
  o For households with one or more children:
    ▪ Raw score zero—High food security
    ▪ Raw score 1–2—Marginal food security
    ▪ Raw score 3–7—Low food security
    ▪ Raw score 8–18—Very low food security

- o For households with no child present:
  - Raw score zero—High food security
  - Raw score 1–2—Marginal food security
  - Raw score 3–5—Low food security
  - Raw score 6–10—Very low food security

Households with high or marginal food security are classified as food se-cure. Those with low or very low food security are classified as food inse-cure.

- Questions HH2 through AD5a comprise the U.S. Adult Food Security Scale.
  - Raw score zero—High food security among adults
  - Raw score 1–2—Marginal food security among adults
  - Raw score 3–5—Low food security among adults
  - Raw score 6–10—Very low food security among adults

- Questions HH3 through AD3 comprise the six-item Short Module from which the Six-Item Food Security Scale can be calculated.
  - Raw score 0–1—High or marginal food security (raw score 1 may be considered marginal food security, but a large proportion of households that would be measured as having marginal food security using the household or adult scale will have raw score zero on the six-item scale)
  - Raw score 2–4—Low food security
  - Raw score 5–6—Very low food security

- Questions CH1 through CH7 comprise the U.S. Children's Food Security Scale.
  - Raw score 0–1—High or marginal food security among children (raw score 1 may be considered marginal food security, but it is not certain that all households with raw score zero have high food security among children because the scale does not include an assessment of the anxiety component of food insecurity)
  - Raw score 2–4—Low food security among children
  - Raw score 5–8—Very low food security among children

(2) **Response Options:** For interviewer-administered surveys, DK ("don't know") and "Refused" are blind responses—that is, they are not presented as response op-tions, but marked if volunteered. For self-administered surveys, "don't know" is pre-sented as a response option.

(3) **Screening:** The two levels of screening for adult-referenced questions and one level for child-referenced questions are provided for surveys in which it is considered important to reduce respondent burden. In pilot surveys intended to validate the module in a new cultural, linguistic, or survey context, screening should be avoided if possible and all questions should be administered to all respondents.

To further reduce burden for higher income respondents, a preliminary screener may be constructed using question HH1 along with a household income measure. Households with income above twice the poverty threshold, AND who respond <1> to question HH1 may be skipped to the end of the module and classified as food secure. Use of this preliminary screener reduces total burden in a survey with many higher-income households, and the cost, in terms of accuracy in identifying food-insecure households, is not great. However, research has shown that a small proportion of the higher income households screened out by this procedure will register food insecurity if administered the full module. If question HH1 is not needed for research purposes, a preferred strategy is to omit HH1 and administer Adult Stage 1 of the module to all households and Child Stage 1 of the module to all households with children.

(4) 30-Day Reference Period: The questionnaire items may be modified to a 30-day reference period by changing the "last 12-month" references to "last 30 days." In this case, items AD1a, AD5a, and CH5a must be changed to read as follows:

AD1a/AD5a/CH5a   [IF YES ABOVE, ASK] In the last 30 days, how many days did this happen?

      _____ days

      [ ] DK

Preface

The following books and articles are useful in explaining and discussing the ongoing debate about the definition of hunger:

Michael Harrington, *The Other America: Poverty in the United States* (New York: Simon & Schuster, 1962); Janet Poppendieck, *Sweet Charity: Emergency Food and the End of Entitlement* (New York: Viking Penguin, 1998); Joel Berg, *All You Can Eat: How Hungry Is America?* (New York: Seven Stories Press, 2008); Mark Nord, Alisha Coleman-Jensen, Margaret Andrews, and Steven Carlson, "Household Food Security in the United States, 2009," Economic Research Service Report 108, US Department of Agriculture, November 2010, 1–44; David Holben, "The Concept and Definition of Hunger and Its Relationship to Food Insecurity," Ohio University, School of Human and Consumer Sciences, 2010, 1–29.

1. Michael Harrington, *The Other America: Poverty in the United States* (New York: Touchstone, 1962), p. 179.
2. President's Task Force on Food Assistance, *Report of the President's Task Force on Food Assistance* (Washington, DC: US Government Printing Office, 1984), p. 34.
3. S. A. Anderson, "The 1990 Life Sciences Research Office (LSRO) Report on Nutritional Assessment Defined Terms Associated with Food Access: Core Indicators of Nutritional State for Difficult to Sample Populations," *Journal of Nutrition* 102 (1990): 1559–1660.
4. See USDA, *Information Bulletin* 93 (March 2012); USDA, "Household Food Security in the United States in 2010"; and Food Research and Action Center (FRAC), "Hunger Data," available at: http://frac.org/reports-and-resources/hunger-data.

Chapter 1   Witnesses to Hunger

1. Gary Bickel, Mark Nord, Cristofer Price, William Hamilton, and John Cook, *Measuring Food Security in the United States: Guide to Measuring Household Food Security* (Alexandria, VA: US Department of Agriculture, Food and Nutrition Service, Office of Analysis and Evaluation, 2000).
2. John T. Cook and Deborah A. Frank, "Food Security, Poverty, and Human Development in the United States," *Annals of the New York Academy of Sciences* 1136 (2008): 193–209.
3. James J. Heckman, "Skill Formation and the Economics of Investing in Disadvantaged Children," *Science* 312, no. 5782 (2006): 1900–1902.

4. Mark Nord, Margaret Andrews, and Steven Carlson, *Food Insecurity in the United States, 2006* (Washington, DC: US Department of Agriculture, Economic Research Service, 2007).

5. Alisha Coleman-Jensen, Mark Nord, Margaret Andrews, and Steven Carlson, *Statistical Supplement to Household Food Security in the United States in 2010* (Washington, DC: US Department of Agriculture, Economic Research Service, September 2011).

6. Deborah A. Frank, Patrick H. Casey, Maureen M. Black, Ruth Rose-Jacobs, Mariana Chilton, Diana Cutts, et al. "Cumulative Hardship and Wellness of Low-Income, Young Children: Multi-Site Surveillance Study," *Pediatrics* 125, no. 5 (2010): e1115–e1123.

Chapter 3   The Grocery Gap: Finding Healthy Food in America

1. See www.peoplesgrocery.org.

2. John Hanc, "A Mobile Oasis in a 'Food Desert,'" *New York Times*, November 1, 2011, available at: http://www.nytimes.com/2011/11/02/giving/a-mobile-food-pantry-in-a -food-desert.html? pagewanted=all.

3. Sylvia Maria Gross, "'Food Deserts' Spread in Rural America," American Public Media, *Marketplace Life*, November 23, 2011, available at: www.marketplace.org/topics/life /food-deserts-spread-rural-america.

4. The USDA's Economic Research Service defined "low access" as more than one mile from a supermarket or large grocery store in urban areas and as more than ten miles from a supermarket or large grocery store in rural areas. See http://www.ers.usda .gov/Data/FoodDesert/documentation.html.

5. Centers for Disease Control and Prevention (CDC), "Number of Americans with Diabetes Projected to Double or Triple by 2050," October 22, 2010, available at: http:// www.cdc.gov/media/pressrel/2010/r101022.html.

6. Christina Bethell et al., "National, State, and Local Disparities in Childhood Obesity," *Health Affairs* 29, no. 3 (March 2010): 347–356; National Council of La Raza, *Key Facts About Childhood Obesity in the Latino Community: A Fact Sheet* (Washington, DC: National Council of La Raza, 2006).

7. Joe Potente, "Remembering the Days of Neighborhood Groceries," *Kenosha News*, December 31, 2011.

8. Ibid.

9. Joe Kane, "The Supermarket Shuffle," *Mother Jones*, July 1984.

10. Pia Sarkar, "Scrambling for Customers: The Supermarket Was Born 75 Years Ago; One-Stop Shopping Has Come a Long Way," *San Francisco Chronicle*, August 4, 2005, available at: http://www.sfgate.com/cgi-bin/article.cgi?f=/c/a/2005/08/04/BUG7PE2 DKH1.DTL&ao=all#ixzz1qF0mpClY.

11. Food Marketing Institute, "75 Facts for 75 Years," available at: http://www.fmi.org /research-resources/fmi-research-resources/supermarket-anniversary-facts.

12. Food Marketing Institute, "Key Facts: Median Total Store Size—Square Feet," available at: http://www.fmi.org/research-resources/supermarket-facts/median-total-store-size -square-feet.

13. PolicyLink, Oakland, CA, "Healthy Food, Healthy Communities: Promising Strategies to Improve Access to Fresh, Healthy Food and Transform Communities," 2011, available at: www.policylink.org/publications/healthyfoodhealthycommunities.

14. Latetia Moore and Ana V. Diez Roux, "Associations of Neighborhood Characteristics with the Location and Type of Food Stores," *American Journal of Public Health* 96 (2006): 325–331.

15. New Mexico Food and Agriculture Policy Council, Santa Fe, NM, "Closing New Mexico's Rural Food Gap," 2006, available at: http://www.farmtotablenm.org/closing_nm _food_gap_4pgs.pdf.
16. Manuel Franco, Ana V. Diez Roux, Thomas Glass, Benjamín Caballero, and Frederick L. Brancati, "Neighborhood Characteristics and Availability of Healthy Foods in Baltimore," *American Journal of Preventive Medicine* 35, no. 6 (2008): 561–567.
17. Sarah Treuhaft, Michael Hamm, and Charlotte Litjens, *Healthy Food for All: Building Equitable and Sustainable Food Systems in Detroit and Oakland* (Oakland, CA: Policy Link, 2009).
18. Alameda County Department of Public Health, "Life and Death from Unnatural Causes in Alameda County, 2008."
19. Carol Horowitz, Kathryn Colson, Paul Hebert, and Kristie Lancaster, "Barriers to Buying Healthy Foods for People with Diabetes: Evidence of Environmental Disparities," *American Journal of Public Health* 94 (2004): 1549–1554.
20. Latetia V. Moore, Ana V. Diez Roux, Jennifer Nettleton, and David Jacobs, "Associations of the Local Food Environment with Diet Quality—A Comparison of Assessments Based on Surveys and Geographic Information Systems: The Multi-Ethnic Study of Atherosclerosis," *American Journal of Epidemiology* 167 (2008): 917–924. A healthy diet was defined using two different measures: the Alternate Healthy Eating Index, which measures consumption of foods related to low risk of chronic disease, and a measure looking at consumption of fats and processed meats.
21. The researchers controlled for age, sex, race, and education. See Troy Blanchard and Thomas Lyson, "Food Availability and Food Deserts in the Nonmetropolitan South," Southern Rural Development Center, April 2006, available at: http://srdc.msstate .edu/publications/other/foodassist/2006_04_blanchard.pdf.
22. Kimberly Morland, Steve Wing, and Ana V. Diez Roux, "The Contextual Effect of the Local Food Environment on Residents' Diets: The Atherosclerosis Risk in Communities Study," *American Journal of Public Health* 92, no. 11 (2002): 1761–1767.
23. J. Nicholas Bodor, Donald Rose, Thomas A. Farley, Christopher Swalm, and Susanne K. Scott, "Neighborhood Fruit and Vegetable Availability and Consumption: The Role of Small Food Stores in an Urban Environment," *Public Health Nutrition* 11 (2008): 413–420.
24. Kimberly Morland, Ana V. Diex Roux, and Steve Wing, "Supermarkets, Other Food Stores, and Obesity: The Atherosclerosis Risk in Communities Study," *American Journal of Preventive Medicine* 30, no. 4 (2006): 333–339.
25. Susan H. Babey, Allison L. Diamant, Theresa A. Hastert, Stefan Harvey, Harold Goldstein, Rebecca Flournoy, Rajni Banthia, Victor Rubin, and Sarah Treuhaft, "Designed for Disease: The Link Between Local Food Environments and Obesity and Diabetes," UCLA Center for Health Policy Research, California Center for Public Health Advocacy, and PolicyLink, April 2008, available at: http://www.policylink.org/documents /DesignedforDisease.pdf; Andrew Rundle, Kathryn Neckerman, Lance Freeman, Gina Lovasi, Marnie Purciel, James Quinn, Catherine Richards, Neelanjan Sircar, and Christopher Weiss, "Neighborhood Food Environment and Walkability Predict Obesity in New York City," *Environmental Health Perspectives* 117 (2009): 442–447.
26. Kristina Sepetys, "Slow Money: The Movement for Sustainable Financing Options for Food and Farming Enterprises in the East Bay," Edible East Bay, spring 2011, available at: http://www.ediblecommunities.com/eastbay/spring-2011/slow-money.htm.
27. Food Marketing Institute, "Supermarket Facts: Industry Overview 2010," available at: http://www.fmi.org/facts_figs/?fuseaction=superfact.

28. Ira Goldstein, Lance Loethen, Edward Kako, and Cathy Califano, "CDFI Financing of Supermarkets in Underserved Communities: A Case Study," Reinvestment Fund, 2008, available at: http://www.trfund.com/resource/downloads/policypubs/CDFIStudy Summary.pdf.

29. Note that the USDA no longer refers to its healthy food access program as the Healthy Food Financing Initiative, but the program mission and design remain the same.

Chapter 6   Food Stamps: Once We Had It Right

1. This article was first published in the *Maine Policy Review* (Winter-Spring 2011). It is reprinted with some minor modifications here with the kind permission of the *Review*'s editor, Ann Acheson, of the Margaret Smith Chase Policy Center.

2. Milo Perkins, "The Food Stamp Plan and the Farmer," statement before the Farm Bureau Fruit and Vegetable Committee, Chicago, 1939, 4.

3. Ibid., 9, 10.

4. Eleanor Roosevelt, "My Day," May 24, 1941, available at: http://www.gwu.edu/~erpapers/myday/displaydoc.cfm?_y=1941&_f=md055895.

5. Janet Poppendieck, *Breadlines Knee-Deep in Wheat: Food Assistance in the Great Depression* (Brunswick, NJ: Rutgers University Press, 1986), 241.

6. American Presidency Project, "John F. Kennedy, Executive Order 10914, January 21, 1961," available at: www.presidency.ucsb.edu/ws/index.php?pid=58853.

7. Funds generated from Section 32 in the USDA's budget are derived from tariffs placed on imported food to the United States.

8. USDA, Agricultural Marketing Service (USDA AMS), *The Food Stamp Program: An Initial Evaluation of the Pilot Projects* (Washington, DC: USDA AMS, 1962).

9. Ibid.

10. USDA, Food and Nutrition Service, "The Food Stamp Act of 1964," available at: http://www/fns.usda.gov/snap/rules/Legislation/pdfs/PL_88–525.pdf.

11. USDA, Food and Nutrition Service, "A Short History of Snap," available at: www.fns.usda.gov/snap/rules/Leglislation/about.htm.

12. George McGovern, *The Third Freedom: Ending Hunger in Our Time* (Lanham, MD: Rowman & Littlefield, 2002), 70.

13. Robert Shrum, *No Excuses: Concessions of a Serial Campaigner* (New York: Simon & Schuster, 2007), 61.

14. Ibid., 62.

15. Kenneth W. Clarkson, *Food Stamps and Nutrition* (Washington, DC: American Enterprise Institute for Public Policy Research, 1975), 65.

16. Ibid., 3.

17. Ibid.

18. USDA, Center for Nutrition Policy and Promotion, "Dietary Guidelines for Americans, 2010," available at: www.cnpp.usda.gov/DietaryGuidelines.htm.

19. Victor Oliveira, Elizabeth Racine, Jennifer Olmstead, and Linda M. Ghelfi, "History of the WIC Program," in *The WIC Program: Background, Trends, and Issues,* Food Assistance and Nutrition Research Report (FANRR) 27, USDA, Economic Research Service, 2002, available at: http://www.ers.usda.gov/publications/fanrr27/fanrr27c.pdf (accessed May 26, 2011), 7.

20. Ibid., 8.

21. USDA, "WIC Farmers' Market Nutrition Program," available at: www.fns.usda.gov /wic/WIC-FMNP-Fact-Sheet.pdf.
22. USDA, "Senior Farmers' Market Nutrition Program," available at: www.fns.usda.gov /wic/SFMNP-Fact-Sheet.pdf.
23. Kenneth Hanson and Elise Golan, 2002. "Effects of Changes in Food Stamp Expenditures Across the US Economy," Food Assistance and Nutrition Research Report (FANRR) 26–6, in *Issues in Food Assistance*, USDA, Economic Research Service, October 2002, available at: http://www.ers.usda.gov/publications/fanrr26/fanrr26–6/fanrr26 –6.pdf (accessed May 26, 2011).
24. Mark Zandi, "Assessing the Macro Economic Impact of the Fiscal Stimulus 2008," Moody's Economy.com, West Chester, PA, 2008, available at: http://www.economy .com/mark-zandi/documents/assissing-the-impact-of-the-fiscal-stimulus.pdf (accessed May 26, 2011), 4.
25. Karen E. Cunnyngham and Laura A. Castner, "Reaching Those in Need: State Supplemental Nutrition Assistance Program Participation Rates in 2008," produced for the USDA Food and Nutrition Service by Mathematica Policy Research, Princeton, NJ, December 2010, available at: http://www.fns.usda.gov/ora/menu/Published/snap /FILES/Participation/Reaching2008.pdf (accessed May 26, 2011), 2.
26. David Swenson, "Selected Measures of the Economic Values of Increased Fruit and Vegetable Production and Consumption in the Upper Midwest," Iowa State University, Leopold Center for Sustainable Agriculture, Ames, IA, March 2010, available at: http://www.econ.iastate.edu/research/other/p11285 (accessed May 26, 2011).

Chapter 7   Today's "Eat More" Environment:
The Role of the Food Industry

1. This chapter is © 2012 by Marion Nestle and Malden Nesheim. Reprinted by permission of the University of California Press.
2. Steven N. Blair and Elizabeth A. Leermakers, "Exercise and Weight Management," in *Handbook of Obesity Treatment*, edited by Thomas A. Wadden and Albert J. Stunkard (New York: Guilford Press, 2004), 283–300; Timothy S. Church et al., "Trends over Five Decades in US Occupation-Related Physical Activity and Their Associations with Obesity," *PLoS One* 6, no. 5 (2011): e19657.
3. K. R. Westerterp and J. R. Speakman, "Physical Activity Energy Expenditure Has Not Declined Since the 1980s and Matches Energy Expenditures of Wild Animals," *International Journal of Obesity* 32 (2008): 1256–1263; CDC, "Physical Activity Trends—United States, 1990–1998," *Morbidity and Mortality Weekly Report* 50 (2001): 166–169.
4. CDC, "Prevalence of Regular Physical Activity Among Adults—United States, 2001 and 2005," *Morbidity and Mortality Weekly Report* 5 (2007): 1209–1212; Jean Adams, "Trends in Physical Activity and Inactivity Amongst US Fourteen- to Eighteen-Year-Olds by Gender, School Grade, and Race, 1993–2003: Evidence from the Youth Risk Behavior Survey," *BMC Public Health* 6 (2006): 57, available at: www.biomedcentral .com/1471–2458/6/57; Sue Y. S. Kimm et al., "Decline in Physical Activity in Black Girls and White Girls During Adolescence," *New England Journal of Medicine* 347 (2002): 709–715; Jim Dollman, K. Norton, and Lynda Norton, "Evidence for Secular Trends in Children's Physical Activity Behavior," *British Journal of Sports Medicine* 39 (2005): 892–897.

5. P. A. Tataranni et al., "Body Weight Gain in Free-Living Pima Indians: Effect of Energy Intake vs. Expenditure," *International Journal of Obesity* 27 (2003): 1578–1583.
6. Ashima K. Kant and Barry I. Graubard, "Secular Trends in Patterns of Self-Reported Food Consumption of American Adults: NHANES 1971–1975 to NHANES 1999–2002," *American Journal of Clinical Nutrition* 84 (2006): 1215–1223.
7. Boyd A. Swinburn, Gary Sacks, and Eric Ravussin, "Increased Food Energy Supply Is More Than Sufficient to Explain the US Epidemic of Obesity," *American Journal of Clinical Nutrition* 90 (2009): 1453–1456.
8. Percentages are calculated using Atwater Values from figures in the USDA Food Availability (Per Capita) Data System, available at: www.ers.usda.gov/data/foodconsumption. These data show no change in the availability of sugars as a percentage of calories from 1980 to 2000. The data sets do not distinguish whole from refined grains, but daily fiber availability increased by five grams per day during that period, perhaps indicating some increase in the availability of whole grains.
9. USDA, Center for Nutrition Policy and Promotion, "Dietary Guidelines for Americans, 2010," available at: www.cnpp.usda.gov/DietaryGuidelines.htm. The NHANES data are analyzed in National Cancer Institute, "Food Sources of Energy Among US Population, 2005–2006," May 21, 2010, available at: http://riskfactor.cancer.gov /diet/foodsources.
10. Cynthia L. Ogden et al., "Consumption of Sugar Drinks in the United States, 2005–2008," NCHS Data Brief 71, August 2011, available at: www.cdc.gov/nchs/data /databriefs/db71.htm.
11. Peter Rupert and Cara Stepanczuk, "Economic Trends: Women in the Workforce," Federal Reserve Bank of Cleveland, March 15, 2007, available at: www.clevelandfed .org/research/trends/2007/0407/03ecoact_031407.cfm.
12. Harold F. Breimyer, *Over-Fulfilled Expectations: A Life in Rural America* (Ames: Iowa State University Press, 1991); USDA, Economic Research Service, "Data Sets: Loss-Adjusted Food Availability: Spreadsheets," updated March 17, 2010, available at: www.ers.usda.gov/data/ foodconsumption/FoodGuideSpreadsheets.htm.
13. Betsy Morris, "The New Rules," *Fortune,* July 24, 2006. Welch's speech was titled "Growing Fast in a Slow-Growth Economy." The shareholder value movement is usually traced to the work of Alfred Rappaport, editor of *Information for Decision Making: Quantitative and Behavioral Dimensions* (Englewood Cliffs, NJ: Prentice-Hall, 1975). The book contains Rappaport's chapter on discounted cash flow, the point of which is to maximize the immediate value of investment projects "subject to the constraint that the earnings of the company must grow at a stipulated rate." See also Boyd A. Swinburn et al., "The Global Obesity Pandemic: Shaped by Global Drivers and Local Environments," *The Lancet* 378 (2011): 804–814.
14. Marion Nestle, *Food Politics: How the Food Industry Influences Nutrition and Health*, rev. ed. (Berkeley: University of California Press, 2007); Marion Nestle et al., "Behavioral and Social Influences on Food Choice," *Nutrition Reviews* 56, no. 5 (1998): s50–s74.
15. R. Rosenheck, "Fast Food Consumption and Increased Caloric Intake: A Systematic Review of a Trajectory Towards Weight Gain and Obesity Risk," *Obesity Reviews* 9 (2008): 535–537; Jennifer M. Potti and Barry M. Popkin, "Trends in Energy Intake Among US Children by Eating Location and Food Source," *Journal of the American Dietetic Association* 111 (2011): 1156–1164; Jessica E. Todd, Lisa Mancino, and Biing-Hwan Lin, "The Impact of Food Away from Home on Diet Quality," USDA Economic Research Report 90, February 2010.

16. USDA, Economic Research Service, "Food Marketing System in the US: New Product Introductions," May 21, 2010, available at: www.ers.usda.gov/Briefing/FoodMarketing System/new_product.htm; Jill Reedy and Susan M. Krebs-Smith, "Dietary Sources of Energy, Solid Fats, and Added Sugars Among Children and Adolescents in the United States," *Journal of the American Dietetic Association* 110 (2010): 1477–1484.

17. Lisa R. Young and Marion Nestle, "The Contribution of Increasing Portion Sizes to the Obesity Epidemic," *American Journal of Public Health* 92 (2002): 246–249; Lisa R. Young and Marion Nestle, "Portion Sizes and Obesity: Responses of the Fast-Food Companies," *Journal of Public Health Policy* 28 (2007): 238–248; Barbara J. Rolls, Erin L. Morris, and Liane S. Roe, "Portion Size of Food Affects Energy Intake in Normal-Weight and Overweight Men and Women," *American Journal of Clinical Nutrition* 76 (2002): 1207–1213; Brian Wansink and Koert van Ittersum, "Portion Size Me: Down-sizing Our Consumption Norms," *Journal of the American Dietetic Association* 107 (2007): 1103–1106; Nicole Diliberti et al., "Increased Portion Size Leads to Increased Energy Intake in a Restaurant Meal," *Obesity Research* 12 (2004): 562–568.

18. Thomas A. Farley et al., "The Ubiquity of Energy-Dense Snack Foods: A National Multi-City Study," *American Journal of Public Health* 100 (2010): 306–311.

19. Carmen Piernas and Barry M. Popkin, "Trends in Snacking Among US Children," *Health Affairs* 29, no. 3 (2010): 398–404; Kiyah J. Duffey and Barry M. Popkin, "Energy Density, Portion Size, and Eating Occasions: Contributions to Increased Energy Intake in the United States, 1977–2006," *PLoS Medicine* 8, no. 6 (June 28, 2011): e1001050.

20. Brennan Davis and Christopher Carpenter, "Proximity of Fast-Food Restaurants to Schools and Adolescent Obesity," *American Journal of Public Health* 99 (2009): 505–510; James E. Painter, Brian Wansink, and Julie B. Hieggelke, "How Visibility and Convenience Influence Candy Consumption," *Appetite* 38, no. 3 (2002): 237–238; Center for Science in the Public Interest, "Dispensing Junk: How School Vending Undermines Efforts to Feed Children Well," May 2004, available at: http://www.cspinet.org /new/pdf/dispensing_junk.pdf.

21. Pablo Monsivais, Anju Aggarwal, and Adam Drewnowski, "Following Federal Guide-lines to Increase Nutrient Consumption May Lead to Higher Food Costs for Consumers," *Health Affairs* 30, no. 8 (2011): 1–7; David Leonhardt, "Sodas a Tempting Tax Target," *New York Times*, May 19, 2009, available at: www.nytimes.com/2009/05/20 /business/economy/20leonhardt.html; David Leonhardt, "What's Wrong with This Chart?" *New York Times*, May 20, 2009, available at: http://economix.blogs.nytimes .com/2009/05/20/whats-wrong-with-this-chart; but see Fred Kuchler and Hayden Stewart, "Price Trends Are Similar for Fruit, Vegetables, and Snack Foods," USDA, Economic Research Service, Economic Research Report 55, March 2008, available at: www.ers.usda.gov/publications/err55/err55.pdf. These USDA economists argue that Consumer Price Index data overstate the rise in the indexed price of fruits and vegetables. Tatiana Andreyeva, Michael W. Long, and Kelly D. Brownell, "The Impact of Food Prices on Consumption: A Systematic Review of Research on the Price Elasticity of Demand for Food," *American Journal of Public Health* 100 (2010): 216–222.

22. AdAgeDataCenter, "100 Leading National Advertisers," *Advertising Age*, June 20, 2010; Brian Wansink and Pierre Chandon, "Can 'Low-Fat' Nutrition Labels Lead to Obesity?" *Journal of Marketing Research* 43 (2006): 605–617; Brian Wansink, *Mindless Eating: Why We Eat More Than We Think* (New York: Bantam, 2006), 1.

23. David A. Kessler, *The End of Overeating* (Emmaus, PA: Rodale, 2009).

Chapter 8   The New Hidden Persuaders: The Digital World of Food Marketing to Children and Teens

1. This research was funded by grants from the Robert Wood Johnson Foundation and the Rudd Foundation. Special thanks go to all my colleagues at the Rudd Center for Food Policy and Obesity and the Berkeley Media Studies Group, who conducted much of this research, especially Andrew Cheyne, Cathryn Dembek, Lori Dorfman, Johanna Richardson, Sarah Speers, and Amy Ustjanauskas.
2. See Better Business Bureau, "Children's Food and Beverage Advertising Initiative," at: http://www.bbb.org/us/childrens-food-and-beverage-advertising-initiative; and Advertising Self-Regulatory Council (ASRC), Children's Advertising Review Unit (CARU), at: http://www.caru.org.
3. Victoria J. Rideout, Ulla G. Foehr, and Donald F. Roberts, *Generation M2: Media in the Lives of Eight- to Eighteen-Year-Olds,* Kaiser Family Foundation, January 2010, available at: http://www.kff.org/entmedia/upload/8010.pdf.
4. Federal Trade Commission (FTC), "Marketing Food to Children and Adolescents: A Review of Industry Expenditures, Activities, and Self-Regulation," a report to Congress, July 2008, available at: http://ftc.gov/os/2008/07/P064504foodmktingreport.pdf.
5. Rideout, Foehr, and Roberts, *Generation M2,* available at: http://www.kff.org/entmedia/upload/8010.pdf.
6. Elizabeth S. Moore, *It's Child's Play: Advergaming and the Online Marketing of Food to Children,* Kaiser Family Foundation, July 2006, available at: http://www.kff.org/entmedia/upload/7536.pdf; Mira Lee, Yoonhyeung Choi, Elizabeth T. Quilliam, and Richard T. Cole, "Playing with Food: Content Analysis of Food Advergames," *Journal of Consumer Affairs* 43, no. 1 (2009): 129–154.
7. Rideout et al., *Generation M2.*
8. Nielsen, *State of the Media: The Social Media Report Q3'11,* 2011, available to subscribers at: http://blog.nielsen.com/nielsenwire/social/.
9. Digital food marketing practices have been described in detail in the Rudd Center for Food Policy and Obesity reports "Cereal FACTS" (www.cerealfacts.org), "Fast Food FACTS" (www.fastfoodmarketing.org) and "Sugary Drink FACTS" (www.sugary drinkfacts.org).
10. Jennifer L. Harris, Sarah E. Speers, Marlene B. Schwartz, and Kelly D. Brownell, "US Food Company Branded Advergames on the Internet: Children's Exposure and Effects on Snack Consumption," *Journal of Children and Media* 6, no. 1 (2012): 51–58.
11. Ibid.
12. General Mills discontinued Millsberry.com at the end of 2010.
13. Harris et al., "US Food Company Branded Advergames on the Internet."
14. CARU, *Self-regulatory* program for children's advertising, available at: www.caru.org/guidelines/guidelines.pdf.
15. FCC, "Children's Educational Television," available at: www.fcc.gov/guides/childrens-educational-television.
16. Rudd Center for Food Policy and Obesity, "Sugary Drink FACTS." These figures are from analysis using data from comScore, www.comScore.com, an online company that tracks internet visitor information.
17. Harris et al., "US Food Company Branded Advergames on the Internet."
18. V. Mallinckrodt and D. Mizerski, "The Effects of Playing an Advergame on Young Children's Perceptions, Preferences, and Requests," *Journal of Advertising* 36, no. 2 (2007): 87–100.

19. See Jennifer L. Harris, Kelly D. Brownell, and John A. Bargh, "The Food Marketing Defense Model: Integrating Psychological Research to Protect Youth and Inform Public Policy," *Social Issues and Policy Review* 3 (2009): 211–271.
20. Harris Interactive, *Trends & Tudes* 3, no. 11 (2004).
21. Center for Digital Democracy, "Commentary on FTC Proposal to Amend Rule to Respond to Changes in Online Technology," 2011, available at: http://www.consumerfed .org/elements/www.consumerfed.org/file/20100630_COPPA_Final.pdf.
22. Amy Ustjanauskas, Bruce Eckman, Jennifer L. Harris, Amir Goren, Marlene B. Schwartz, and Kelly D. Brownell, "Focus Groups with Parents: What Do They Think About Food Marketing to Their Kids?" Rudd Center for Food Policy and Obesity report, May 2010, available at: http://www.yaleruddcenter.org/resources/upload/docs /what/reports/RuddReport_FocusGroupsParents_5.10.pdf.
23. Moore, *It's Child's Play*.
24. Rudd Center for Food Policy and Obesity, "Fast Food FACTS." These figures are from analysis using data from comScore.
25. Rudd Center for Food Policy and Obesity, "Sugary Drink FACTS." These figures are from analysis using data from comScore.
26. Shar VanBoskirk, "US Interactive Marketing Forecast, 2011 to 2016," August 24, 2011, available at: http://www.forrester.com/US+Interactive+Marketing+Forecast+2011+To +2016/fulltext/-/E-RES59379?docid=59379.
27. These figures are from analysis using data from comScore.
28. *Consumer Reports,* "That Facebook Friend Might Be Ten Years Old, and Other Troubling News," June 2011, available at: www.consumerreports.org/cro/magazine-archive /2011/june/electronics-computers/state-of-the-net/facebook-concerns/index.htm.
29. Amanda Lenhart, Kristen Purcell, Aaron Smith, and Kathryn Zickuhr, "Social Media and Mobile Internet Use Among Teens and Young Adults," Pew Internet and American Life Project, February 3, 2010, available at: www.pewinternet.org/Reports/2010 /Social-Media-and-Young-Adults.aspx.
30. These figures are from analysis using data from comScore.
31. Nielsen, "How Teens Use Media: A Nielsen Report on the Myths and Realities of Teen Media Trends," June 2009, available at: http://blog.nielsen.com/nielsenwire/reports /nielsen_howteensusemedia_june09.pdf.
32. These figures are from analysis using data from comScore.
33. Fuse and the University of Massachusetts, "Fuse's Teen Advertising Study: Spring 2009," May 2009, available at: http://www.fusemarketing.com/pdfs/Fuse_UMASS _Teen_Advertising_Study.pdf.
34. Niall Harrison, "Meet the Top Twenty Brands on Facebook," TNW Magazine, July 4, 2011, available at: www.thenextweb.com/socialmedia/2011/-07/04/meet-the-top-20 -brands-on-facebook/.
35. Rudd Center for Food Policy and Obesity, "Fast Food FACTS."
36. Rudd Center for Food Policy and Obesity, "Sugary Drink FACTS."
37. Rudd Center for Food Policy and Obesity, "Cereal FACTS."
38. Kellogg Company, "2010 Annual Report," 2011, available at: http://annualreport2010 .kelloggcompany.com.
39. Jonathan Mildenhall, Vice President for Global Advertising Strategy and Content Excellence, Coca-Cola Company, quoted in "New Global Ad from Coca-Cola Unites Teens Through Music," March 14, 2011, available at: http://www.thecoca-colacompany .com/dynamic/press_center/2011/03/uniting-teens-through-music.html.

40. Johanna Richardson and Jennifer L. Harris, "Food Marketing and Social Media: Findings from 'Fast Food FACTS' and 'Sugary Drink FACTS,'" 2011, available at: http://www.yaleruddcenter.org/resources/upload/docs/what/reports/FoodMarketingSocialMedia_AmericanUniversity_11.11.pdf.

41. Amanda Lenhart, Rich Ling, Scott Campbell, and Kristen Purcell, "Teens and Mobile Phones," Pew Internet and American Life Project, April 20, 2010, available at: www.pewinternet.org/~/media//Files/Reports/2010/PIP-Teens-and-mobile-2010-with-topline.pdf.

42. Nielsen, "US Teen Mobile Report: Calling Yesterday, Texting Today, Using Apps Tomorrow," October 14, 2010, available at: blog.nielsen.com/nielsenwire/online_mobile/u-s-teen-mobile-report-calling-yesterday-texting-today-using-apps-tomorrow/.

43. VanBoskirk, "US Interactive Marketing Forecast, 2011 to 2016."

44. Ingrid Lunden, "Report: Video Accounts for Half of All Mobile Traffic; Android Biggest for Mobile Ads," TechCrunch, February 22, 2012, available at: techcrunch.com/2012/02/22/report-video-accounts-for-half-of-all-mobile-traffic-android-biggest-for-mobile-ads/.

45. Nielsen, "Kids Today: How the Class of 2011 Engages with Media," June 8, 2011, available at: blog.nielsen.com/nielsenwire/consumer/kids-today-how-the-class-of-2011-engages-with-media/.

46. These figures are from analysis using data from comScore.

47. Rudd Center for Food Policy and Obesity, "Fast Food FACTS."

48. Rudd Center for Food Policy and Obesity, "Sugary Drink FACTS."

49. Kerri Panchuk, "Pizza Hut Sees $7M in Sales from iPhone App," Dallas Business Journal, August 13, 2010, available at: www.bizjournals.com/dallas/stories/2010/08/16/story3.html?b=1281931200 3792111.

50. Rudd Center for Food Policy and Obesity, "Sugary Drink FACTS."

51. American Academy of Pediatrics, "Sports Drinks and Energy Drinks for Children and Adolescents: Are They Appropriate?" Pediatrics 127, no. 6 (2011): 1182–1189.

52. Kellogg Company, "Apple Jacks Race to the Bowl Rally," available at: http://itunes.apple.com/us/app/apple-jacks-race-to-bowl-rally/id421398910?mt=8.

53. Sonya A. Grier and Shiriki Kumanyika, "Targeted Marketing and Public Health," Annual Review of Public Health 31, no. 1 (2010): 349–369.

54. Rudd Center for Food Policy and Obesity, "Cereal FACTS."

55. Rudd Center for Food Policy and Obesity, "Fast Food FACTS" and "Sugary Drink FACTS."

56. Natalie Zmuda, "How Coke Is Targeting Black Consumers," Ad Age, July 1, 2009, available at: http://adage.com/article/the-big-tent/marketing-coke-targeting-african-american-consumers/137716/; Coca-Cola Company, "As Inclusive as Our Brands: 2009 US Diversity Stewardship Report," 2010, available at: Origin.thecoca-colacompany.com/citizenship/pdf/2009_Diversity_Report.pdf.

57. Karlene Lukovitz, "Coke Extends Bet Partnership into the Store," MediaPost, July 18, 2011, available at: www.mediapost.com/publications/?fa=Articles.showArticle&art_aid=154215.

58. Ustjanauskas et al., "Focus Groups with Parents."

Chapter 9   The ABCs of School Lunch

1. PL 396, June 4, 1946, 60 Statutes 231.

2. Both the income eligibility levels and the reimbursement rates are adjusted each year based on the Consumer Price Index. For updated information, see USDA, "National School Lunch Program," October 2011, available at: http://www.fns.usda.gov/cnd/lunch/aboutlunch/NSLPFactSheet.pdf.
3. Elizabeth Lloyd-Richardson et al., "Two-year follow-up of an Adolescent Behavioral Weight Control Intervention," *Pediatrics* 130, no. 2, August 1, 2012.
4. Ironically, a recent intensive analysis of school cafeteria revenues found that in many schools à la carte items were being sold at prices that did not actually cover their full costs. They appeared to food service directors to enhance revenues because the income from their sales was usually balanced against the price paid to acquire them, without any allocation of the labor or management costs involved in handling them.
5. Dorothy Pannell-Martin, *School Foodservice Management for the Twenty-First Century*, 5th ed. (Alexandria, VA: inTEAM Associates, Inc., 1999), 8, 9.
6. Katherine Ralston, Constance Newman, Annette Clauson, Joanne Guthrie, and Jean Buzby, *The National School Lunch Program: Background, Trends, and Issues*. USDA, Economic Research Service, ERR-61, July 2008.
7. USDA, Food and Nutrition Service, "Erroneous Payments in the National School Lunch Program and School Breakfast Program: Summary of Findings," November 2007.

Chapter 14   Getting Off the Anti-Hunger Treadmill

1. See Regional Food Bank of Oklahoma, "Our Mission Is Fighting Hunger . . . Feeding Hope," available at: http://www.regionalfoodbank.org/ (accessed January 28, 2012).
2. According to Feeding America, food banks distribute more than 3 billion pounds of food annually. Using the USDA estimate that the average American eats 4.7 pounds of food per day, I calculate 4.7 × 45 million × 7 days/month × 12 months = 17.7 billion pounds.
3. USDA, National Institute of Food and Agriculture, "Program Synopsis: Community Food Projects," available at: http://www.nifa.usda.gov/funding/cfp/cfp_synopsis.html (accessed February 14, 2012).
4. Jeanette Abi-Nader et al., "The Activities and Impacts of Community Food Projects, 2005–2009," Community Food Security Coalition, October 2010, available at: http://www.foodsecurity.org/pub/CPF_Activities_Impacts_2005–09.pdf (accessed February 14, 2012).
5. Ken Regal, personal communication, March 2010.

Chapter 15   Childhood Hunger: A Battle That Can Be Won

1. Annie E. Casey Foundation, "Kid's Count" report, 2012.

Chapter 16   Beyond the Charity Myth

1. Bob Arnebeck, "Yellow Fever in New York City, 1791–1799," paper presented at the 26th Conference on New York State History, Syracuse, NY, June 9–11, 2005.
2. "The Yellow Fever Visitation—Terrible Scenes in New Orleans and Memphis," *Frank Leslie's Illustrated Newspaper*, September 28, 1878, Philip S. Hench Walter Reed Yellow Fever Collection, University of Virginia, available at: http://yellowfever.lib.virginia.edu/reed/.

NOTES

3. See Malaria Site, "History of Malaria During Wars," available at: http://www.malaria
site.com/malaria/history_wars.htm.
4. John Pintard, letter to his daughter, July 13, 1832, displayed in the New-York Historical Society exhibit "Plague in Gotham: Cholera in Nineteenth-Century New York,"
April 2008.
5. World Health Organization, "Yellow Fever: Fact Sheet," 2011, available at: http://
www.who.int/mediacentre/factsheets/fs100/en/ (accessed January 21, 2012).
6. CNN, "UN Reports Cholera Outbreak in Northern Iraq," August 30, 2007.
7. Mark Doyle, "Haiti's Cholera Row with UN Rumbles On," *BBC News,* December 14,
2011, available at: http://www.bbc.co.uk/news/world-latin-america-16180250 (accessed
January 21, 2012).
8. World Health Organization, "World Malaria Report 2011: Fact Sheet," December
2011, available at: http://www.who.int/malaria/world_malaria_report_2011/WMR
2011_factsheet.pdf (accessed January 21, 2012).
9. CDC, "The History of Malaria, an Ancient Disease," available at: http://www.cdc.gov
/malaria/history/eradication_us.htm; CDC, "Elimination of Malaria in the United
States (1947–1951)," available at: http://www.cdc.gov/malaria/about/history/elimination
_us.html; National Center for Zoonotic, Vector-Borne, and Enteric Diseases (ZVED),
Division of Parasitic Diseases, "Biology/CDC Malaria," April 23, 2004.
10. Nick Kotz, "Hunger in America: The Federal Response," Field Foundation (New York),
1979.
11. Kevin Bonsor, "How Fire Engines Work," How Stuff Works, available at: http://science
.howstuffworks.com/fire-engine.htm (accessed August 3, 2008).
12. Feeding America, "Hunger Study 2010," available at: http://feedingamerica.org/hunger
-in-america/hunger-studies/hunger-study-2010.aspx (accessed January 21, 2012).
13. New York City Coalition Against Hunger, "Not Too Big to Fail: As NYC Hunger
Soars, Feeding Programs Close Due to Government Cuts: Annual Hunger Survey
2011," available at: www.nyccah.org/node/1352.
14. Janet Poppendieck, *Sweet Charity: Emergency Food and the End of Entitlement* (New
York: Penguin Books, 1998), 201–229.
15. The value of a grocery bag of food as estimated by the South Texas Food Bank and
based on USDA, Food and Nutrition Service, "Food Stamp Program: Average Monthly
Participation by State (Households)," data as of November 30, 2007, available at:
http://www.fns.usda.gov/pd/summary_excel-data.xls.
16. "Americans' Approval of Congress Drops to Single Digits," *New York Times,* October
25, 2011, available at: http://www.nytimes.com/interactive/2011/10/25/us/politics
/approval-of-congress-drops-to-single-digits.html.

Chapter 19 Seven Steps to Ending Child Hunger by 2015

1. Adapted and updated from a paper by Food Research and Action Center, "Seven Steps
to Ending Child Hunger by 2015," July 1, 2009.

– 288 –

Reyes, Daniel, 163
Rice subsidies, 68
Richardson, Renee, 218–219
Rigby-Hiebert, Carol, 148–149
Ronald McDonald, 111
Roosevelt, Eleanor, 81
Rosa Parks Elementary School
    (Indianapolis), 231
Rudd Center for Food Policy and Obesity,
    107, 109–110
Rural areas, food deserts in, 47, 48, 50–51

Safety net, 30
Safeway, 49
St. Mary's Food Bank (Phoenix), 138–139
St. Paul's Presbyterian Church (San
    Angelo, Texas), 149
Sampson, Al, 146–147
Samuels, Melanie, 149–150, 151
School breakfast programs, 16, 17,
    216–217
  in Alsup Elementary School, 41–43
  increasing participation in, 237–238
  in New York City, 160, 165–167
School Meals Coalition, 167
School meals programs, 10, 16, 17
  access to, 191–194
  free or reduced price, 124–125,
    126–127, 131–132, 237–238
  increasing access to, 193–194
  issues confronting, 123
  legislation on, 60–64
  nutrition standards for, 125–126,
    130–131
  percentage of children enrolled in,
    190–191
  reform of, 73–74, 133
  universal free school meals, 133,
    165–167
  See also National School Lunch
    Program (NSLP); School breakfast
    programs
Schumacher, Gus, 92
Second Harvest, 139
SEE-LA, 179
Select Committee on Nutrition and
    Human Needs, 84
Senate Hunger Committee, 84

Senior Farmers' Market Nutrition Program
    (SFMNP), 88–89
SFMNP. *See* Senior Farmers' Market
    Nutrition Program (SFMNP)
Shanley, Joann, 162
Shareholder value movement, increase in
    availability of calories in American
    diet and, 102
Share Our Strength, 157, 189, 193, 194
Shenk, John, 151
Shore, Bill, 189, 197
Shore, Debbie, 189
Silverbush, Lori, 5, 11–12
Simmons, Sonya, 159–160, 173
Simon, Daniel Bowman, 92, 94
Skittles, 116
Smucker's, 183
Snack foods
  marketed as healthy, 105
  marketed to children, 108
  ubiquity of, 104
Snacking, 104
SNAP. *See* Supplemental Nutrition
    Assistance Program (SNAP)
SNAP Gardens, 94
"The SNAP Vaccine: Boosting Children's
    Health" (report), 29
Snickers, 121
Sobe, 118
Social media, food marketing to children
    via, 115–117
Soda/soft drinks
  food stamps and, 83–84
  marketed to children, 108, 113, 116,
    117–118, 120, 121–122
  as source of calories in American diet,
    100, 101
Soup kitchens, 8, 38, 137, 138, 207, 208
Southland Baptist Church, 148
South Texas Food Bank, 209
Soybeans
  crop insurance on, 70–71
  subsidies for, 68
Special Supplemental Nutrition Program
    for Women, Infants, and Children.
    See WIC (Special Supplemental
    Nutrition Program for Women,
    Infants, and Children)

I believe that a good story well told can truly make a difference in how one sees the world. This is why I started Participant Media: to tell compelling, entertaining stories that create awareness of the real issues that shape our lives.

At Participant, we seek to entertain our audiences first and then invite them to participate in making a difference. With each film, we create social action and advocacy programs that highlight the issues that resonate in the film and provide ways to transform the impact of the media experience into individual and community action.

Forty-two films later, from *An Inconvenient Truth* to *Food, Inc.,* and from *Waiting for "Superman"* to *The Best Exotic Marigold Hotel* and *Lincoln,* and through thousands of social action activities, Participant continues to create entertainment that inspires and compels social change. Through our partnership with Public-Affairs, we are extending our mission so that more of you can join us in making our world a better place.

Jeff Skoll, founder and chairman
Participant Media